The Bathroom

THE BATHROOM

A Social History of Cleanliness and the Body

Alison K. Hoagland

History of Human Spaces

An Imprint of ABC-CLIO, LLC

Santa Barbara, California • Denver, Colorado

Library of Congress Cataloging-in-Publication Data

Names: Hoagland, Alison K., 1951- author.
Title: The bathroom : a social history of cleanliness and the body / Alison K. Hoagland.
Description: Santa Barbara, California : Greenwood, An Imprint of ABC-CLIO, LLC, [2018] | Series: History of human spaces | Includes bibliographical references and index.
Identifiers: LCCN 2018019067 (print) | LCCN 2018021735 (ebook) | ISBN 9781440852671 (ebook) | ISBN 9781440852664 (hardcopy : alk. paper)
Subjects: LCSH: Bathing customs–United States–History. | Bathrooms–United States–History. | Hygiene–United States–History.
Classification: LCC GT2845 (ebook) | LCC GT2845 .H63 2018 (print) | DDC 391.6/4–dc23
LC record available at https://lccn.loc.gov/2018019067

ISBN: 978-1-4408-5266-4 (print)
      978-1-4408-5267-1 (ebook)

23 22 21 20 19   1 2 3 4 5

This book is also available as an eBook.

Greenwood
An Imprint of ABC-CLIO, LLC

ABC-CLIO, LLC
130 Cremona Drive, P.O. Box 1911
Santa Barbara, California 93116-1911
www.abc-clio.com

This book is printed on acid-free paper ∞
Manufactured in the United States of America

CONTENTS

PREFACE: THE PERSONAL AND THE PUBLIC IN THE AMERICAN HOME

The bathroom sits at the intersection of personal behavior and public influence in the American home. An intensely private space, the bathroom is where the user locks the door and performs personal functions alone. At the same time, the external influences on the function and appearance of the bathroom are numerous—technological change, public infrastructure, political intervention, fashion, consumerism, ideals of cleanliness, and so on. Paradoxically, the notion that the bathtub, sink, and toilet should be concentrated in one room was a result of late–19th-century beliefs about disease that had been discredited by the time bathrooms were becoming universal features of American houses. Yet the three-fixture bathroom persisted through the 20th century as a desirable aspect of genteel living, reflecting social status in its separation, size, and decoration.

Privacy is a key theme that runs through this book. The functions performed in the bathroom—which reflect personally held, culturally influenced ideas about the body—are generally performed alone. Greater wealth and status permit homeowners to attain increased privacy from not having to share their bathrooms with as many people and from locating bathrooms out of view of guests. Multiple bathrooms in a house and their location next to bedrooms, with a more public so-called powder room for guests, ensure this privacy. Privacy even appears in our euphemisms.

The *bathroom* takes the name of the least-offensive function that occurs within, although relieving oneself (another euphemism) occurs there far more frequently. "Going to the bathroom" thus describes relief and has nothing to do with bathing. Employing these euphemisms is another way in which a user's true purpose is disguised.

The public aspect of the bathroom appears in the many social issues that impinge upon it, such as the changing interpretation of cleanliness and hygiene. After the Civil War, sanitarians' belief that disease emanated from filth caused them to be extremely wary of the toilet, which introduced into the home threats to personal health. They recommended that plumbing fixtures be concentrated in one room, that sewage be moved rapidly out of a house through small-diameter pipes, that pipes be exposed, and that bathrooms be ventilated. By the end of the 19th century, germ theory held that disease came from personal contact and that such simple acts as hand-washing were more important for health than environmental cleanliness. At the municipal level, concern for the drainage of low-lying, miasmic areas gave way to an interest in water purity.

Modernization also characterizes the development of the bathroom. The role of scientific expertise, new technology, new materials, relation to larger systems, and an efficient and automatic operation represented modernity in early-20th-century America. Vitreous china and enameled cast iron, both materials developed in the late 19th century, formed bathroom fixtures that functioned and endured; the materials and the fixtures themselves have changed little over more than a century, yet the bathroom still appears to be one of the most modern rooms in the house.

This book examines the bathroom in the American house. Public bathrooms offer an interesting, though separate, set of insights into the past, but they will not be dealt with here. The American bathroom in the house merits study because for decades, if not most of the 20th century, the proliferation, technological prowess, and cleanliness of the bathroom offered an ideal for European and other nations. This book considers the bathroom from its coalescence as a three-fixture room in the house, beginning in the late 19th century, up to the present.

The first chapter sets the context by examining ideas surrounding cleanliness from the ancient world forward. While not a comprehensive overview, this survey tracks an up-and-down course rather than an ever-cleaner trajectory. After a peak of interest in bathing in ancient Rome, the nadir of bathing in the 16th century was followed by a new interest in the 17th and 18th. The scene then shifts to the United States. Although bathtubs and flushing toilets were available in the early 19th century, their use was not widespread, and the bathroom, as a room, was slow to take shape.

The next three chapters consider important elements of bathroom development from the last half of the 19th century until World War I. Chapter 2 discusses the sanitarians of the 1870s and 1880s, who were highly influential on the development of the bathroom. Their gradual concession to germ theory and public hygiene was a major shift, although one that left the bathroom intact. Chapter 3 considers the technology of the three fixtures, which was mostly established by the end of the 19th century, while standardization and mass production in the early 20th century brought their prices down. Chapter 4 looks at infrastructure, or how public investment influenced the bathroom. Case studies of Memphis and Baltimore illustrate the scientific and political debates about water and sewer systems.

Chapter 5 considers the uneven distribution of the bathroom, to the extent that even as late as 1940, barely a majority of Americans had a three-fixture bathroom. The two lagging populations were the urban poor, who were often ignored by the politically powerful, and the rural population, for whom the installation of indoor bathrooms was often a personal, strategic decision. A brief look at government housing programs in the 1930s reflects the expectations surrounding bathrooms.

Privacy is the subject of chapter 6, which tracks where bathrooms were placed and how many there were, from the mid-19th century until after World War II. House plans provide one of the source materials for this investigation, and although most compilations of plans are prescriptive rather than reflective of buildings that have been built, they indicate norms. As the three fixtures became consolidated in bathrooms, the room moved closer to bedrooms, out of public sight. The half-bath known as a powder room then arose to serve guests, keeping them out of family areas.

The next two chapters look at the selling of the bathroom in the 1920s and 1930s. Chapter 7 examines sanitary-ware catalogs and advertisements to see how the bathroom was pitched to consumers. No longer solely a place of utility, the bathroom was sold as a place of style, on which prospective customers needed to be advised. Chapter 8 discusses the advertising of items for personal care, as concerns about hygiene were usurped by self-consciousness about appearance and body odor. Subtly instructing customers on how to use the products, the ads also encouraged people to spend more and more time in the bathroom, as personal grooming became more complicated.

The last two chapters consider the bathroom from after World War II to the present. Chapter 9 looks at the growth of the bathroom, both in numbers and in size, as the bathroom went from a site for new materials and ergonomics to a place of luxury and sensuousness. The last chapter identifies current political issues and social trends reflected in the bathroom, including water conservation, universal access, and germophobia.

As personal and private as the bathroom may seem, it is also a place where outside forces wield great influence. As such, it becomes an intriguing vehicle to see ideas about sanitation, cleanliness, hygiene, privacy, social status, consumerism, and much more expressed in tangible form. How the three-fixture bathroom became the norm for Americans, and what happened after it did, involves an exploration of changing ideas about privacy, cleanliness, and modernization.

ACKNOWLEDGMENTS

The bathroom turned out to be a fascinating and wide-ranging topic, and I have enjoyed my time pondering the smallest room in the house, despite all the teasing from friends. My first thanks goes to James Ciment, who approached me about writing this book. I am also grateful to fellow scholars, friends, and family who helped along the way: Chris Bell, Alison Bradford, Larry and Pat Burdick, Betsy Cromley and Curt Lamb, Jamie Jacobs, Carol MacLennan, and Mark Schara, with special thanks to my perceptive readers and critics, Catherine Bishir and Al Chambers. For help with research, my thanks go to the staffs of the Library of Congress, the J. Robert Van Pelt and John and Ruanne Opie Library at Michigan Technological University, and the Hagley Museum and Library. I also appreciate the opportunity to view historic bathroom fixtures at the Plumbing Museum in Watertown, Massachusetts, and the Kohler Design Center in Kohler, Wisconsin; at the latter facility, my thanks to Angela Miller, archivist, for producing critical documents.

In 1934 my grandparents, Philip J. and Esther Ward Kimball, renovated an early 19th-century stone farmhouse in Centerville, Delaware, installing modern bathrooms. I remembered those bathrooms from occasional stays at their house when I was a child, and I was pleased to return to that house during the research for this book, more than forty years after my grandparents had died. The bathroom fixtures were still there: baby-blue ones in the guest bathroom and, in the master bathroom, the height of modernity and fashion: black fixtures. It was not until I researched this book that I understood the significance of those colors, but I had long remembered them.

CHRONOLOGY

Ca. 4000s BCE	Chinese settlements use bamboo pipes to carry water.
Ca. 2000s BCE	Houses in Mohenjo-daro, in the Indus Valley, contain bathing rooms that drain into a sewer, which empties into a river outside of the city walls.
Ca. 1000s BCE	Houses on Crete have water closets flushed by water that drains into a sewer.
Ca. 800s to 500s BCE	Ancient Greeks have public bathing houses.
Ca. 600s to 300s BCE	At Olynthus, Greece, about a third of the houses have bathing rooms adjacent to the kitchen fire.
700s BCE to 400s CE	Rome has 1,000 public baths, some of them massive, with sequences of heated spaces. Latrines over sewers are located in public toilets, as well as in the bathhouses. The public sewer, like the aqueducts, is an engineering achievement.
200s CE to 1500s	Christianity tolerates bathing but not as a means of bringing pleasure. Ascetics adhere to a state of being unwashed.
600s	Islam is founded. The religion encourages bathing, so believers build elaborate bathhouses.
1500s to ca. 1700	Europeans spurn bathing, seeing the skin as porous. Instead, they achieve cleanliness through wiping the skin, for which linen is the most desirable material.

1594	John Harington, godson of Queen Elizabeth I, develops a water closet.
1700s	Bathing reappears, both in public bathhouses and in private houses of the elite. By the end of the century, personal cleanliness is a marker of class.
1775	Alexander Cummings, in Great Britain, patents the first water closet with a valve. He also introduces the S-shaped trap.
1790s	Public baths appear in New York and Philadelphia.
1801	Philadelphia's water system, driven by steam pumps, goes into operation. President Thomas Jefferson has water closets installed in the White House.
1823	In Philadelphia, 401 private houses have bathtubs.
1829	Tremont Hotel opens in Boston with eight water closets and eight bathing rooms.
1836	Astor Hotel opens in New York with a bath and a water closet on each floor.
1840	John Hall publishes first architectural plans showing houses with bathtubs and water closets.
1840s and 1850s	Advice manuals encourage bathing.
1847	Thomas Maddock immigrates from England with the technical knowledge to make sanitary pottery ware. Established in Trenton, New Jersey, his company continues in the family until 1929.
1853	Mount Vernon Hotel in Cape May, New Jersey, offers a bath in every room.
1860	All of the 16 largest cities in the United States have waterworks.
1861–1865	During the Civil War, U.S. Sanitary Commission urges hygienic practices at army installations.
1868	Henry Moule receives a patent for an earth closet, which uses dirt to cover excretions. The earth closet enjoys modest popularity for a decade or two.
1869	Massachusetts establishes first state board of health.
1870s	J. L. Mott Iron Works of New York develops a process to enamel cast iron.

1870s and 1880s	Sanitarians alert the American public to the dangers of sewer gas, arguing that disease is caused by polluted air that is not always noticeable. As a result, sanitarians encourage isolation of bathroom fixtures into one ventilated room with exposed pipes.
1875	Standard Manufacturing begins production of cast-iron sanitary ware, making one to two tubs a day.
1879	Congress establishes the National Board of Health, charging it with advising on epidemics that spread across state lines. The board lasts for only four years. Procter & Gamble introduces Ivory soap.
1882	New York and Washington adopt first plumbing codes.
1880s and 1890s	Germ theory gains ascendancy, as scientists prove that disease comes from microscopic organisms and does not arise spontaneously. Emphasis of disease prevention shifts away from general environment to personal hygiene.
1888	Baltimore adopts an ordinance requiring every new dwelling of four or more rooms to include a bathroom with a bathtub.
1889	Pears' soap puts an endorsement from Henry Ward Beecher on the front page of the *New York Herald*, pioneering the celebrity endorsement.
1890s	Gas-fired hot-water heater comes on market, replacing the coal stove as the source of heat for water.
Ca. 1897	Municipalities begin treating drinking water with filtration.
1900	Standard Sanitary Manufacturing Company produces 150 tubs a day.
1901	New York's Tenement Act requires flush toilets, one for every two families, in new construction.
1902	Public health official Charles V. Chapin declares the end of the theory that disease arises from environmental filth.
1906	Construction begins on a sewer system for Baltimore, the last major American city to build one.
1908	Universal Sanitary Manufacturing Company introduces slip casting, which permits batch production of sanitary pottery. The Statler Hotel in Buffalo offers "a room and a bath for a dollar and a half," touting the private bathroom connected to every bedroom.

1909	In Trenton, 34 firms, employing 5,000 workers, make sanitary ware.
1910	Manufacturers agree on five-and-a-half-inch spacing for screws anchoring the hinge of the toilet seat. Standard introduces Ivorite-coated toilet seats, replacing exposed wooden seats.
Ca. 1910	Municipalities begin treating drinking water with chlorination.
1910s and 1920s	The New Public Health focuses on contagion as the source of disease.
1911	Kohler Company develops double wall for tubs, replacing roll rim. Woodbury uses sex to sell its soap, with the tag line, "A Skin You Love to Touch."
1914	Smith-Lever Act provides matching funds for U.S. Department of Agriculture extension services, including those that advise on improvements to homes. Ten years later, 50,000 rural families have installed water systems, and 15,000 have built sewer systems according to recommendations.
1915	Universal Sanitary introduces the Dressler tunnel kiln, reducing firing times for sanitary ware.
1919	The Cecil B. DeMille film *Male and Female* depicts Gloria Swanson taking a luxurious bath.
1920s	Mixer taps, which combine hot and cold water so that they come out of one spout, gain popularity.
1922	Sanitary-pottery workers embark on bitter strike in Trenton.
1923	Federal antitrust suit breaks up monopoly of sanitary-pottery manufacturers.
1926	National Bureau of Standards issues standards for vitreous-china fixtures. Universal Sanitary introduces colored bathroom fixtures, with Standard Sanitary and Kohler following soon after.
1929	The Metropolitan Museum of Art exhibits a bathroom with black Kohler fixtures in an arrangement designed by Ely Jacques Kahn.
1930s	Electric water heaters come on market.
1931	National Bureau of Standards establishes colors for sanitary ware.
1933	U.S. Division of Subsistence Homesteads begins to oversee construction of 99 semirural communities, all with houses with indoor bathrooms. The U.S. Public Works Administration begins to oversee construction of 20,000 urban row houses and apartment buildings, all with indoor bathrooms.

1935	U.S. Resettlement Administration is established. It oversees the construction of three greenbelt towns, all with houses with indoor bathrooms. In another program, it oversees the construction of 17,000 units for rural dwellers but drops the requirement for indoor bathrooms. Rural Electrification Administration begins to help cooperatives bring electricity to farms, providing an easy means of pumping water.
1940	Census shows that only 55 percent of Americans have full plumbing facilities.
1941–1945	Five million World War II recruits stay in temporary barracks that have indoor bathroom facilities.
1947–1951	William Levitt builds 17,500 houses, all with one indoor bathroom, in his community on Long Island.
1953	Joseph Eichler, a California developer, claims to be the first to offer two bathrooms to middle-class purchasers in his Fairmeadow project near Palo Alto.
1959	Baltimore's last public bathhouse closes.
1960	Only 62 percent of farm dwellers have indoor toilets.
Early 1960s	Fiberglass-reinforced plastic bathtub-showers come on the market.
1960s	Sunken tubs, saunas, and hot tubs gain favor.
1966	Alexander Kira's study of the bathroom charges that it has been designed more for plumbers than for users. He publicizes people's behavior in the bathroom and suggests ergonomic fixtures.
1967	Kohler introduces the "Bold Look of Kohler" marketing campaign.
1968	Roy Jacuzzi markets a whirlpool bath for relaxation.
1972	Clean Water Act prohibits pollution of waterways. The Washington Suburban Sanitary Commission requires toilets to consume no more than 3.5 gpf (gallons per flush).
1978	California is the first state to require low-flow toilets, consuming no more than 3.5 gpf.
1989	Massachusetts is first state to mandate ultra-low-flow toilets, or those that consume no more than 1.6 gpf. Toto, a Japanese firm, begins production in the United States of the Washlet, which combines toilet and bidet along with hands-free design.

1990   Only 1 percent of Americans do not have full plumbing facilities. The bathroom has doubled in size since 1970, 70 square feet compared to 35. The Americans with Disabilities Act introduces people to accessible design in all commercial facilities.

1993   Diane von Furstenberg publishes *The Bath*, which positions the bathroom as a place for solitude, serenity, and luxurious materials.

1994   Energy Policy Act of 1992 goes into effect, limiting sale of toilets to the ultra-low-flow standard of 1.6 gpf.

1999   Caroma, an Australian firm, introduces the dual-flush toilet, providing either a 1.6- or 0.8-gallon flush.

2014   California restricts toilets to high-efficiency standard, or 1.28 gpf.

Chapter 1

CLEANLINESS: PRECEDING THE BATHROOM

An interest in cleanliness preceded the modern bathroom by millennia, not just centuries. A brief look around the world, especially in the Western tradition, will show the varying attitudes toward the functions that eventually became located in the bathroom. The trajectory of ever-greater interest in personal cleanliness in the West is not a straight one; the ancient Romans' obsession with bathing was not equaled until the 20th century. Different motivations for cleanliness help explain this uneven path, as one rationale gained ascendancy at one time, while another ruled at another time. The impulse toward cleanliness could be driven by medical considerations, including personal hygiene; pleasure, such as relaxation or regeneration; religious inspiration, aligning a clean body with a clean soul, for instance; and social customs, such as gatherings in bathhouses. All these motivations play into the interest in bathrooms in the United States today, but in the past, they dictated very different behaviors. Furthermore, cleanliness was not always achieved with water or even steam. Expanding the understanding of cleanliness helps to question the inevitability of the bathroom as it exists today.

Evidence of water control for personal use in early cultures survives, but it is difficult to determine the underlying attitudes toward cleanliness that this might have implied. Chinese settlements had some sort of plumbing involving pipes made from bamboo in the fifth millennium BCE (Carter 2006, 24). In the third millennium BCE, the houses in Mohenjo-daro in the Indus Valley in present-day Pakistan included a bathing room with a bathtub that drained into a cesspit and then into a sewer main, which emptied into a river outside the city walls (Carter 2006, 25). The Minoan civilization on the island of Crete, dating from around 2000 BC, had not only bathtubs and a sewer system but also water closets (Giedion [1948] 2013, 629). The latter had wooden seats and were flushed by rainwater, which was stored in cisterns and transported in terra-cotta pipes and then drained into a sewer (Carter 2006, 27). These civilizations valued cleanliness, exhibiting some technological prowess to achieve it, but the philosophy behind it is unclear.

For ancient Greeks, cleanliness was part of a philosophy of life that included exercise, work, diet, and sleep. Greek baths were closely tied to the gymnasiums, where physical exertion took place. The baths were not places to luxuriate but were more likely cold showers, located (e.g., in the gymnasium of Priene, built in the fourth century BCE) between the exercise facilities and the semicircular exedra, which accommodated philosophical discussions (Giedion [1948] 2013, 630). Outside the gymnasiums, Greeks built aqueducts to serve public fountains, where water was available to all. In their houses, evidence for warm baths exists, such as the remains at Olynthus (seventh to fourth century BCE), where bathrooms, built at the back of the kitchen fire, were found in about a third of the houses. These were hip baths, in which a servant poured water over the bather, who sat in a shallow tub (V. Smith 2007, 79).

It was the Romans, though, who brought bathing to a high art. The opulent public bathhouses reflected the meaning that Romans gave to the bath—a daily occurrence, performed with others, in which the sensuous experience of the bath was paramount. Exercise was also involved, as a diversion or as a prelude to the bath, but did not occupy the same importance as it did to the Greeks. Instead, the bath itself was the object. The complexity of the public bathhouses, involving water, heat, a progression of bathing spaces, and latrines, indicates the significance that Romans ascribed to their baths.

Aqueducts brought water into Rome. In the first century CE, three tanks distributed water, with 40 percent of it going to public purposes, including military camps, public fountains, public troughs, and fifteen sets of baths and latrines. By the third century CE, Rome had 1,000 public baths to serve its population of 1 million (V. Smith 2007, 104). Within each bathhouse, a cistern stored the water until needed.

Each of the large public bathhouses, or *thermae*, offered a progression of interconnected bathing rooms, beginning with the *tepidarium*, or medium-heat room, to the *caldarium*, or hot room, and ending with a cold plunge in the *frigidarium*. Other rooms offered dry heat and steam heat, but most bathers lingered in the caldarium and frigidarium, where they would soak leisurely, converse with their fellow bathers, and receive massages. These rooms were lavishly appointed, with marble finishes and mosaic floors.

The grandest baths, those of Caracalla (215 CE) and Diocletian (284–305 CE), were massive, with soaring, two-story spaces. In general, the large public bath complex stretched over several city blocks, with rational plans, symmetrical composition, deft use of light, and voluminous, impressive spaces. These were some of the most sophisticated buildings of the Roman Empire. The engineering that made them possible was also noteworthy. The hypocaust heating system consisted of floors raised on short pillars so that heat could circulate underneath. The heated air then circulated in the walls, which enabled the rooms to be heated to different temperatures, before it vented below the eaves. A nearby furnace heated the air, as well as the water that filled the baths (Yegül 2010, 17–18, 103, 81–86).

The baths were open to all, attracting people from across the social spectrum. No areas within seem to have been reserved for higher-ranking patrons; instead, bathers would have mixed freely. Women were also welcome at baths, although perhaps at different times than men. Nudity would have been common, although simple tunics might have also been worn. The Roman baths' subsequent reputation as scenes of erotic behavior is difficult to verify, but it is likely that some baths permitted the mixing of genders and that sexual activity took place (Yegül 2010, 27–34).

More significantly, the baths were an important part of the daily routine of most males. Visited in the afternoons, the baths would have encouraged relaxation, socializing, and the exchange of information. Full immersion in both hot and cold baths was typical. Pleasure would have played a large part in the experience.

Latrines also formed part of bathhouses and stood on their own in public toilets called *foricae*. These multiseat facilities with accommodations for as many as 100 people appeared in the first two centuries BCE and into the first century CE and grew more luxurious in the second century CE. They were located over a branch of the main sewer, which washed away the deposits. Windows high in the walls illuminated them. A trench in front of the seat contained running water, perhaps to rinse out the sponge that, attached to the end of a stick, Romans used to wipe their anal areas. Intended to be used by many people simultaneously, the foricae might have also had a mix of social classes. It is unclear if women used them at the same time as men or if they used them at all. Houses also had private toilets, which tended to have only one seat and drained into a septic tank, not a public sewer. Nearly every house in Pompeii and Herculaneum (both destroyed in 79 CE) had a private toilet, while only a tenth of them had private baths (Koloski-Ostrow 2015, 26, 85, 31, 120).

The Cloaca Maxima, or great sewer, facilitated the cleansing of the foricae in Rome. The sewer, which may have been constructed as early as

Latrines at Ostia Antica, near Rome, Italy, ca. first century CE. A sewer ran underneath to wash away the deposits. (Andy Chisholm/Dreamstime.com)

600 BCE, was improved and added to through the centuries. Intended to drain the swamps of Rome and the streets after storms, its primary purpose was not to serve the foricae. The water brought in through the aqueducts eventually drained into the sewer, after use, and its quantity helped move the sewage through the pipes, into the Tiber River. Like the aqueducts, the sewer was one of the major engineering achievements of ancient Rome.

With all these resources expended on water—getting it, using it, and disposing it—it is clear that water was very important to Romans. Personal hygiene seems to have been a by-product, not the main purpose, of the baths; the social and pleasurable aspects seem to have been more highly valued. The engineering and display of water also seem to be a form of conspicuous consumption, something that a prosperous and powerful empire was able to do. As the empire declined, cities were unable to maintain the infrastructure that the large public baths required, and bathing fell out of favor (Yegül 2010, 98, 199; Carter 2006, 31; V. Smith 2007, 102).

While Romans valued the prosperity and leisure that bathing and bathhouses represented, other cultures found different virtues in bathing. Most forms of religion incorporate ritual washing, seeing water as a purifier. Judaism requires handwashing at various times, including before breaking bread at supper. Full-body immersion is also required for men in relation to certain holidays and for women after menstruation and childbirth. Islam requires washing before each of the five daily prayers. Full-body immersion is part of the Christian rite of baptism, at least with many denominations. The examples are endless, but they indicate an important attitude toward water and cleanliness: that it played a role in religious observance.

Religions also offered guidance on excretions. Deuteronomy, one of the oldest books of the Bible, mandated that there be a place for relief outside an encampment and that people cover their excretions with dirt (23:11–12). Muslims reserved the left hand for cleansing after defecation and forbade its use in eating. Hindus were directed to defecate first thing in the morning (Koloski-Ostrow 2015, 467). Instructions such as these suggest that what is perceived today as good hygiene was once an aspect of ritual purification.

Some religious adherents did not see bodily cleanliness as important as cleanliness of the soul. Judeo-Christian asceticism, reacting against the excesses of Rome, held that bodily cleanliness was a distraction. Saint Paul advocated moderate asceticism for the masses and advanced asceticism for the ardent, but Christianity swung between the moderate and radical ascetics beginning in the third and fourth centuries CE (V. Smith 2007, 126–35). In the more moderate version, bathing was acceptable as long as the purpose was not to bring pleasure to the bather. For more radical ascetics, the state of being unwashed encouraged the achievement of grace and godliness (Yegül 2010, 206).

Islam, rising in the Middle East after the seventh century CE, encouraged bathing. Influenced by both Roman and Byzantine traditions, Muslims maintained customs of full-body immersion in water, as well as steam and hot-air baths, which apparently originated in Russia and Finland and spread to Syria in the third century CE. Their elaborate bathhouses, called *hammams*, included a progression of spaces, domed *caldaria*, and steam baths. The hammams were religious places, complementary to the mosque, and endowing a hammam was viewed as an act of charity (Giedion [1948] 2013, 634–35, 641–43). As these bathing traditions spread throughout the Middle East, Christians held onto their disdain for bathing, as well as other forms of opposition to Islam. When bathing regained popularity in the 19th century in the West, so-called Turkish baths with oriental themes reflected the romanticization of the Muslim's maintenance of bathing customs. In New York City in 1897, 62 public steam baths had Russian or Turkish themes (Yegül 2010, 226–30).

Through the Middle Ages, Europeans continued to spurn bathing, at least as a public display. Although "a thousand years without a bath" may be overstating the case, a growing rejection of bathing by the end of the Middle Ages arose. But during the Middle Ages, people continued to bathe, some at the public steam baths and bathhouses of Paris; others, at home, if servants were available to heat and carry the water; others, in rivers and lakes; and monks, in monasteries equipped with baths. The public steam baths apparently continued the licentiousness evident in Rome, with communal facilities, mingling of the sexes, and pleasure as an emphasis. Their reputation as places of dissipation and social instability, along with the spread of syphilis and the appearance of successive waves of plagues, led government officials to ban them by the middle of the 16th century (Vigarello 1988, 28, 32; Yegül 2010, 218).

Medical reasons also factored into this shift at the end of the Middle Ages. By the 16th century, Europeans tended to see the skin as porous, and heat and water only enabled poisons to penetrate the body. Cleanliness then became detached from water. Smells could be removed by wiping them away, particularly with scented linen (Vigarello 1988, 9, 17). And wearing linen next to the skin could also aid in cleanliness, as well as display it. The upper classes increasingly wore fresh white linen as a sign of status. This discovery of linen as a cleaning agent was deemed an advance of civilization. In his 1624 treatise on the construction of houses, the French doctor Louis Savot did not see the need for baths: "We can more easily do without than the ancients, because of our use of linen, which today serves to keep the body clean, more conveniently than could the steam-baths and baths of the ancients, who were denied the use and convenience of linen" (quoted in Vigarello 1988, 60). Hands and faces—visible parts of the body—were kept clean, but with wiping rather than with washing.

By the beginning of the 18th century, cleanliness achieved by bathing was at a low point. But as that century wore on, a new interest in bathing arose, especially among the upper classes. A public bath appeared on the Seine in Paris in 1761. Public fountains offered water to all, sometimes with laundry tanks nearby. Among the upper classes, baths in houses became more common, and cleanliness became a sign of refinement. Baths also became more private, as specialized rooms appeared (Vigarello 1988, 103, 185, 100, 110).

Privies also appeared more often in the houses of the elite. Unlike close stools, which were lidded portable boxes with removable receptacles for excretions, the privy in a fixed place in its own room, with a valve to prevent odors from spreading, indicated a new interest in hygiene as well as privacy (Vigarello 1988, 110). The British were developing flush toilets by the last quarter of the 18th century (V. Smith 2007, 234). The French called these toilet rooms *lieux à l'anglaise*, acknowledging the English origin (and perhaps suggesting the origin of the British word "loo") (Vigarello 1988, 110; Bryson 2010, 355). In France, the bidet for washing the genital and anal areas appeared after 1740 (Vigarello 1988, 105). In upper-class houses, the several rooms adjacent to the bed-chamber for washing and hygiene were decorated in rococo designs, indicating a renewed approach to bathing as a sensual pleasure. Both in England and in France, the ability to harness water supplies resulted in displays, not only in the cascades and fountains found in gardens, but also in basins, baths, and water closets inside the house. Nonetheless, piped water was rare even in the houses of the elite in the 18th century, although servants made close stools and baths feasible for the privileged. The English preferred the large but expensive plunge

The close stool of Franz Joseph I, emperor of Austria (1830–1916), is in the collection of the Kammerhof Museen der Stadt Gmunden. The close stool, a cross between a privy and a chamber pot, was portable but required emptying. (Fine Art Images/Heritage Images/Getty Images)

bath, a deep but narrow pool, while the French liked the tub bath, and the elegant and sometimes frivolous designs of their bathrooms suggest the pleasure that they took in them (Girouard 2000, 225, 252, 232).

Increasingly, though, baths consisted of cold-water experiences, taking them out of the realm of the pleasurable. Both medical and religious reasons account for this. The skin was still seen as porous, but new theories held that, instead of letting toxins in, the skin could also help to expel them from the body. Dirt got in the way of this process (Bryson 2010, 353). But hot water opened the pores too much, so cold water was preferred. The Catholic Church had wavered in its advice on bathing, sometimes seeing it as an element of civility and other times as evidence of vanity, but the Protestant Reformation, reacting against the excesses of the Catholic Church, leaned toward a modified asceticism. Plain clothes, lightly ornamented churches, temperance, and moderation were encouraged. John Wesley, the founder of Methodism, is credited with coining the well-known phrase "cleanliness is next to godliness"; the actual quote from his 1778 sermon was "Slovenliness is no part of religion. Cleanliness is indeed next to Godliness" (Bryson 2010, 353). Juxtaposing cleanliness to slovenliness indicates that this was not necessarily a reference to bathing but that a certain tidiness of person was seen as a reflection of inward grace. Cold baths, then, provided a suitable amount of denial of pleasure along with a degree of cleanliness. They also served to distinguish hardworking ascetic Protestants from pampered, decadent aristocrats (Vigarello 1988, 98).

At the end of the 18th century, cleanliness acquired a closer identification with hygiene. The appearance of illness and epidemics in dirty, malodorous places was too much to ignore, so cleanliness of place was recognized as a public benefit. Municipal water systems and street cleaning grew in importance, with the emphasis on the improvement of the atmosphere rather than personal cleanliness, particularly of the poor. The elites, with the means to bathe more frequently, did so, leading personal hygiene to reflect class distinctions (Vigarello 1988, 146, 152–54, 159–60). The theory that illness resulted from moral weakness was supplanted by the idea that poverty itself caused illness, due to the harmful environment of crowded urban living conditions. Efforts at improvement, to be effected by private charitable organizations, not public agencies, were directed at places, not individual people (V. Smith 2007, 265–79).

Also at this point, at the end of the 18th century, attitudes toward cleanliness in the young United States began to diverge from those in Europe. Americans had adopted European modes of behavior—such as those articulated in *The School of Good Manners*, published in New England in 1715, in which Eleazar Moody reprinted older French and English books on civility—including, "Come not to the Table without having your Hands and Face washed, and your Head combed" (quoted in Bushman and Bushman 1988, 1219). But the birth of the United States coincided with an interest in gentility among the rising middle class. One of the markers of gentility was personal cleanliness, at least of the face and hands. Prescriptive literature guiding genteel behavior spelled out the necessity of washing the visible parts of the body, as well as polite conversation, neatness of dress, sitting up straight, and other aspects of civility. That citizens of the early republic should be encouraged to behave like European aristocracy in their personal deportment might have been ironic, but it also gave them a power: anyone could achieve social respectability. Following a few rules enabled members of the middle class to elevate themselves socially. It also enabled them to look down on those who chose not to participate in this coded behavior. The poor remained unrespectable by choice, not happenstance, in this view because they refused to wash themselves and observe other niceties. The middle class was thus able to consolidate its status in a fluid society (Bushman 1993, xv–xvi, 409–15).

While cleanliness might have been the preferred state, the prevalence of bathing in the late 18th and early 19th centuries is difficult to determine. In 1799, Elizabeth Drinker, a well-to-do 65-year-old Philadelphian, took a shower in the backyard of her Philadelphia house and recorded in her diary that "I bore it better than expected, not having been wett all over att once, for 28 years past" (quoted in Bushman and Bushman 1988, 1214). On the previous occasion, in 1771, she was visiting mineral baths at Bristol, Pennsylvania, and likewise had had to work up her nerve. As a member of the gentry, she would have had the wherewithal to take a bath, marshaling servants to heat and carry the water, but she apparently chose not to do so. Instead, she would have washed parts of her body in a sponge-bath fashion (Bushman and Bushman 1983, 1214–15).

Elizabeth Drinker's experience reflects bathing customs that were on the cusp of change. The opportunities for bathing in public places were numerous. In the 1820s, President John Quincy Adams swam daily, nude, in the Potomac River (Seale 1986, 1:166). Rivers and mineral springs had always been popular places for bathing, either in establishments or unofficially. Public baths, appearing in Philadelphia and New York in the 1790s, emphasized cleanliness rather than the rejuvenation one would find at a mineral spring. In the early 19th century, public baths and showers spread to nearly every eastern city (K. Brown 2009, 200). Hotels, too, began to include baths, in a sign of rising expectations. The Tremont Hotel in Boston opened in 1829 with eight water closets on the ground floor and eight bathing rooms in the basement (Hoy 1995, 14). In 1836, New York's Astor Hotel provided a bath and water closet on each floor. By 1853, the Mount Vernon Hotel in Cape May, New Jersey, offered baths in every room (L. Wright [1960] 2000, 234). These opportunities to bathe in public places would have most likely been used on occasion, not as a regular event. Even taking a dip in a nearby river was possible only seasonally in most places.

Bathing in private homes remained uncommon. Without running water, heating and carrying gallons of water was laborious, obviously most feasible in households with servants. Municipal water systems piped water to the edge of the property. Philadelphia, which had a water system, counted 401 bathtubs in private houses in 1823 (K. Brown 2009, 207–8). But even without a municipal water supply, cisterns storing rainwater in the attic or wells in the yard provided water that could be pumped with hydraulic rams or force pumps. Even though it was possible to have a bathtub supplied by running water, bathing was confined to the households of the wealthy or industrious. For a daily bath to become the norm, more than just technology needed to be in place. Cleanliness had to become a desirable habit, not only a sign of gentility.

By the 1840s, a number of reform movements were sweeping the United States. Temperance, abolitionism, and religious awakening were among the nationwide movements that absorbed Americans. To some, the belief that the United States was capable of improvement and that citizens had it within their power to effect change was one of the redeeming virtues of the nation. To others, reform played out on a more personal level, and health was one area of concern. Beliefs about cleanliness accorded with those in the 18th century, which emphasized the role that the skin played in ridding the body of filth. Accumulations on the skin were seen as an impediment to the proper elimination of wastes (Bushman and Bushman 1988, 1222–23). William Buchan, whose book *Domestic Medicine* was published in London in 1769 and in 17 American editions before 1800, noted, "When that matter which ought to be carried off by perspiration, is either retained in the body, or re-absorbed from dirty clothes, it often occasions cutaneous disease, fever, etc." (quoted in Bushman and Bushman 1988, 1224). Personal cleanliness was the solution.

In the 1840s and 1850s, a number of advice manuals encouraged bathing. Catharine Beecher's 1842 *Treatise on Domestic Economy* gave a long rationale that echoed Buchan's 18th-century view of the skin as an agent in "throwing off," through perspiration, "those waste and noxious parts of the food not employed in nourishing the body." But, because "the skin has the power of absorbing into the blood particles retained on the surface," washing the skin daily was imperative (118–19). In the late 1850s, this same view of the skin as performing an important function prevailed, with a slight shift. In 1858, Edward L. Youman's *Hand-Book of Household Science* noted that the skin "is an organ of drainage, with a double function; co-operating with the kidneys, on the one hand, to relieve the system of water, and with the lungs on the other, to extrude its gases." The residue left by the "twenty or thirty ounces" of perspiration must be removed, not because it might be reabsorbed—oils took care of that—but because it might obstruct the pores (431–32).

Because of this identification of oils on the skin, soap arose among the recommendations for bathing, first appearing in manuals in the 1850s. Youman's *Hand-book of Household Science* contained a long passage, quoting a Dr. Wilson, on how to wash one's face in a basin: Soap the hands and then rub the hands on the face. Do not use a towel to apply soap, and do not forget to rinse (434). E. G. Storke's *The Family and Householder's Guide*, published in 1859, insisted that "washing the face, hands, and arms, once a day, with soap and water," would be sufficient for people who do not get very dirty, but workmen would need to wash more often (179).

Another issue often discussed was the temperature of the water. Cold-water baths had been recommended in the 18th century for helping with blood circulation, by contracting the vessels when cold and then opening them when warm and when being rubbed vigorously by a towel. This was thought to be good for blood flow (Bushman and Bushman 1988, 1222). Hot water would open the pores, exposing them to noxious elements, and so it was to be avoided. In the early 19th century, cold water gained popularity as a curative in itself. Hydropathy, which became popular in the 1840s, used cold water in various bathing regimens, along with exercise and temperance. As a curative, it engaged the patient in the healing process and fed into the enthusiasm for self-improvement and reform (Ogle 1996, 12).

There were dangers associated with cold-water bathing, though, and Catharine Beecher recommended it only for "persons in good health, and with strong constitutions" (120). Within a decade or two, the enthusiasm for cold-water bathing began to wane. In 1859, E. G. Storke noted that the cold bath "was at one period very generally considered as a tonic," but he called that belief "altogether unfounded." A warm bath was best "for insuring personal cleanliness and for promoting the health and functions of the skin" (176). Increasingly, the pleasurable aspects of baths were identified as reasons to take one. Cold water might produce "an invigorated feeling, and a warm glow on the skin" (Beecher 1842, 120). If so, "the pleasurable sensation is such that the daily bath is not likely to be omitted," so cold bathing was permissible (Lyman and Lyman 1859, 351). But a warm bath, it was finally recognized, "will be found to impart a feeling of refreshment, to improve the strength, and to render their spirits lighter and more cheerful" (Storke 1859, 177). George Templeton Strong, who installed a bathtub in a building behind his New York house in 1843, expressed those lighter spirits when he described his bathing experience: "I've led rather an amphibious life for the last week—paddling in the bathing tub every night and constantly making new discoveries in the art and mystery of ablutions" (quoted in Bushman and Bushman 1988, 1225).

The frequency of bathing depended on the availability of facilities. Catharine Beecher bemoaned the fact that "there is no civilized nation which pays so little regard to the rules of health, on this subject [cleanliness], as our own. To wash the face, feet, hands, and neck, is the extent of the ablutions practised by perhaps the majority of our people" (120). Caroline Gilman's 1840 advice manual described a "hand bath" in great detail, maintaining that the whole body could be washed satisfactorily without immersion. Although she simplified her advice, saying, "You have nothing to do but to remove your clothing and apply the water to your whole body with your hands; and then rub your skin dry," she amplified her advice with options as to temperature of the water, employment of brushes, amount of water, and how to protect the floor or carpet (61). In 1859, Joseph and Laura Lyman's manual advised "as a general rule for cool weather, a full bath twice in a week will be found sufficient to secure the highest degree of health and comfort" (350).

The popularity of bathing after about 1840 can also be seen in published house plans, which included separate rooms for tubs as well as water closets. Water closets—mechanisms that used water to carry away excretions— were on the market by the late 18th century. Like bathtubs, they could function without a municipal water supply or sewer system, but their cost and intricacy limited their ownership to the well-to-do and ingenious. As the next chapter will explore, their desirability was not assured. This critical element of the modern bathroom underwent a long process to gain acceptability.

Nonetheless, architectural plan books began including both bathtubs and water closets. John Hall's plan book, *A Series of Select and Original Modern Designs for Dwelling Houses*, published in 1840, was the first American tome to include these facilities in houses. They were always separate from each other, in rooms located at the rear of the building, with the water closet most distant from the living areas. Catharine Beecher's *A Treatise on Domestic Economy*, from 1842, did not include any water closets. But she did lay out an elaborate area in the backyard that provided for a "bathing-room" piped to a pump and boiler, which were also connected to the adjoining kitchen, so that "great quantities of hot and cold water can be used, with no labor in carrying, and with very little labor in raising it," assuming the water was coming from a well or underground cistern. Nearby, at the rear of the yard, were two well-ventilated privies (276).

That same year, Andrew Jackson Downing's book of house plans and garden designs, *Cottage Residences*, included water closets in a couple of plans. He explained that because the water closet was small—it "does not actually require a space larger than 3 by 4 or 5 feet"—it could be put any-where: "it may therefore be introduced in the first or second story of almost every house," although he pictured it in only two of the nine designs in the book. Downing included a diagram and a lengthy description of a water closet that he had taken from the work of John Claudius Loudon, a Scot-tish horticulturist (107–8). On one plan, Downing located the water closet at the end of the second-floor wing of a servants' quarters, suggesting by its placement not that this was for the use of servants, but rather that it be situated as far away as possible from polite company. At the other end of the servants' quarters, closest to the main bedrooms, was a bathing room, which, being located over the kitchen, could be "supplied with hot water by pipes leading to a boiler in the kitchen below" (141). Downing's next book, *The Architecture of Country Houses*, published in 1850, included more bathtubs and water closets, especially in the more expensive designs. The most common treatment was a second-floor room with a tub and a water closet, but he also placed water closets on the first floor, near the kitchen in one case, and next to a boudoir in another (288, 308, 326, 350, 322, 339). In 1846, the popular magazine *Godey's Lady's Book* published a model design that included a water closet, but it was reached from the backyard, similar to the designs that included privies, with no internal connection to the rest of the house ("Model Cottages" 1846, 134).

In the 1850s, architectural plan books continued to advise the installation of bathrooms, placing them ever closer to bedrooms, if only for the convenience of the sick. C. P. Dwyer's 1856 manual argued that cottages of "the better class" should have a bathroom near the bedchambers, "for the special benefit of invalids," implying that bathing had a role in curing illness (115). The architect Minard Lafever (1856) also saw a medical benefit to baths, arguing that an "apparatus for bathing" should be available in every house and in large houses on every floor on which there were bedrooms, "for the better preservation of the health of the inmates." He included a detailed discussion of how to provide running water where public waterworks were not available. He also advised water closets, "shower-baths" over tubs and a sink in every bedroom as well as in the bathroom (426–27). By contrast, the Philadelphia architect Samuel Sloan was less enthusiastic about bathing. For several years, beginning in 1860, he provided house designs that ran monthly in *Godey's Lady's Book*, but only about half of them contained bathrooms or water closets. Several of them had both, in a room on the second floor.

These plan books indicate the uneven acceptance of piped bathtubs and water closets. Not necessities, they were optional features of plans that were themselves only suggestions. Slowly the water closet made its way to the second floor, adjacent to the bathtub, at least as an acceptable consideration for a new house. Despite available if imperfect technology, the bathtub and water closet were only hesitantly adopted on a personal level. As public policy, though, cleanliness gained adherents.

Because of the 18th-century identification of filth with disease, lack of cleanliness became identified with epidemics. With this, cleanliness became a public issue, expanding far beyond the personal. Yellow fever epidemics of the 1790s sparked two different reactions among doctors, who formed separate organizations based on their beliefs. Members of the

College of Physicians held that the disease was brought to the United States by ships from disease-ridden foreign areas, while Academy of Medicine members thought the disease originated in "putrid exhalations" from low-lying areas in cities. Both of them recognized that public health required the involvement of government, either to quarantine disease-bearing ships or to clean urban neighborhoods of filth. The latter approach saw public cleanliness as a virtue. As one newspaper article observed in 1798, "All the large towns are turning their most serious attention to maintaining CLEANLINESS in their houses, yards, and streets. Their suffering experience has not been learned in vain" (quoted in Blake 1956, 9). The urban poor were urged to clean themselves and their surroundings as a matter of public health.

Civic cleanliness—the idea that this should be the responsibility of local government—caught on slowly. Personal waste continued to be viewed as a nuisance, not a health threat, and the disposal of it was left to the individual, who utilized cesspools and manure pits or ladled the waste from privy vaults with pails. Sewer systems were used for draining streets, which helped remove the dead animals, garbage, and standing water that were seen as a cause of disease, not for the removal of personal waste. Street cleaning became recognized as a municipal function. Attitudes toward the responsibility for disease shifted slowly. While cholera epidemics in the 1830s had been seen as a moral failing, particularly affecting the impoverished, by the 1860s, cholera was viewed as a social problem, something of concern to the larger society (Melosi 2000, 39, 59).

The interest in public health in the 1860s also derived from experiences during the Civil War. The example of Florence Nightingale during the Crimean War allowed for a role for women and civilians in the area of health, sparked by the high rate of deaths from disease among the troops (Hoy 1995, 31). With the onset of the Civil War in the United States, the U.S. Sanitary Commission formed as a semiofficial auxiliary to the army to urge hygienic practices at army installations (Melosi 2000, 66). The commission raised money for supplies, provided more than 15,000 volunteer nurses, and undertook inspection and statistics-gathering programs, emphasizing the prevention of disease. Although antiseptic practices were not recognized, general cleanliness, in an attempt to reduce disease-causing filth, helped improve conditions in camps and hospitals (Hoy 1995, 37, 61). After the war, the thousands of women who had worked for the sanitary commission went back to their cities and towns, spreading the word of public hygiene. Furthermore, the sanitary commission's experience showed that centralized planning and concern for cleanliness benefited public health, laying the groundwork for greater civic involvement after the war.

The growing imperative of cleanliness—necessary for personal health, social acceptability, and public welfare—had a number of physical expressions in the first half of the 19th century in the United States. More and more private homes installed bathing facilities and water closets; in 1849, 3,500 bathtubs were counted in private houses in Philadelphia, out of the 15,000 that were supplied with municipal water (Wilkie 1986, 650). Meanwhile, more municipalities undertook to provide water to their citizens, sometimes including public outlets that were free to the poor. Municipal sewer systems, while not intended for personal waste, undertook to eliminate general filth in parts of cities. The stage was set for a broad sanitary reform movement after the Civil War.

In the 19th century, Americans found many reasons to espouse cleanliness in the name of health, both personally and politically. Religious imperatives had less effect on personal behavior regarding cleanliness. At the same time, the pleasurable aspects of a warm bath began to be promoted. Although the technology was available, the modern bathroom did not begin to take shape until the political, in the form of sanitary reform, affected the personal, in the design of that most private space, the bathroom.

Chapter 2

SANITATION: CREATING THE BATHROOM

There is no inherent need for the three fixtures now identified with the bathroom—toilet, sink, and tub—to be in one room. Water and sewer pipes could extend anywhere, and there is no advantage, other than economy, to have them run to and from the same room. Instead, the creation of the bathroom as a three-fixture space was due to now-discredited theories of disease and contamination. Sanitarians of the 1870s and 1880s alerted the public to the dangers of "sewer gas"—so successfully that the modern bathroom still takes the form advocated by these public health proponents. The creation of the bathroom is a story of newly recognized professionals, conflicting scientific theories, and how they affected the home.

The introduction of bathroom functions into the home was not new—washbasin, chamber pot, and bathtub had brought these functions indoors a long time earlier. What was new was the connection of these functions to larger systems—water and sewer. With this, fears arose of unseen hazards. Some of these concerns (such as the purity of drinking water) were justified, while others (such as safety from sewer gas), even if not justified, were no less sincere. But validated in retrospect or not, late–19th-century thinking affected the creation of the bathroom.

Concern about infectious diseases produced many theories on their transmission. By the middle of the 19th century, scientists focused on environmental filth. The miasmatic, or zymotic, theory held that putrefaction of substances produced gases, or a miasma, conducive to the spontaneous generation of elements that caused diseases in humans. As one scientist observed disapprovingly, "dirty clothes, bad smells, damp cellars, leaky plumbing, dust, foul air, rank vegetation, swamps, stagnant pools, certain soils, smoke, garbage, manure, dead animals, in fact everything physically, sensorially, esthetically, or psychically objectionable, were lumped together as 'unsanitary' . . . and were regarded as a sort of general 'cause of disease' to be condemned wherever found, 'for fear of epidemics'" (Hill [1916] 1920, 9). One solution was the removal of stagnant water, and municipal governments saw to the drainage of low-lying areas of cities, while homeowners concerned themselves with soggy basements. Another was the disposal of human excretions, and cities built sanitary sewage systems at an increased rate.

The introduction of water closets into houses had brought noxious effluvia into the home, overwhelmed earthenware sewer lines, and overflowed cesspools. A pernicious effect of indoor plumbing was sewer gas—the gas that emanated from sewers, entering houses through drains in fixtures or by leaky sewer lines running underneath the house. As the 1881 publication *Sewer Gas and Its Dangers* held, in cities like Chicago "sewer-gas is the cause of more physical suffering, and the cause of more diseases, than any other one thing" (G. Brown 1881, 17). Sewer gas—a combination of all of the gases of the putrefying elements in the sewer—was invisible and could be odorless, heightening the sense of danger. Unlike other miasmatic effects, in which the poor bore the brunt of the infectious diseases, sewer gas exposed the wealthy—those most likely to have plumbing in their houses—to disease (Wingate 1883, 172). From the late 1860s until the 1890s, sewer gas was seen as a deadly threat to the healthy home.

The combination of domestic threat and municipal connections called for new expertise. Sanitarians, including doctors, civil engineers, and others from allied fields, took a new interest in public health, forming the American Public Health Association in 1872. Sanitary engineering, a profession that arose in the late 1870s, combined engineering and science to protect the public health (Tarr 1984, 248). By 1883, sanitary engineers were seen as a profession occupying the middle ground between architects and contractors (Stone 1979, 298). Also a part of this new sanitary professionalism was the creation of state boards of health to oversee water quality, beginning with Massachusetts in 1869 (Tarr 1984, 241).

The public shared a concern about sewer gas, perceiving it as a direct threat, and sanitarians published articles in such popular journals of the day as *Ladies Home Journal, Popular Science Monthly*, and *Sanitary Engineer*, which was founded in 1877 by plumbing manufacturer Henry C. Meyer and directed at the public as much as plumbers. Because sewer gas entered houses, homeowners took an interest, and many argued that it was a wife's particular duty to be cognizant of the plumbing in her house. Mrs. H. M. Plunkett's 1885 book, *Women, Plumbers, and Doctors; or, Household Sanitation*, claimed on its title page that it would show that "if women and plumbers do their whole sanitary duty, there will be comparatively little occasion for the services of the doctors." Plunkett asserted that "women are more interested in preventive medicine and household hygiene than men" (10). One group not called on to solve the problem of sewer gas were architects. As one sanitarian sniffed, "It might be expected that our architects would give special heed to sanitary requirements, but thus far they have been too busy with the aesthetic side of their profession" (Wingate 1883, 179; Adams 1996, 42).

Plumbers had the skill to secure the house from sewer gas, but, according to the sanitarians, they were inherently untrustworthy and needed close supervision. Plumbers, whose name derived from the Latin term for lead, were workingmen—plumbing was a trade, not a profession. Plumbers learned their craft through apprenticeships, not in school. One critic charged that "the number of plumbers competent to do good work is small . . . The mass of the trade are grossly ignorant of scientific principles, and are influenced too strongly by mere considerations of profit." Although he conceded that good plumbers "have been snubbed by architects, cramped by customers, their motives distrusted and their intelligence belittled," there did seem to be a class prejudice at work (Wingate 1883, 178). Not only were sanitarians from the upper classes, the homeowners likely to have a bathroom in the 19th century were as well. Most of the sanitarians' advice was directed at ensuring that plumbers did the right thing through close supervision. Cities began adopting regulations for plumbing beginning in the early 1880s, specifically to ensure that this happened.

Sanitarians in the United States initially followed British precedent. There, in the 1840s, Edwin Chadwick had surveyed the sanitary condition of the poor and advocated environmental sanitation, promoting the "sanitary idea" that filth produced disease. American cities adopted the idea that a clean water supply and effective sewage disposal systems would improve health (Stone 1979, 288; Melosi 2000, 12). After the Civil War, the more specific focus on sewer gas also echoed the British writers. Col. George E. Waring Jr. led the charge in the United States, becoming the leading proponent of sanitary facilities and raising the status of sanitary engineering. Waring trained as an agricultural chemist and worked as an agricultural and drainage engineer with Frederick Law Olmsted and Calvert Vaux on the creation of Central Park in New York. After serving as a cavalry officer in the war, Waring traveled in Europe and, after returning to the United States, began publicizing the dangers of poor drainage and sewer gas (Cassedy 1962b, 163–64). William Paul Gerhard, born and educated as a civil engineer in Germany, worked for Waring in the early 1880s and went on to become the best publicist of the sanitarian movement. His book, *House-Drainage and Sanitary Plumbing*, first published in 1882, went through multiple editions. In the seventh, published in 1898, he was still insisting that sewer gas was a scourge and ventilation was the answer. Although sewer gas could enter the home through any plumbed fixture, and kitchen sinks and bathtubs were just as suspect as water closets, attention naturally focused on the water closet because it was this fixture that necessitated the connection to a sewage system. Two solutions presented themselves: not to have an indoor water closet, which meant the continued use of the privy, or using a material other than water to cover up the excreta. Before the water closet became available, people had relied on privies or, in more cases than we would like to believe, nothing at all. One sanitarian suggested in 1870 that in much of the United States, "the corn-field and the thicket are the only retreat provided" (Waring 1870, 27). So a privy was certainly an improvement. A privy, or outhouse, is an enclosed space, usually wooden, with a seat and a vault underneath to catch the deposits. In rural areas, the vault could be a simple hole in the ground, and once it was full, the privy could be moved to a site over a new hole. At Fort D. A. Russell in Wyoming, an 1887 inspection revealed that the ground behind the barracks and officers' quarters was "honey-combed with abandoned and filled up pits" (quoted in Hoagland 2004, 187). At that point, the post had been occupied for only twenty years. In urban areas, however, there was little space for moving a privy, so the vaults, constructed of brick, were intended to be emptied. This unpleasant job involved ladling the contents into a "night cart," which then rumbled through the city, often spilling its contents. By the late 1840s, hand-operated pumps and closed wagons had improved this chore (Worthington 1990, 453).

There were then two aspects of privies that concerned public health officials. One involved privies that were not emptied regularly and allowed to overflow. Tenement landlords, in particular, were deleterious in this regard. Overflowing privy vaults and cesspools contributed to the miasmatic air that sanitarians feared, although the openness of the surroundings meant that the evil gases were soon dissipated. An intermediate solution, such as that employed at an 1864 tenement house in New York City, was a multicompartment wooden privy, with a brick vault below. Piped water washed the contents of the vault into the city's sewers. This presaged New York's Tenement House Act of 1867, which required that privies be connected to sewers, where available. The act also mandated one toilet or privy for every twenty residents (Dolkart 2006, 47, 60).

The second drawback to privies was the hazard of locating them near wells. Like cesspools, which received waterborne sewage, privy vaults were rarely completely sealed. Both were likely to contaminate the water supply. As sanitarian William Paul Gerhard described the privy, "It rivals with the leaching cesspool in nastiness and danger to health. It pollutes the soil, taints the water in the well and contaminates the air of the neighborhood. A privy must always receive unqualified condemnation" (Gerhard 1884, 44).

Furthermore, reluctance to use the privy due to its distance from the house resulted in health problems. For those hesitant to use the privy, chamber pots served as temporary solutions, especially at night, but they had to be emptied frequently. Privies were preferred during the day, but Gerhard noted that "in cold weather and during rain-storms persons are liable not to use it when they ought to, and trouble of the digestive organs is sure to follow, as every physician knows. This is especially the case with females and with delicate children. Sick persons and invalids may suffer severely from exposure to the weather" (Gerhard 1882, 153). A further problem with privies was that they were highly visible and that modest women were therefore reluctant to use them. As Waring noted, "If the walk [to the privy] is exposed to a neighboring work-shop window, the visit will probably be put off until dusk" with a "pernicious" effect on her health (1870, 27).

Users had slightly different objections to privies than public health officials. For the users, simple convenience was more important. Generally, privies' separation from the dwelling meant that they were either too far away or too close. In 1913, Mrs. Fred Lebeau, who occupied a house in northern Michigan owned by the copper-mining company where her husband worked, asked company management to install a toilet in her house, citing a litany of problems with the privy. First, she cited her handicapped daughter, who was on crutches due to "tuberculosis of the bone" and a cast on her foot. Then she mentioned her own infirmity: "And another thing I have the same sickness in my right hand. It is seventine weeks. It is that I do not work with it, I have my hand rapped up like a broken arm." Her housework was difficult to accomplish: "You can see just one hand to do the work. And the care of seven children. The oldest one aged 13 years is sick since one year." She also took in two boarders out of need: "So that I can pay the expenses of my washing outside and a dressmaker to repare the clothes of the family. You see it is very hard for me to do my work" (quoted in Hoagland 2011, 29). The care of seven children and two boarders was complicated not only by her infirmity, but by the distant privy, which was even more difficult for a girl on crutches.

If too close, however, the privy's smell reached the house, especially in hot weather. At the same company, other tenants pleaded for indoor toilets because, as James H. Berryman noted, "the out side toilet makes

The earth closet was invented by Reverend Henry Moule in the 1850s, about twenty years before this model was produced. Rather than using water to carry away waste, the earth closet used dry earth to cover the waste and mitigate the odor. (SSPL/Getty Images)

an awful odor at this time of the year"; Philip Miller explained that "the old one [privy] which we have now is about 12 to 13 ft. away from the kitchen, which makes a very bad smell in the summer time and brings many flies"; and Alex A. Brown claimed "the out house cause[s] such an awful smell in the warm weather on account of the box [vault] leaking" (quoted in Hoagland 2011, 28). No one wanted to be too close to the privy, but if it were too far away, it was inconvenient.

The other method that did not rely on water for sewage disposal was the earth closet. Invented in England by Rev. Henry Moule in the late 1850s, it received a patent in the United States in 1868. One of the investors in the company that produced it was sanitarian George Waring, who became a steadfast supporter of the system. A number of other patents for earth closets were issued in the United States as well (Sipe 1988, 27–28, 32).

Basically, the earth closet used earth instead of water. Behind the seat was a reservoir of dry earth; when the user pulled a lever, earth covered the deposits. A trap door allowed the mixture to fall to a holding space below. The moisture- and odor-absorbing capacity of the dry earth was seen as its greatest asset, permitting the device's usage inside the house. As Waring trumpeted, "A properly constructed Earth-Closet may be kept in constant use in an unoccupied room. It is absolutely free from odor. There is an entire absence of the depressing, headachy effect that always accompanies the water-closet or night-chair" (1870, 16). Waring particularly encouraged the earth closet's use in sick rooms, for invalids with limited mobility. The portable earth closet had a small receptacle below, similar to a metal drawer. Other built-in earth closets had large concrete holding tanks on the floor below. An intermediate, stationary version had a tank the size of a chamber pot. Eventually, though, the holding tank of whatever size would have to be cleaned out, the earth spread out and dried. It could then be used again—as much as six times, according to the literature—or spread on gardens as fertilizer (Sipe 1988, 30–31). Waring even promoted its sale to neighboring farmers. But the earth closet's greatest attribute was that it was not connected to pipes and therefore not a vehicle for sewer gas.

The earth closet's primary drawback was the labor entailed in maintaining it. The used earth would have to be removed and new earth put in the reservoir, perhaps as often as once a day. The dirt that was removed would then have to be dried, either in a greenhouse-like arrangement outside or in a pan beneath the stove. The earth closet also created dust, because the dirt was dry when it was poured into the tank. Waring also encouraged the use of ashes, especially for city dwellers with limited access to dirt, but ashes would have been even dustier. The disposal of the dirt or ashes in urban areas was an additional problem. Finally, the earth closet was apparently not as odor-free as advertised (Sipe 1988, 34–35).

Although earth closets continued to be manufactured into the 20th century, they were never hugely popular. Much more appropriate for rural situations than for settled areas that would soon receive piped water and sewer, earth closets had a brief surge of popularity in the early 1870s. But as William Paul Gerhard wrote in 1884, "It is certainly much cheaper to have a properly managed earth-closet and to confine the plumbing in the house to a kitchen sink, a force-pump, a tank and a kitchen boiler. Certain advantages, however, of an indoor water-closet, as regards comfort, convenience and health, must be conceded" (45–46). Waring himself realized that the public preferred water closets and marketed his earth closets for situations where water closets were not appropriate. He continued to caution the public about sewer gas even when it was clear it would not make them turn to the earth closet as a solution (Cassedy 1962b, 165; Handlin 1979, 463).

The convenience of the indoor bathroom overrode any concerns that Americans might have had about it. Easy to reach in any weather and not requiring any physical removal of excreta, the bathroom and in particular the indoor toilet became increasingly popular during the last quarter of the 19th century. The question then became how to mitigate the evil effects of sewer gas, and for this, the sanitarians had ample advice. Their recommendations became so ingrained in the public mind that they continued to be followed long after germ theory had changed the calculus for a sanitary home. The sanitarians' alarm about sewer gas helped shape the modern bathroom.

Ventilation was the cardinal rule for combatting sewer gas. The waste pipes needed to be vented, and the soil pipe, extending above the roof, was found to be the best solution. This pipe should be accompanied by a fresh-air inlet near the bottom, which had the additional advantage of preventing siphonage, which happened when a change in air or water pressure emptied traps of their water, rendering them ineffective (Gerhard 1882, 58–59; Ogle 1996, 129). In addition, the bathroom itself should be on an exterior wall so that it could have a window. Fresh air to dispel the gases was vital.

Next, the sewer gas should not be permitted to enter the room from the drains. Traps in each drain should close off the sewer. The S-shaped trap, which left water completely blocking the pipe to prevent any gases from rising up, proved to be the most effective. Although initially there were doubts about the efficacy of water in preventing the penetration of sewer gas, this was proved wrong around 1880, when water became recognized as the best sealant. Plugs for basins were an additional protection (Gerhard 1882, 59, 133–34; G. Brown 1881, 166; Ogle 1996, 132).

Getting the sewage out of the dwelling as smoothly as possible was also desirable. As one sanitarian advised, "Not an atom of filth should be allowed to cling to the sides of waste-pipes" (G. Brown 1881, 220–21). Heavy cast-iron pipes replaced porous earthenware ones. In the early 1880s, screw-jointed wrought-iron pipes began to replace cast-iron ones, which had been joined with lead caulking (Stone 1979, 297). To determine if there were gas leaks, a plumber could add peppermint oil to the exterior soil pipe and see if the odor were detectable inside the house.

Keeping the pipes open and accessible was less a convenience to the plumber than a means of dispelling sewer gas. No longer should pipes be enclosed behind walls or in wooden casings (G. Brown 1881, 217). Gerhard advised that the collection of pipes serving a bathroom "be as plain and as open—which does not necessarily mean unsightly—as possible. Keep all pipes outside of walls or partitions, have them where you can constantly see them . . . Dispense with woodwork as much as possible" (1884, 46). Gerhard even quoted Waring's description of the ideal water closet: "made of white earthenware, and standing as a white vase in a floor of white tiles, the back and side walls being similarly tiled, there being no mechanism of any kind under the seat, is not only most cleanly and attractive in appearance, but entirely open to inspection and ventilation. The seat for this closet is simply a well-finished, hardwood board resting on cleats a little higher than the top of the base, and hinged so that it may be conveniently turned up, exposing the closet for thorough cleansing" (Gerhard 1882, 196). As Harriet Plunkett observed approvingly in 1885, "There is a growing fashion of arranging all fixtures in what is called the 'open' manner, i.e., with no wood casings about them at all. The bath-tubs stand up on feet, the lavatory-slabs are supported on metallic brackets, and the whole arrangement leaves no dark corners to become filthy" (119). Plunkett may have been overly optimistic, though; contemporary illustrations do not indicate that the open style of fixtures and pipes, much less white fixtures and tiles, became widely adopted until the early 20th century. Kitchens and laundry rooms—places occupied by servants—adopted open pipes and unenclosed sinks long before bathrooms. A room used by the family, such as a bathroom, had to maintain conventions of style and not appear overly utilitarian. Several decades would pass before the stripped-down aesthetic advocated by Plunkett would be widely acceptable.

Because sewer pipes were inherently dangerous, sanitarians advised concentrating the fixtures to eliminate long runs of sewer pipes. William Paul Gerhard echoed the advice of British sanitarian S. Stevens Hellyer when he advised, "Plumbing fixtures should be concentrated in a house as much as possible in vertical groups, so as to render necessary only few vertical stacks of soil and waste pipes, and to avoid long horizontal runs of pipes, which are objectionable, between floor-joists—first, because they necessitate the cutting of beams; second, because they prevent the running of waste-pipes with proper fall" (Gerhard [1882] 1898, 112; Hellyer [1877], 1893, 143–45). The shorter the pipe, the more likely it was to be flushed out completely after each use. In a publication oriented to less expensive houses, which would have only one bathroom, Gerhard advised that "the bathroom should be as nearly as possible directly over the kitchen, so that one waste pipe and one line of vent pipe may answer for both" (1884, 46).

The effect of this advice was to advocate for the modern bathroom—three fixtures in one room. Washbasins in bedrooms were inadvisable, as were bathtubs in dressing rooms or water closets in convenient nooks. The three fixtures should be concentrated to eliminate long runs of sewer pipes. They should also be removed from the bedroom, where the oblivious resident would be inhaling poisonous fumes all night long. Gerhard advised "remove plumbing fixtures from sleeping rooms, as sewer-gas, entering these through leaky joints or defective traps and fixtures, would be much more dangerous to persons inhaling it during sleep than during hours of active exercise" (1882, 123). Fixtures previously scattered around the house should be brought into one manageable room.

And for some sanitarians, one room should suffice. Along with concentrated fixtures, sanitarians also advised fewer of them. As Gerhard advised, "It is much better to have only one water-closet in a house, used constantly by all its occupants, and therefore frequently flushed, than to have half a dozen or more, each used only a little" (1882, 122). The location of this room was also an issue. "In view of the great danger to health from defective plumbing," it made sense to some to locate the bathroom "in an annex, separated from the living and sleeping-rooms of the house" (Gerhard 1882, 113–14). But then the convenience inherent in having an indoor bathroom would be lost, because its proximity, especially as opposed to the privy, was one of its selling points. Instead, Gerhard recommended separating the water closet from the bathroom, "such as is common in Europe, but little known in this country" (1882, 123). While Americans readily adopted some advice from the sanitarians, and eventually adopted others, the separation of the toilet from the rest of the bathroom was one that they never warmed to. Instead, the more common solution was the one offered by an architect in the popular 1882 book *The House That Jill Built, after Jack's Had Proved a Failure*: "There is one bath-room for all the chambers of the second floor, not too remote but somewhat retired, and having no communication with any other room" (Gardner [1882] 1896, 177).

In their association of sewer gas with infectious diseases and their broader belief in disease agents arising from putrefying filth, the sanitarians were soon forced to confront new evidence in disease transmission. Germ theory emerged from the work of such scientists as Robert Koch, Louis Pasteur, and Joseph Lister in the 1860s and 1870s. Identifying microscopic organisms as causes of disease, they developed the field of modern microbiology and found ways to combat harmful bacteria. These microorganisms could be in the water or air, but they always came from a previous case of the same disease; they could not generate spontaneously (Tomes 1998, 32). The theory did not immediately revolutionize disease prevention, but once the bacilli of typhus, cholera, and tuberculosis were identified in the early 1880s, the evidence became convincing. Germ theory would demand new behaviors and arrangements, but it was several decades before a broad swath of Americans accepted it and altered their behavior as a result.

The rise of germ theory meant that not only was there a shift from putrefaction to germs as the cause of disease; it also meant that there was a shift from sanitarians to scientists as the authorities, as well as a shift from general sanitation to personal hygiene as a public concern. Germs could be identified only in a laboratory, so it was bacteriologists, epidemiologists, and collectors of vital statistics who framed the next approaches to public health. Charles V. Chapin, the superintendent of health in Providence, Rhode Island, for nearly 50 years, was the acknowledged leader of this field. Heralded as "the great American pioneer of modern public health,"

Chapin trained as a medical doctor, but his greater contribution was in bacteriology and epidemiology and in publishing his findings widely (Hill [1916] 1920, 7).

With the rise of the contagionist theory, environmental sanitation was no longer the primary solution. Worrying about the air, particularly odorless components of the air, as the sanitarians had done, justified a concern beyond one's own house. Beginning with Chadwick's work in Great Britain in the 1840s, water and sewage became a municipal concern, not just individual. The sanitarians of the post–Civil War period in the United States pushed for clean water, highly confined sewage systems, and regulation of plumbers, all in the name of public health. Harriet Plunkett argued for the public element of public health: "Whether we live in the country, and our neighbor's cess-pool leaks into our well, or he spreads a morbific fertilizer on his land where the poisonous effluvia can enter our windows; or in the city, where his decayed or ill-made waste-pipe, laid next our wall, lets the sewer-gas into our house, or a choked and broken drain infects our soil—we have a direct interest in his house and grounds" (1885, 203).

Germ theory promoted a public health that was more directed at hygiene, or individual cleanliness. Water contamination, especially by fecal matter, continued to be a real concern, and broad public actions were still the realm of the new public health professionals. But diseases that had been proven to spread through spit or coughing meant that personal behaviors had to be changed. Other people could be hazardous, and germs could be found on public transportation or at public gatherings (Tomes 1998, 92). Germs were also thought to lurk in dust and dirt, so thick carpets and overstuffed furniture fell out of favor (McClary 1980, 34). Cleanliness became much more important, especially in the bathroom. Easily cleaned tile floors and walls, as well as smooth earthenware and enameled iron fixtures, were recommended for bathrooms.

The filth theory and germ theory had elements that overlapped, so the shift to new ways of thinking was gradual. Like sewer gas, germs were invisible and ubiquitous. Harriet Plunkett, in incorporating germ theory into the older sanitary science, held that disease germs emanated from the sewers. She knew that "fermenting organic filth can not generate the typhoid poison," but she still felt that it helped it develop: "it has a vast influence in developing the seeds when once planted" (131, 144). There was nothing that the sanitarians did to which the contagionists could object; even Charles Chapin acknowledged that "advocates of the filth theory did much good." He applauded their "efforts to secure better water, to build good sewers and drains, and promptly remove excreta from dwellings" and called these actions "true sanitation" (1902, 239).

But in 1902, Chapin declared victory for the contagionists, publishing an article titled "The End of the Filth Theory of Disease" in which he stated flatly, "We know that the gaseous emanations from decaying matter do not produce specific disease" (236). He then mentioned a number of infectious diseases and showed that in each case, mere filth, or putrefying material, was not the cause.

A decade later, contagionists shifted their approach to emphasize contact infection and the possibility of a healthy carrier, in a movement called the New Public Health. Dangers from sewer gas, dust, and fomites (inert objects that harbored germs) were played down as advocates of contagionism attempted to rid public health policy of the last vestiges of 19th-century sanitarianism. As Hibbert Winslow Hill wrote in 1916 in *The New Public Health*, "The old public health was concerned with the environment; the new is concerned with the individual. The old sought the sources of infectious disease in the surroundings of man; the new finds them in man himself" (8). He also noted, " 'Defective plumbing,' such a nightmare twenty years ago, has been conclusively shown to have nothing to do with disease-generation or disease-propagation whatever, unless perchance there be an actual gross leakage of infected sewage" (12). Gradually, isolating the sick became more important than ridding the environment of dust and dirt (Tomes 1998, 237–39).

The virtue of sanitation, though, continued to stay

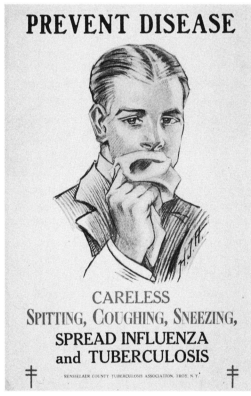

PREVENT DISEASE

CARELESS
SPITTING, COUGHING, SNEEZING,
SPREAD INFLUENZA
and TUBERCULOSIS

RENSSELAER COUNTY TUBERCULOSIS ASSOCIATION, TROY, N.Y.

By the early 20th century, scientists had convinced Americans that germs caused disease, which was spread by personal contact. General filth was no longer seen as a cause of illness. Public service advertisements were created to educate Americans on how to avoid spreading germs. (National Library of Medicine) with Americans, finding its way through articles and advertisements into the public psyche (McClary 1980, 43). The bathroom would be a place of hard surfaces—enameled iron and vitreous-china fixtures, tiled walls and floors, unornamented and easily cleaned. Advice from the anticontagionist sanitarians, however, would also continue to influence the public: three fixtures would be concentrated in one room, pipes would be exposed, fixtures would have traps, and the room would have a window. Many factors other than scientific theories helped form the modern bathroom, but ideas about sanitation and hygiene were critical influences.

Chapter 3

TECHNOLOGY: FURNISHING THE BATHROOM

The technology of the three basic bathroom fixtures was in place by the 1890s and has not changed much since. Sink, bathtub, and toilet were developed incrementally, not invented by one person, and originated mostly in Great Britain, which led the world in pottery and iron industries, the two critical materials for bathroom fixtures. Once American industries had mastered the British models, they continued to develop the designs. Mechanization of the production process and such government actions as standardization and trust-busting caused prices to drop in the 1920s, enabling fixtures to become available to a greater portion of the population.

In the United States, the materials of these new fixtures became a battleground between the industries that produced them. Both the vitreous-china producers and the producers of enameled cast iron entered the bathroom-fixture business, and both argued that they had the superior product. Before turning to the form and function of each fixture, a brief overview of these two industries shows that technical improvements to the materials, mechanization of production, and consolidation in the industry contributed to the growing availability and popularity of bathroom fixtures.

With earthenware and porcelain containers serving in washstands and as chamber pots, the pottery industry had a role in bathrooms before there were fixtures. Earthenware, however, was porous and easily stained, so it was the development in the United States of vitreous china in the 1890s that positioned American pottery makers to dominate parts of the sanitary-ware market (A. Maddock 1962, 113–14). Vitreous china is earthenware that has been fired, coated with a vitreous glaze, and then fired again. The vitreous coating, which contains glass powder, makes the object tougher, denser, and shinier. Most importantly, the material is waterproof and stain resistant. Initially, vitreous china was prone to warping and splitting, but those deficiencies were remedied over time. Porcelain, a higher-grade clay fired at a high temperature to render it impermeable, also continued to be popular for some bathroom fixtures.

Thomas Maddock, a potter who immigrated to the United States from England in 1847 with some technical knowledge, claimed to be the first to manufacture sanitary ware in America. By 1873, he made basins and bowls for water closets, but such was the superiority of British imports that his retailer insisted that he stamp them as having been made in Staffordshire (T. Maddock 1910, 19–23; A. Maddock 1962, 213). Trenton, New Jersey, where Maddock located his business, which continued in his family until 1929, became the heart of the sanitary-pottery industry in the United States. There, dozens of small firms—by 1909, 34 firms employing 5,000 workers—produced sanitary ware in small batches (Stern 1994, 125). The employees were highly skilled craftsmen organized into unions. The management of these companies organized into the Sanitary Potters Association in order to fix prices, a stranglehold that was broken by a federal antitrust suit in 1923.

Half of the workforce in the sanitary-pottery industry were pressers, skilled craftsmen who pressed clay into molds. A single item such as a toilet might require sixteen different pieces into which clay had been pressed; after drying for a day, the components were stuck together, allowed to dry for several weeks, and then fired in a beehive kiln for more than a week. Two innovations helped to streamline the process. German potters developed slip casting, in which the clay was poured into molds, eliminating much of the skill. The Universal Sanitary Manufacturing Company in New Castle, Pennsylvania, introduced this process in the United States in 1908, employing unskilled, nonunionized workers as it shifted from batch production to bulk production. In Trenton, managers introduced the new technique slowly, building new plants that employed nonunionized laborers. The second technological change involved firing. Loading a kiln and controlling the temperature traditionally required skilled workers. Universal introduced the gas-fired Dressler tunnel kiln, developed in England, in 1915, eliminating the need for skilled workers, reducing staff, and cutting firing times from several days to as little as fifteen hours (Stern 1994, 144–47, 166). The tunnel kilns needed to run continuously, at close to full volume, to be profitable, facilitating the shift to bulk production and consolidation in the industry.

Greater efficiency, though, came at a cost for skilled workers, who embarked on a bitter industry-wide strike in 1922. Management refused to deal with the union, in some cases for as long as ten years (A. Maddock

1962, 322). One economist estimated that in 1927 a sanitary-pottery company would need two-thirds of the labor to produce ware and half the labor to fire it that it did in 1922. For the consumer, however, these technological changes resulted in more affordable sanitary ware. Six years after the strike, retail prices had dropped 37 percent (Stern 1994, 215).

The other industry vying for the sanitary-ware market was cast-iron producers. Cast iron lent itself easily to sinks and tubs, but over time it rusted, despite the application of paints. In the 1870s, J. L. Mott Iron Works of New York developed a process of enameling cast iron by reheating an already-cast item and then sprinkling a vitreous compound over it (Winkler 1989, 18). Once it cooled, the item had the same rust resistance as vitreous china. Although called "porcelain enamel," no porcelain was involved. The difficulty with enameled cast iron was that the enamel and the cast iron expanded and contracted at different rates—a problem for an item that was designed to be filled with hot water. By the late 1880s, better techniques for enameling began to address this issue. Enameled cast iron was not as durable or stain resistant as vitreous china, but the milder use of a bathtub, as compared to a kitchen sink, say, made it suitable for the former use. The development in 1926 of acid-resistant enamel, which stood up to extensive cleaning, paved the way for the complete dominance of enameled cast iron in the production of bathtubs.

When Standard Manufacturing began producing cast-iron sanitary ware in 1875 in Pittsburgh, it was able to make one or two cast-iron tubs a day (Winkler 1989, 18). The company introduced enameled cast iron in 1883. In 1899, Standard Manufacturing merged with several other companies to form Standard Sanitary Manufacturing Company, which then dominated the enameled cast-iron sanitary-ware industry. By 1900, Standard Sanitary was producing 150 tubs a day (Rodengen 1999, 34).

Enameled cast iron was not as suitable for toilets, due to their complex design. By 1927, nearly all bathtubs in the United States were made of enameled cast iron, while nearly all toilets were made of vitreous china. Sinks split the industries, with vitreous china taking between a quarter and a half of the market, despite the fact that it cost three-fourths again as much as cast iron (U.S. Department of Commerce 1931, 816–17; Gries and Ford 1932, 222). Savvy producers of cast-iron sanitary ware diversified their product line by acquiring sanitary potteries. J. L. Mott, which in 1881 had imported from Staffordshire all of the sinks and toilet bowls offered in its catalog, acquired the Trenton Fire Clay and Porcelain Company in 1902 (Winkler 1989, 18). Standard Sanitary acquired the Great Western Pottery Company of Ohio in 1913 (Rodengen 1999, 34). The Kohler Company, founded in Sheboygan, Wisconsin, in 1873 as a foundry making cast-iron agricultural implements, produced iron water troughs and hog scalders, to which feet could be added to make a bathtub, or so its catalog copy suggested. By the mid-1890s, Kohler shifted its focus to enameled cast-iron sanitary ware (Moskowitz 2004, 70). In 1925, it acquired a sanitary-pottery company in Trenton, operated it there for two years, and then moved operations to a new plant in its company town of Kohler, near Sheboygan. With the major sanitary-ware companies producing both enameled cast-iron and vitreous-china products, the industry consolidated into fewer companies that dominated the sanitary-ware industry.

Of the three basic fixtures in the bathroom, the sink is the simplest. Deriving from a bedroom washstand, which was a table or cabinet with an earthenware bowl on it or sunk into it, its connection to earthenware is clear. A well-equipped washstand had a bowl in which to wash; a large pitcher to provide wash water; a smaller pitcher for drinking water; a brush vase to hold toothbrushes; a soap container; a mug; a chamber pot stored in the cabinet of the washstand, removed at night for convenient use; and a slop jar, also in the cabinet of the washstand, into which used water from the washbasin would be poured (A. Maddock 1962, 137). The washstand itself would be of wood construction, perhaps with a marble slab top and backsplash. The bedroom washstand was of course predicated on domestic servants to deliver the water and take away the contents of the chamber pot and slop jar. Houses without servants were likely to have a washbowl in or near the kitchen, the source of hot water. At the lowest end of the spectrum, people washed in containers that served other purposes, such as frying pans or horse troughs.

With the advent of piped water, the washstand became a fixture, and, for reasons discussed in the previous chapter, that fixture was most often placed in the bathroom. The idea of a round porcelain bowl continued, now sunk into a marble slab and served by water faucets. A marble backsplash could be added, and the basin could be elaborately decorated. Marble had drawbacks, though, in that cleansers would pit and stain it, and the joint between the bowl and the slab provided a space for dirt to lodge. By about 1900, the porcelain basin and marble slab combination fell out of favor, and one-piece alternatives entered the market. Enameled cast iron had the advantage that it could provide large slab space around the basin, which was more difficult with vitreous china, but the enamel was prone to chipping. Solid porcelain sinks, another alternative, were heavy and their glaze would craze. In 1904, a method was developed to overcome the warping to which large objects of vitreous china were subject, and vitreous-china sinks became more viable. Vitreous china is impervious to acids, except for hydrochloric acid, and holds up well over time (A. Maddock 1962, 292–94). Both enameled cast iron and vitreous china featured one-piece construction, avoiding any seams where germs might be found. The sinks hung on the wall or were placed on pedestals or thin legs, minimizing the construction underneath so that the floor could be easily cleaned (Allen 1907, 227). By 1911, the oval basin had replaced the round one.

The common term in America for this fixture in the early 20th century was "lavatory," although "sink" grew in popularity through the 20th century and is more common today. In Great Britain, however, "lavatory" today refers to the whole room—a three-fixture bathroom—and "basin" denotes the sink. In the 19th century, "sink" was more commonly used to refer to a depression in the ground filled with water and also denoted a latrine.

Faucets were essential for conveying the piped water to the sink. The type of handle tended to indicate what sort of mechanism it manipulated. The first faucet to become popular had a Fuller ball valve, in which a lever handle moved a conical soft-rubber disk against or away from a metal seat to control the flow of water. The rubber element needed maintenance, though, and the water flow was hard to regulate, so these valves lost popularity in the 1920s. Compression valves usually had a cross handle that controlled a stem that threaded into the valve body, moving a hard-rubber disk against or away from a metal seat. Appearing in the 1890s, compression valves are basically the faucet technology that is universally used today (Bock 2001, 49). Faucets and related visible piping were originally brass, which takes constant maintenance and is feasible only with domestic servants. As a result, vitreous-china handles, minimizing the exposed metal, became popular. Nickel plating also solved the exposed-brass problem, but nickel too needed polishing, and if scrubbed too often, the nickel wore off and exposed the brass underneath. Finally, in the 1920s, chromium plating, which did not require polishing, appeared (Bock 2001, 48–49).

Sinks, as well as tubs, required a means of keeping the water in the bowl, and by the 1930s, the two recommended means were chain and plug and "pop-up waste," which operated by lifting a knob on the slab of the sink. As early as 1882, sanitarian William Paul Gerhard had expressed concern about the chain and plug in tubs, because that "device gets unclean from soapsuds," and lingering dirt in the bathroom was the sanitarian's worst fear. Fifty years later, the chain and plug were deemed "somewhat old-fashioned for lavatories" (Gries and Ford 1932, 221).

The final improvements to faucets were mixer taps, which combined hot and cold water so that they came out of one spout. Available in the 1890s, they did not become widely used until the 1920s. People may have simply preferred to fill a basin and shave or wash from it, rather than leave the water running (Bock 2001, 50). Standard Sanitary's 1919 catalog had no mixer taps, but in its 1923 catalog, nearly half of the lavatories

A roll-rim tub with vitreous-china faucet handles. Photo by James W. Rosenthal, Washington Place, Honolulu, Hawaii, 2007. (Library of Congress)

were equipped with a "combination hot and cold water fitting"; by 1927, most of the sinks pictured in its catalog had combination faucets. The deep basin, still common today, reflects the outmoded custom of filling a sink and washing from it. In fact, if people use running water to shave or wash, they do not need to fill a basin, although it may conserve water to do so.

As one writer noted in 1907, "A good ever-present supply of hot water is one of the necessities for the full enjoyment of a bath room" (Cutler 1907, 171). Initially, fixtures in the kitchen provided the piped hot water. Cold water from outside was piped into the boiler, which only stored the water, despite its name. From the bottom of the boiler, water was piped to an iron container called a "water back," on the back of the coal-fired, cast-iron stove. From the top of the water back, the heated water was piped back to the boiler. Pipes carried the hot water from the top of the boiler to fixtures in the house as needed (Ogle 1996, 70). The disadvantages of this system were spelled out in a catalog for its replacement, the gas-fired water heater:

> The Old Way, with Water-back and Boiler. The amount of hot water available at one time is limited to about one-half the capacity of the boiler. Unless there has been a hot fire burning for at least two hours there is no hot water on hand. . . . It takes at least two hours to heat water enough to take a bath. Wastes fuel by heating up range and everything near it, only a small part of which heat is transferred to the water. Costs more per gallon of water heated. Seldom ready when wanted. Makes work with dirt with coal and ashes. Water never hot in the middle of the night, when, if wanted at all, is wanted in a hurry. (Monarch 1905, 3)

By the end of the 19th century, the gas-fired hot-water heater came on the market. Its advantages were heralded by the same catalog:

> "The New Way, with Monarch Water Heaters. No limit to the quantity available. Any amount ready as fast as it can be drawn. Causes no heat anywhere except in the water, where it is wanted. It takes thirty seconds. Saves fuel by absorbing into the water all heat produced. Costs less per gallon of water heated. Always ready. No work, no dirt. Hot water ready night and day. It can be removed from rented houses as readily as any other stove" (Monarch 1905, 3).

Initially located in the kitchen, just as their predecessors had been, gas-fired water heaters were increasingly located in basements, along with furnaces. In the 1930s, electric water heaters began to compete with gas (Cowan 1983, 94).

The tub is similar to the sink except that its large size demands certain considerations. Marble was the height of luxury, although extremely rare; porcelain was also highly prized, but its fragility, great weight, and considerable expense left it in the realm of the wealthy. Vitreous china was also extremely heavy, even if such a large piece could be cast without warping. Cast iron, having been used for troughs and other large containers, became the preferred material. Once an effective enameling began to replace paints in the 1880s, enameled cast-iron tubs dominated the market. Set on feet, the tub with one rounded and sloped end, called the French pattern, was the most common form by 1911, and without feet is still the most common form today.

Enameled cast-iron tubs were initially encased in wood, as their sheet-metal predecessors had been. The development of the roll rim obviated the need for wood casing and also eliminated the dirt-collecting seam between wood and metal. Affordable tubs would be enameled on the inside and painted on the outside with white enamel paint (Keene 1911, 82). The feet and roll rim posed a problem, though, in that it was difficult to clean underneath and behind the tub. Manufacturers provided a ring base to cover and eventually replace the feet (Allen 1907, 220). In 1911, Kohler fabricated a tub with a rim or apron that extended to the floor, making a double wall. The other sides could be attached to the bathroom wall, providing an efficient use of space with clean lines and no dark corners to harbor germs. Nonetheless, the single-shell roll rim remained on the market, sold by the major manufacturers into the late 1930s. Manufacturers offered tubs in lengths ranging from four and a half to six feet, although five feet became the most popular (Gries and Ford 1932, 217; Giedion [1948] 2013, 704).

The flush toilet is a considerably more complicated fixture, using water to clean out the receptacle. The development of the toilet—called the "water closet," even in America, until well into the 20th century—was the work of many hands, proceeding incrementally. One type of water closet relied on movable parts to remove the waste with water. Generally credited with the first of these was Sir John Harington, godson of Queen Elizabeth I, who in 1594 developed a water closet with a seat with a pan underneath, an overhead cistern to create a rush of water, and a valve to release waste water. It did not catch on (Yee 1975, 72). More popular was the pan closet, which had a hinged metal pan above an earthenware bowl filled with a few inches of water. A handle would tip the pan, spilling its contents into the water, but it was hard to keep the pan clean, and the pan did not prevent air from the sewer line from entering the room (Yee 1975, 72; Stone 1979, 304). In 1775, Alexander Cummings, a Scottish watchmaker, patented the first water closet with a valve. When a handle was pulled, water both entered the bowl and left it through a flap-like valve at the bottom of the bowl. Cummings also introduced an S-shaped pipe at the bottom of the bowl that created a seal, preventing odors from reentering. A few years later, Joseph Bramah, a cabinetmaker, improved upon Cummings's valve, and although his version was complicated and noisy, he successfully produced and sold it. The Bramah remained on the market for more than a century (Carter 2006, 153–55; Yee 1975, 72). English plumber Thomas Crapper was one of many who patented improvements to the water closet, and although his name is memorable, excrement was called "crap" long before Thomas Crapper developed water closets (Penner 2013a, 98).

Americans were somewhat slow to adopt these new water closets. Popular in the United States was the most basic type, the hopper, which had a conical bowl and was flushed by jets of water that entered under the rim, spiraling down to rinse the bowl. Without much water surface to receive waste, though, the hopper was difficult to keep clean. Pan closets were widely used in this country until the end of the Civil War, when valve closets began to take over. Thomas Maddock gave some sense of the hierarchy when he quoted an 1877 British publication: "The valve water closet apparatus is chiefly fixed, in good houses, for private and visitors' use and the pan closet for servants' use" (T. Maddock 1910, 80). The primary drawbacks of these were that the movable parts did not hold up well over time and that the flap or pan was difficult to keep clean. Because none of these toilets operated by discharge of water from a tank, they were connected directly to the water supply.

Instead of relying on mechanical parts to control the flush, the next type of toilet used the force of the water to flush the waste. Englishman T. W. Twyford developed the all-earthenware washout closet in about 1870. In this, the flush emptied the bowl, but without much force; as one critic wrote, the flush "gravitates through the trap in a most unselfish way, taking little or nothing with it" (quoted in L. Wright [1960] 2000, 202). In 1885, Twyford improved on his own work and designed his new washout closet to be exposed, not enclosed in wood, with the mechanical parts that regulated flushing in the water tank high above the bowl (L. Wright [1960] 2000, 205; Yee 1975, 72). In 1889, D. T. Bostel, also British, developed the washdown closet, which had a larger body of water in the bowl and brought the flushing water in at the rim (Gottfried and Jennings [1985] 2009, 281).

In about 1870, J. R. Mann developed the siphonic closet, which divided the incoming water so that part entered the bowl through a pressure jet near the bottom, while the other part entered at the rim. When flushed, the water at the bottom of the bowl started the emptying process by suction, and when the bowl was empty and air entered the bowl, the siphonic action stopped (Gottfried and Jennings [1985] 2009, 281). Much quieter than the washdown and washout closets, it also did not need the rush of water created by gravity, so high tanks were no longer necessary (L. Wright [1960] 2000, 204). The siphonic jet closet was slow to catch on, however, and did not become common in the United States until the 1890s. Still, the washdown type, sometimes made of enameled cast iron, was available into the 1930s, offering an alternative that was one-quarter the price of a siphon-jet vitreous-china model (Gries and Ford 1932, 218–19). Through the 20th century, Great Britain and Europe generally used the washdown closet, while North America and Asia favored the siphonic jet closet (Carter 2006, 165).

The introduction of water into the bowl of the toilet ran into a problem with the round bowl, which is that the centrifugal force of the water might cause it to splash over the sides. A "save-all tray" was required to catch this overflow. Charles Harrison of New York solved this problem in 1877 when

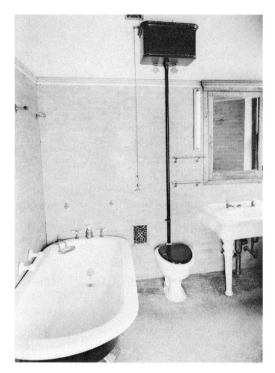

The Edward E. Ayer House in Chicago, Illinois, featured a bathroom with a roll-rim tub, toilet with raised tank and pull chain, and sink with two faucets. Photo by Harold Allen, 1964. (Library of Congress)

he patented the oval bowl, whose shape broke the centrifugal force. His invention sped the acceptance of the washout, washdown, and siphonic jet toilets. The oval bowl is still favored today (Winkler 1989, 19).

The washout and washdown toilets required water tanks to intensify the force of the rushing water. Some tanks operated with siphonic action, which began with the pulling of a chain. The tank, at first positioned on the wall high above the toilet, was made of sheet metal encased in wood, succeeded by enameled cast iron. Earthenware tended to sweat when cold water was brought into warm rooms, but vitreous china did not have the same drawback.

With the siphonic jet, which did not rely on the force of incoming water, tanks were brought down to the same level as the toilet. With the enlargement of the water-supply pipe, other types no longer required the additional height (Allen 1907, 233). By 1903, Standard Sanitary's catalog asserted that "the low tank combinations are conceded to be the most modern fixtures" (56). By 1922, sanitary potters had developed a "closet combination," in which the tank was integrated with the toilet (A. Maddock 1962, 291).

A consensus on the height of the toilet seat was achieved early in the 20th century. The 19th-century toilet seat tended to be 16 or 17 inches high, but this was reduced to 14 or 15 inches. This accommodation may have been for children, but a concern that the higher seat "tightens up the abdominal muscles, and hinders the peristaltic action of the intestines" also argued for a lower height (Gries and Ford 1932, 218; A. Maddock 1962, 288). In 1966, Alexander Kira's groundbreaking ergonomic study of the bathroom recommended a semisquat toilet whose height would be

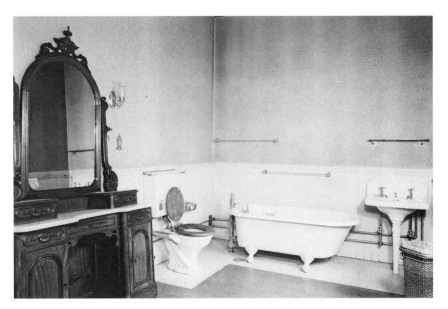

The second Harrison Gray Otis House in Boston, Massachusetts, featured a bathroom that included a low-tank toilet, a roll-rim tub, and a pedestal sink with two faucets. Photo by George M. Cushing, 1967. (Library of Congress)

9 inches in order to facilitate the most physiologically sound posture for defecation (Kira 1966, 61–68).

Even after toilets were freed from their wooden casings, the seats of the washdown, washout, and siphonic jet toilets were still wood, set on small rubber disks that rested on the vitreous china. By 1910, Standard introduced its Ivorite seats, in which a pyroxylin, or nitrocellulose, material was sprayed onto wood. Advertised as nonporous, nonstainable, and acid-proof, the new seats were a glossy white, not given to fading or cracking. By 1910, manufacturers agreed on a standard spacing of the holes for the hinge at five and a half inches on center so that seats were replaceable and interchangeable (T. Maddock 1910, 114).

In the first decade of the 20th century, the bathroom often contained more than three fixtures. In the 1907 book *Sanitation in the Home*, Chicago sanitary engineer Jonathan K. Allen mentioned the foot bath tub, sitz bath tub, nursery bath tub, shower bath, and bidet, all of which appear in contemporary catalogs (221–24). By Allen's description, the foot bath tub, 26 by 21 inches, 15 inches high, was designed for the "restful and tonic effect of a foot bath" (221). The sitz, or hip, bath, measured 30 by 27 inches, 13 inches high in front and rising to 21 inches in back. The user

The Ivinson Mansion in Laramie, Wyoming, featured a bathroom with a double-walled tub and a needle shower. Photo by Jack E. Boucher, 1974. (Library of Congress)

would sit in the bath with legs out over the front, leaning against the back. Besides serving as a substitute for the foot bath tub and being a convenient place for bathing small children, Allen also mentioned "the distinctive use for women," without explanation (221).

The shower bath, with the water pouring down from a perforated head, had a receptor, or shallow tub, on the floor, with a waterproof curtain surrounding the user. Allen noted that shower baths could also be placed in tiled alcoves, with a waterproof curtain instead of a door (222). The regular bathtub could also serve as the receptor, again with a waterproof curtain. Water could be plumbed into the wall, or else a rubber tube would run from the tub's faucet to the shower head (Allen 1907, 222; Keene 1911, 80). Allen also mentioned a rain bath, which had larger and lower-velocity drops than a shower bath, and a needle bath, which delivered water in jets from several rows of pipe around the body, as well as from above (222).

Showers proved a hard sell for women. The Standard catalog attempted to win them over in 1906: "Women frequently object to the use of a shower bath on account of the wetting of the hair. In order to overcome this, we

This bathroom inside the Whittier Mansion in San Francisco, California, featured a roll-rim, footed tub with an embossed design on the outside, a heavily ornamented bidet, and a toilet with a raised tank and pull chain. Photo by Jack E. Boucher, 1960. (Library of Congress)

furnish, free of charge, with each 'Standard' Portable shower, a rubber cloth cap of the highest grade and quality through the use of which this wetting is obviated." The catalog also noted that women should find showers useful: "To most women the shampooing of their hair is a tedious and vexatious task, but not so if they use a shower bath" (67). Catalogs pictured women demurely peeking out of shower curtains. By the 1930s, a government publication declared that "the shower is used more today than ever before" (Gries and Ford 1932, 219).

Allen dismissed urinals for the home as superfluous as well as likely "to become offensive." Bidets he saw as expensive and redundant to a sitz bath (224). Bidets never really caught on in the United States, despite their popularity in Europe. Americans often associate the bidet with sex-related cleansing of genitalia, but, as the Maddock catalog of 1927 explained delicately, "the bidet fixture is an appliance designed to maintain for the user a constant state of cleanliness of the private parts. Its most important use is that of a rectal bath. . . . The bidet is usually installed alongside of the water closet. In using the bidet it is not necessary to undress. The clothing is in the same position as when using the water closet" (cited in A. Maddock 1962, 301; Kira 1966, 10). Nonetheless, bidets were never popular in the United States, and the standard bathroom equipment remained three fixtures.

Beyond fixtures, bathrooms also had accessories. The medicine cabinet—"either built in or attached to the wall"—was one of Jonathan Allen's recommendations in 1907. He advised that "the best ones have shelves of thick glass with a plate glass mirror on the door" (236). Glass shelves supported on nickel-plated brackets were both sanitary and sleek. In the first decade of the 20th century, towel racks and hooks, soap cups, drinking-glass holders, and toothbrush racks were all present, some made of vitreous china, others of brass with a nickel-plated finish, later with chrome.

The setting for these fixtures reflected the aesthetics of the fixtures as well as the latest ideas on sanitation. In the late 19th century, the heavy wooden cabinets that encased the plumbed fixtures were complemented by wooden floors, curtains, carpets, and dim lighting. Sanitarians' push to expose pipes, have white surfaces, and equip bathrooms with light and ventilation resulted in a new appearance for bathrooms. Once exposed, the fixtures could be molded into elaborate shapes, but this drew the ire of sanitarians: "Floral and architectural patterns in deep relief cover the exterior of many of their closets; even recumbent lions, and swans in full sail, with closet-basins on their backs, and other incongruous combinations, are being produced, so that it is almost impossible for a servant, however cleanly disposed, to keep such closets clean" (Hellyer [1877] 1893, 237). Straight lines and smooth surfaces were much preferred. The new fixtures were glossy white, with manufacturers competing for the whitest finish, but a border trim could be added to the bathtub, shower receptacle, sitz tub, and foot bath tub. By 1906, Standard offered eight different designs of borders that could be applied to its fixtures.

Color could be found in the walls, floors, or stained-glass windows. Jonathan Allen recommended tile for the walls because it was "impervious to vapor." The tile also offered some ornamentation to the room: "In no place may fancy tiling be used more appropriately than here. Frequently the entire interior of the bathroom is lined with art tile of costly and elaborate workmanship" (214). As a cheaper alternative, he suggested enameled sheet metal, although others suggested white enamel paint on woodwork or waterproof wallpaper (214; "Bath-Room Fixtures" 1905, 44). Tile also served for the floor, particularly mosaics in a range of color. Allen suggested "a pattern border with solid center over which rugs may be laid." Cheaper alternatives were oil-finished wood, wood parquetry, linoleum, and cement mixed with sawdust, which "gives a slightly flexible and warm floor" (215). Linoleum in a tiled pattern was suggested as early as 1905 ("Bath-Room Fixtures" 1905, 44).

Although sanitarians recommended a bathroom with hard surfaces, impervious to water, they did not have to be white. The 1906 Standard catalog recommended tile floors and wainscot, if not the whole wall, but said, "It is preferable not to make the bath room all white, as it gives a cold, cheerless appearance, and does not add any to its sanitary effectiveness" (57). Catalogs in the 1920s showed bright white fixtures against dark and pastel-colored walls. The introduction of colored fixtures in the late 1920s—a technological achievement of its own—will be discussed in chapter 7.

Besides taste and marketability, another of the many influences on bathroom technology was government regulation. In the United States, the federal government's role was limited, as health and safety concerns were addressed at the municipal level. Bathroom fixtures were dependent upon plumbing, and because of the danger perceived in piping sewage out of the house, municipal plumbing codes regulated plumbing early on. By 1882, New York and Washington had plumbing codes; by 1884, Philadelphia, Boston, and San Francisco had joined them (Gerhard 1882, 230). In most cases, plumbers had to submit plans for approval, inspectors examined the work as it proceeded, inspectors examined the plumbing again just before it was enclosed, and sometimes they tested the pipes with pressure or with oil of peppermint (Gerhard 1882, 231).

A national plumbing code could not be enforced, but it could serve as a guideline for localities. Simplification was a watchword of the Department of Commerce under Herbert Hoover, who served as secretary from 1921 to 1928. Hoover, a mining engineer, brought an interest in efficiency, elimination of waste, and simplification to the job. In 1921, the Department of Commerce brought together a Building Code Committee, composed of practicing engineers and plumbers. Relying on the practitioners' experience, as well as tests performed by the Bureau of Standards, which were delineated in 200 pages of a report, the committee issued its draft recommendations in 1922. After wide circulation and revisions according to comments, the Department of Commerce issued the final report in 1928. The government could regulate only for issues of health and safety, and the science had changed so much since the early municipal plumbing codes that many of the regulations on the books were thought unnecessary.

Primarily, the report urged simplification, presenting a recommended plumbing code that was shorter than many then in existence. Significantly, the report laid out "basic plumbing principles," which included a supply of pure water, a connection to a public sewer, a private water closet for each family in a multifamily dwelling, unenclosed fixtures of smooth nonabsorbent materials, and adequate lighting and ventilation in water-closet rooms.

The report also waded into long-simmering controversy when it proved reluctant to abandon old ideas about sewer gas. While noting that bacteriologists had established that disease-producing bacteria are rarely found in the air from sewers and drains, the committee nonetheless maintained that "health may be influenced by factors which do not cause specific diseases, for there are chemical and physiological as well as bacteriological factors involved" and that sewer air should be considered threatening to the health of a building's occupants until further research proved otherwise (U.S. Department of Commerce 1929, 7, 13–15, 17).

The report also noted that the standardization of plumbing materials and fixtures was a public benefit but not oriented toward health and safety; therefore, it could not be required under law (U.S. Department of Commerce 1929, 10). Plumbers had long sought standardization in their field; as early as 1905, the National Association of Master Steam and Hot Water Fitters had developed standards for the dimensions of pipes and fittings and weights of materials that they hoped manufacturers would adopt ("Work of Standardization" 1905, 34). Standardization finally gained acceptance with the Progressive Era emphasis on efficiency.

Within the Department of Commerce and Bureau of Standards, Herbert Hoover established a Division of Simplified Practice to bring together industry experts to develop standardized conventions. By 1928, these committees had developed standards for such items as brass lavatory and sink traps; hot-water storage tanks; wrought-iron and wrought-steel pipes, valves, and fittings; and staple vitreous-china plumbing fixtures (U.S. Department of Commerce 1929, 207). The development of the vitreous-china code began in 1925 when a group of manufacturers requested the division's help in developing standards, which it issued in 1926 (U.S. Department of Commerce 1930, 21). Providing a means for grading the quality of vitreous-china fixtures, the code defined vitreous china as a material that would pass the "red-ink test," which involved immersing a piece of china in red ink for an hour. The ink should not show through the glaze or seep more than 1/8 inch into the china (4). The publication also provided dimensional standards for eight kinds of water closets, two tanks, three kinds of lavatories (one of them, the straight-front lavatory, in six different sizes), and two urinals (8–9). The height of the toilet was fixed at 15 inches, with an allowance for "juvenile bowls" at 13 inches (10–12). Lavatories were to be 31 inches to the top of the basin, and on sinks smaller than 24 inches across, a soap-dish depression on the left side was required (14–17, 7).

The Staple Vitreous China report hailed its own work by noting that the benefits that large consumers traditionally had were now available to the small consumer, by "lowering the price by reason of broadening the field of supply." It also enabled consumers to replace fixtures more easily. Manufacturers likewise benefitted from "the well-known economies" of mass production (22). Adoption of the standards was purely voluntary on the part of the manufacturers, but it enabled them to limit their range of products. The vitreous-china standards reflected common practice in the design of the fixtures and fixed the designs of sanitary ware for decades.

In 1934, a committee of the President's Conference on Home Building and Home Ownership looked back over the past half century and concluded that "the plumbing industry has taken advantage of the opportunities that the 'Machine Age' has created and has utilized them to the fullest advantage in improving manufacturing methods, as well as the quality, the appearance, the sanitary aspects, and the efficiency of the fixtures and materials that go to make up a plumbing system" (Gries and Ford 1932, 160). The report expressed some doubt as to whether colored fixtures were a "passing fad" or worth the investment, but it pointed with pride to the efficiency of fixtures that filled with water and emptied rapidly, that were extremely sanitary, and that were even relatively quiet, out of manufacturers' concern for "the nerves of the user" (Gries and Ford 1932, 161). An artifact of mass production, standardized in materials and dimensions, and designed in sleek sanitary styles, the bathroom of 1930 could be said to epitomize the Machine Age.

Chapter 4

INFRASTRUCTURE: CONNECTING THE BATHROOM

While it was possible to have a bathroom without connections to a larger municipal infrastructure, densely built areas such as cities increasingly turned to public systems of water and sewerage in the 19th century. These systems drew individual houses into larger networks, just as electricity and gas supply systems were doing at the same time. Dense living meant that, like one's connection to neighbors through the spread of disease, one was also connected to them through the systems meant to halt that disease: water and sewer. The very private space of a bathroom led to participation in the public sphere of infrastructure.

The provision of piped-in water in urban areas happened much more smoothly than the construction of sewerage facilities. In no city, though, did they happen together; water invariably preceded sewers, usually by decades, until its effects demanded the provision of a sewerage system. Water and sewer services required modernization on a different level than the individual bathroom, but modernization nonetheless: central-ized authority, automatic operation, efficiency, technology, and scientific expertise.

Before piped-in water was available, city dwellers procured water for themselves or partook of the few common outlets. Residents drew water from wells and springs, either on their own property or public ones in the street. They also captured rainwater in cisterns. Particularly in the busi-ness sections of the city, local government provided cisterns and wells for fire suppression as being in the common interest. Failing these sources, city dwellers could pay to have water delivered by wagon to their houses. Given the difficulties inherent in these different methods of obtaining water, households typically consumed only three to five gallons per day (Tarr 1984, 228).

The provision of piped water to houses changed their residents' relationship to the physical environment, the public sphere, and new technologies. First, a source of clear, pure water had to be available. That source often shifted as urban areas grew. Second, the technology had to be present: a pump and a distribution network. Steam engines and cast-iron pipes, both technologies imported from England, provided the essential ingredients, but holding ponds and reservoirs were also necessary (McMahon 1988, 26). The complexity of the urban piped water system, which crossed public and private land and required a great deal of capital, meant that municipal responsibilities stretched the role and capacity of ill-equipped city governments (Ogle 1996, 328). For such a broad public venture, a shift in thinking was required among citizens—not only to believe that something so challenging was within the capability and purview of municipal government, but also that a water system was a necessary and desirable reason to shed long-standing concerns for individualism and the privacy of the home.

Infectious disease spurred the creation of the first water system in the United States. Philadelphia suffered epidemics of yellow fever in the 1790s, with the summer of 1793 being particularly deadly, killing about a twelfth of the population of 50,000 (Blake 1956, 37). Elected officials took steps to improve the water supply; not knowing that yellow fever is spread by virus-carrying mosquitoes, they believed the problem was in the water itself. The city contracted with English-trained engineer Benjamin Henry Latrobe to design a water system that drew on river water rather than individual wells. He proposed two steam engines: one to power pumps to pull water out of the Schuylkill River and send it about a mile to the center of the city and the other to elevate the water there so that it could be distributed by gravity throughout the city. By 1801, the system was operational.

Philadelphia's residents connected so slowly to the water supply that the system operated at a deficit for many years. The city offered free water for three years to those who had helped underwrite the cost of construction through subscriptions to water loans. And, cognizant of its duty to the poor, the city also offered free water from public hydrants in poor areas (Ogle 1996, 329). But other residents resented paying for something that they had always obtained for free. By 1814, nearly 3,000 households took water from the new system (Melosi 2000, 35).

Philadelphia's water system required constant improvement. The steam engines were balky and needed to be replaced. The city was also growing. In 1815, the city built a new pumping station at an upriver site known as Fairmount, about two miles from the city. Because Fairmount was on a hill, the water needed to be pumped only once, up out of the river; then gravity carried the water to residents. The steam pumps first installed there

Benjamin Henry Latrobe designed the pump house in Centre Square, Philadelphia, as shown in this 1807 etching by George E. Blake. Steam pumps lifted water from the Schuylkill River and sent it to this pump house, which elevated the water so that it could flow by gravity to houses throughout the city. (Library of Congress)

were replaced with water-powered ones in the 1820s. The wooden pipes that had carried water throughout the city were replaced by cast-iron pipes imported from England beginning in 1817.

Despite its technical difficulties, Philadelphia's pioneering water system was a success, and other municipalities followed suit. New York, Boston, Detroit, Cincinnati, and other cities developed waterworks over the next half century. By 1860, all of the 16 largest cities in the United States had waterworks (Tarr 1984, 231). Most of these were privately built. The difficulties in financing capital improvements publicly, which in most cities required authorization from state legislatures, made contracting with a private company more feasible. In 1830, 80 percent of the 45 waterworks then in operation were privately run (Melosi 2000, 36). But then the tide began to shift, as private companies proved to be not up to the task. Never as profitable as private investors wanted, the companies preferred to supply areas that provided the greatest returns. Poor neighborhoods and elevated areas received meager service (Blake 1956, 76). As public health became a concern that seemingly could be improved by better drinking water, city governments became more willing to see the provision of water as their proper sphere. And as cities grew larger and more densely inhabited, the purity of water from individual wells was more likely to be compromised by nearby privy vaults. Also, cities increasingly needed water for their own use, not only for fire suppression but also for street cleaning, which was viewed as another disease-prevention strategy. By 1880, the United States had 599 municipal waterworks, just over half of them privately run (Melosi 2000, 74). Twenty years later, only 9 of the 50 largest cities still had privately run water systems (Schultz and McShane 1978, 393).

With the provision of convenient, piped-in water, Americans increased their water consumption dramatically, overwhelming existing accommodations for sewage disposal. In Chicago, residents used 33 gallons per day per person in 1856, a figure that rose to 144 gallons by 1882, while Detroit consumers went from 55 to 149 in the same time span. These numbers include industrial uses, and consumption dropped once metering was introduced (Tarr 1984, 231). Meters faced widespread resistance from consumers, not surprisingly, and were introduced gradually, beginning in the late 19th century (Melosi 2000, 123–26). Water was flowing into—and out of, in a tainted state—houses like never before. Those with the means enthusiastically adopted the water closet. Perhaps a quarter of urban households had water closets by 1880, which often discharged into cesspools in the yard (Tarr 1979, 162). Although cesspools could be emptied on a regular basis, and the "odorless excavator" helped mechanize this process, overflowing cesspools created a recognized health hazard. The excess might drain into the house's basement or even the neighbor's basement.

Many cities prohibited households from connecting their cesspools to the city's drains, which were designed for storm water and usually drained into the nearest body of water. City governments understood street drainage to be their bailiwick, because they focused on facilitating the conduct of business, which meant keeping the streets passable. Open gutters became covered as cities developed, but these storm sewers also received the products of manure-strewn streets, as well as dead animals and other offal. They were not equipped to accommodate household sewage as well.

The widely adopted solution to the problem of household sewage was the water-carriage sewer system, in which water moved the excreta from each household to a common outlet. For an example of how to do this, Americans turned once again to England, where Edwin Chadwick had suggested a water-carriage sewer system in the 1840s. Chadwick's system was based on the idea that the sewers would be essentially self-cleaning, due to the water flowing through them. As a believer in filth as a cause of disease, Chadwick was concerned that sewage not remain in the pipes but be rapidly transported away from residents. He also suggested that the sewage be used to fertilize crops, thereby enabling the system to pay for itself. Although Chadwick's plan was not adopted wholesale when London finally installed sewers in the late 1850s, his ideas nonetheless influenced Americans.

The development of a sewer system had many challenges. First, it was a large capital expenditure. The system involved pipes from households and then lateral pipes, which fed into collector sewers, which fed into mains, which in the early years discharged into a body of water and, later in the early 20th century, into a treatment plant. The system usually depended on gravity, but if the topography did not comply, the sewage had to be lifted by pumps (Engler 2004, 181). The small-diameter lines were constructed of vitrified clay pipe, the larger ones of brick (Tarr 1988, 166).

A sewer system was also quite different from the individual collection of excreta that had preceded it. The sewage disappeared almost automatically, not requiring human action. It was also capital-intensive, rather than labor-intensive. And, like the provision of water, a sewer system drew the individual into a larger collective endeavor, dependent on a centralized authority. No longer was sewage the sole responsibility of the householder.

Despite the enormous cost, cities built sewers for several reasons. The initial capital expenditure was great, but sewers required little subsequent labor, compared to the physical emptying of cesspools and transporting of sewage, providing savings in the long run. Second, a system that removed the sewage immediately from the vicinity was far more sanitary than existing procedures involving privy vaults and cesspools. Third, a city with such a modern and healthful improvement as a municipal sewer would attract business and residents (Tarr 1979, 311–12). In the 1850s, Jersey City, Chicago, and Brooklyn installed sewer systems (Tarr 1984, 237). The real growth occurred, though, beginning in the 1870s, encouraged by the sanitarians. By 1907, every American city, save one, had a sewer system, and that one, Baltimore, had a system under construction (Schultz and McShane 1978, 395).

Although a great triumph of public health, municipal sewers did not happen without struggles. Two major questions needed to be resolved: how to design the sewer and what to do with its end product. The first question, whether to combine street and household waste in one sewer or keep them separate, is illustrated by the case of Memphis, Tennessee, and was resolved by the end of the 19th century. The second, whether to treat the sewage and to what degree, is illustrated by Baltimore's experience. Both

Most American cities built sewer systems in the late 19th century. This excavation is for a sewer system in Nebraska, ca. 1889. (Library of Congress)

of these debates consumed public health officials nationwide, and these case studies show how changing understandings of environmental health influenced sewage systems.

Memphis, a port city on the Mississippi River, was familiar with yellow fever epidemics, but the one in 1878 was particularly severe, killing more than 5,000 people in a city with a population of 30,000. So many people fled the city during the epidemic that estimates were that only 19,500 people lived there that summer, of whom 17,600 contracted yellow fever. The following summer, yellow fever returned but killed fewer than 500 due to the immunity the residents had developed (National Board of Health 1880, 431). The subsequent desire for action brought in the federal government, elevating the discussion of Memphis's sewers to the national stage.

Congress established the short-lived National Board of Health in 1879, with its primary concern being epidemics spread across state lines, particularly through shipping, and especially up the Mississippi River from New Orleans. The three federal agencies with medical officers were the Marine Hospital Service, the U.S. Army, and the U.S. Navy, and it was the infighting among the representatives of these agencies that doomed the National Board of Health just four years after its inception (Smillie 1943, 925; Michael 2011, 128). But in 1879, at its founding, the devastating effects of disease in Memphis led the National Board of Health to investigate, make recommendations, and publish its findings. The National Board sent to Memphis a team of three professionals, headed by John Shaw Billings, formerly with the U.S. Army's Surgeon General's Office. They were joined by Col. George E. Waring Jr., the sanitarian, who had gone from promoting earth closets to water closets to sewer systems. The committee began its work in November and issued its report on March 1, 1880.

First, the board oversaw a house-to-house inspection and issued a report on sanitary conditions. Inspectors examined 10,873 structures, 6,386 of them dwellings; only 398 of them had water closets. Memphis had 5,914 privies, less than half of which they termed "clean." The report found that the drinking water was polluted, privies were located in the basements of nearly 500 houses, a third of the basements were damp or wet, and most of the 374 sinks had no traps (National Board of Health 1880, 433). The source of drinking water for the city was the highly polluted Wolf River, wells, or cisterns collecting rainwater, some of which were located in basements, perilously close to privy vaults. The board made nine recommendations, including changing the source of the piped water. Providing ventilation in order to dispel sewer gas and other effects of putrefaction was also a concern, so the board advised "opening, ventilating, and chilling" all the houses in the city and instituting building regulations that would include elevating all houses at least two feet off the ground. To remove materials contaminated by illness, the board advised destroying rags and surplus bedding and tearing down nearly 500 buildings. To effect better drainage, the streets should be paved with gravel, and concrete curbs and gutters should be constructed. The slow-moving Bayou Gayoso, which cut through the city, not only failed to flow at times, but during high water, the river backed up into it, so the board suggested that a dam be built to prevent this. The bayou was also the recipient of much sewage, including that from privies that lined its banks, so the board advised the city to acquire the land on either sides and create a park. The board also recommended hiring a "competent sanitary officer" (National Board of Health 1880, 418–19; Peterson 1979, 90).

The most expensive recommendation was that the city build a sewer system along the lines of that recommended by George Waring. At the time of the survey, Memphis had only four and a half miles of private sewers, with 215 connections (National Board of Health 1880, 428). The main decision for city authorities was whether to build a combined system, which would

handle both storm water and household sewage in the same pipes, or to seg-
regate the two sources of waste in a separate system. The combined system
would cost more than $1,000,000; the separate one that Waring proposed
would cost $225,000 but would do nothing to cope with storm water (Tarr
1979, 317). Better gutters and street cleaning, he believed, would take care
of the runoff from storms. The essential advantage of his separate system,
as Waring saw it, was that small, smooth earthenware pipes would carry
the household sewage away from the house rapidly. Ever fearful of sewer
gas, Waring latched onto this aspect of Chadwick's plan for London. He
forbade the house connections to be larger than four inches in diameter
and the lateral sewers six inches. At the head of each branch, he installed
flush tanks, which would fill with city water and flush automatically about
once a day, in order to clean out the sewer. His system also dispensed with
manholes, the usual access from the street down to the pipes (National
Board of Health 1880, 418). Most other American cities had built combined systems, reasoning that it was cheaper to build one system than two
parallel ones, one for storm water and one for sewage. And many engineers
did not think that the sale of sewage for agricultural use would justify the
expense it took to build a separate system (Tarr 1979, 314).

Probably attracted by the low price of Waring's plan more than its
sanitarian-inspired features, Memphis officials immediately engaged Waring to oversee construction of this system. The recent establishment of
the Taxing District of Shelby County, a commission form of government,
enabled them to raise the funds required for construction, which began
in January 1880 (Ellis 1964, 65). By June 1, the onset of the yellow fever
season when all construction work stopped, about 20 miles of sewers had
been laid and were operational (Wrenn 1985, 345). By December 31, 1881,
Waring's plan had been substantially completed, with about 30 miles of
sewer lines and nearly 8,000 building connections (Ellis 1964, 66; Wrenn
1985, 345). Five years later, the system had 43 miles of sewers at a total
cost of $291,000 (Ellis 1964, 66).

Because Waring patented certain features of this system and proceeded
to sell his system to other municipalities, he had an interest in defending its
unique qualities. In response to a description of his system in the *Transactions of the American Society of Civil Engineers*, Waring claimed several
new features for his system: the complete separation of household waste
from rain water; the provision for automatic flushing; the small diameter
of the pipes; and the elimination of mortar joints in brick pipes, which
tended to catch material, by substituting vitrified pipe. The small size of
the pipes had led residents to complain of items getting caught in the pipes,
causing obstructions. But Waring went on to highlight what he saw as the

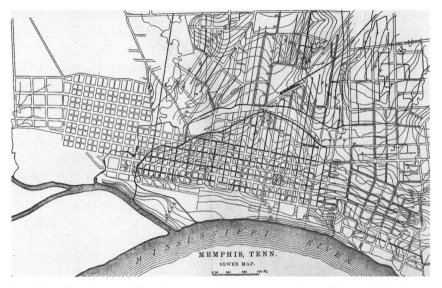

MEMPHIS, TENN.
SEWER MAP.

Deadly yellow fever epidemics spurred the construction of Memphis's sewer system in the early 1880s. Sanitarian George E. Waring Jr., who designed and promoted the system, included this map in a Census Bureau report from 1886. (City of Memphis, Tennessee)

"fundamental benefits" of his system, which were deeply intertwined with his belief in the deleterious effects of sewer gas. His system ensured the movement of "filthy accumulations in catch-basins and in sewers too large to be cleansed by their natural flow," preventing "foul and dangerous gases resulting from the decomposition of this filth." Speed was essential in moving this material away from houses, and he claimed that sewage moved from the most remote house on the sewer line into the Mississippi River in two hours. One observer said, " 'Sewer gas' is unknown there" (Odell 1881, 47, 52).

In 1882, Waring revisited his accomplishment in the pages of the *American Architect and Building News*. He noted that many of the other recommendations, beyond his sewer system, had not been carried out, and he did not want his reputation to suffer if disease returned to Memphis. The only fault he acknowledged in his system was that it was not big enough. He had planned for water consumption at 40 gallons per person per day or 250 gallons per household but found that households were consuming 2,300 gallons per day. He attributed this to the foul water supplied from the Wolf River by a private company, which required some flushing before use. But he also alluded to deliberate overconsumption of this unmetered water: "the company is not popular among the people, and . . . many leave their taps running in order to increase the cost of pumping" (143). The problem of water supply was finally solved in 1887 by the drilling of an artesian well, which produced clear, good-tasting water. The city immediately contracted with a private company to supply the city (Ellis 1964, 69).

In 1884, Waring again defended his system in Memphis. The absence of manholes was becoming a glaring omission, leaving the sewer system with no access points. Whenever city workers had to dig down to reach the sewer system, they installed a manhole. Waring insisted that they had been omitted only for the sake of economy and not at his recommendation (27). Furthermore, Memphis's public health improved markedly after the installation of his sewer system, although the new source of water probably contributed as well. In 1872, Memphis had a death rate of 46.6 per thousand, the worst in the nation. By 1889, that rate was reduced to 21.5 (Ellis 1964, 72).

Six years after completion, the *Engineering and Building Record* (successor publication to *The Sanitary Engineer*) sent respected engineer Rudolf Hering to inspect the Memphis sewer system. Hering had also toured sewerage facilities in Europe in an effort to determine the efficacy of the separate and combined systems. His conclusion was that local conditions should determine the selection. The combined system worked better in larger cities, which had to contend with storm water, while the separate system suited smaller cities better (Tarr 1979, 318–19). The empirically inclined Hering found no advantage to the ability of Waring's separate system to whisk sewage away from a house; mortality rates were similar in places that had separate and combined systems (Cassedy 1962b, 170).

In his examination of the Memphis sewers, Hering was extremely critical of Waring's "novelties," or new features. Hering noted that overflow pipes had to be provided because of the heavy use of the system. He also suspected that residents had installed "surreptitious connections" to carry rainwater away from their houses and yards. Second, he found the flush-tanks unnecessary, because the terrain was generally sloping. Third, the omission of manholes was "a failure." Moreover, the small, four-inch household pipes caused frequent stoppages, as did the six-inch pipes in the laterals. Hering concluded that "what was new cannot be called good, and what is good cannot be called new" (1887, 739).

Undeterred, Waring continued to promote the separate system of sewerage, offering his services as a consulting engineer, traveling all over the United States and Europe, and turning his attention to sewage treatment, which he argued was better effected in a separate system (Waring 1894, 943). He served as commissioner of street cleaning for New York City from 1895 to 1898. In 1898, the army sent Waring to Havana, Cuba, as part of a commission to advise on campsites for U.S. troops and offer recommendations on the sanitary condition of the city. Ironically for someone who had devoted his life to combatting the "filth diseases," Waring died of yellow fever contracted in Cuba, soon after his return to New York in 1898 (Cassedy 1962b, 171, 173–74).

The effort to build a sewerage system in Baltimore, the last major American city to obtain one, illustrates the difficulty of getting an electorate to commit to such a substantial expense. This was a widespread problem in 19th-century American cities, which were not organized for major capital undertakings. That power remained in the state government, which authorized bond issuances and municipal charter changes. The local governments were decentralized, with weak mayors and strong councilmen. Baltimore's campaign to obtain sewers also involved the debate over how, or even if, to treat sewage, at a time when the scientific understanding of treatment methods was rapidly changing.

Water was comparatively easy for Baltimoreans to obtain. A private company provided Baltimore's water until 1854, when the city acquired the company and continued to draw water from Jones Falls, which ran through the city. As the city expanded after the Civil War, though, it experienced water shortages and was forced to look elsewhere. In 1881, a new facility opened on Gunpowder Falls, about 11 miles from the city center, and continued to serve the city for the next 40 years (Anderson 1977, 67). By the late 1890s, water consumption was calculated at 95 gallons per person per day, although this probably included industrial uses (*Report of the Sewerage Commission* 1897, 14).

The rise in water consumption after the improvement of the water supply in 1881 spurred discussions of a comprehensive sewer system. Baltimore was blessed by its topography: the terrain rose 500 feet from the harbor to the far edge of the city, facilitating waterways that ran down to the harbor, so the stagnant pools of other cities were not as frequent here as in flatter cities. Waters ran into the Patapsco River, a broad arm of the Chesapeake Bay that served Baltimore's busy harbor. Although the harbor was legendarily malodorous, the politically powerless people who tended to live closest to it could do nothing about it. Baltimore also escaped the devastating epidemics that other cities experienced in the late 19th century. Still, the desirability of a sewer system was obvious to many, foremost for the good it would do for public health. And in a competitive industrial economy, Baltimore's boosters sought to promote a modern sewer system as one more reason to bring business to the city of half a million people.

There were many objections to providing this infrastructure. Baltimore, like many American cities in the 19th century, had a weak municipal government ruled by machine politics. The state government controlled the city's ability to raise money through bonds. Various interest groups lobbied against a sewer system: night scavengers who profited from the collection of the products of privy vaults and cesspools, as well as their subsequent sale as fertilizer; the wealthy elite who had private sewer systems; businessmen who opposed higher taxes; good-government groups that did not want large contracts reinforcing the machine's control; and oystermen who did not want a system pumping sewage into the sensitive waters of the bay (Euchner 1991, 278–85; Crooks 1968, 93). Baltimore had the biggest oyster-packing industry in the world; in 1880, 48 packing houses processed 7.2 million bushels of oysters (Boone 2003, 157).

To overcome all of these objections and find the political will to build a major infrastructural project took a lot of work and an unusual event. The poorly functioning municipal government was reorganized with a new charter in 1898, which gave more power to the mayor. In 1899, the elite citizens of the city formed the Municipal Art Society and began lobbying for improvements along the City Beautiful lines promoted by the Chicago World's Fair of 1893, hiring Frederick Law Olmsted to develop a plan for Baltimore's parks. Another of their projects was a municipal sewer system. Also at the end of the century, the political machine's hold ended when a reformist candidate was elected mayor. But it was the devastating event of the fire of 1904 that turned the tide. On February 7, a fire raged through downtown, destroying 70 city blocks of 1,526 buildings, although fortunately killing no one. The fire shook Baltimoreans, and they began to pull together. As the editor of the *Baltimore News* proclaimed on the day after the fire, "We shall make the fire of 1904 a landmark not of decline but of progress" (quoted in Crooks 1968, 142). The next year, a referendum included a vote on a symbol of that progress—a $10 million bond for a new sewer system. It passed by a 3–2 margin.

Once Baltimoreans had decided to build a sewer system, the next question was what kind. In 1893, the Baltimore mayor had appointed a Sewerage Commission, which brought in as consulting engineers Samuel M. Gray of Providence and Rudolf Hering of New York. The two engineers, agreeing on their findings, issued one report in late 1896. Their first recommendation was that Baltimore construct a separate system, due less to the declining fears of sewer gas than to the fact that the city had already built 30 miles of storm drains at a cost of $4 million (*Report of the Sewerage Commission* 1897, 10). Given that this infrastructure was already in

The devastating fire in downtown Baltimore in 1904, which leveled 70 city blocks, caused Baltimoreans to rethink the importance of infrastructure and civic investment to their city. One result was the construction of a sewer system—the last major American city to build one. (Library of Congress)

place, it made no sense to tear that up and start anew; nor was it possible to use the storm drains for household sewage.

The heart of the consultants' report addressed what to do with the sewage once it had been collected. The report explored three options. The first was dilution, or dumping it into a large body of water and counting on the diluting effects to render it harmless. The Patapsco River was not considered for this outlet, but a more distant site on Chesapeake Bay was. The second option was chemical precipitation, which the consultants thought was inadvisable. The third option, which the consultants favored, was filtration through sand and irrigation of crops, for which they found a site in Anne Arundel County, south of the city, which they thought would be suitable. The Sewerage Commission, however, overruled its consultants, afraid that the electorate would never support the additional cost of the filtration scheme. Construction of the first part of the system, serving 330,000 people, would cost about $3.8 million for the dilution scheme and $5.7 million for the filtration one. Furthermore, the operation and maintenance costs of the latter were much higher: $173,000 a year as opposed to $58,000 for the dilution scheme (*Report of the Sewerage Commission* 1897, 49). The commission hired additional consultants to explore currents in the bay to determine the best place to deposit the sewage and settled on a site east of the city.

Objections arose, though, from the oyster industry. Reflecting recent research about the transmission of disease, dilution no longer seemed as benign as before. In 1893, after a group of students at Wesleyan University in Connecticut contracted typhoid fever after eating oysters, scientists proved definitively that the disease could be transmitted through tainted oysters (Capper, Power, and Shivers 1983, 86). Although Chesapeake oysters were not implicated, a reputation for clean waters became even more important to Maryland's oyster industry. As a result, the mayor asked the Sewerage Commission to explore filtration and treatment options. The commission engaged a Board of Advisory Engineers consisting of Gray, Hering, and Frederic P. Stearns, a prominent Boston engineer, who oversaw soil tests in Anne Arundel County, south of the city, to see if it was appropriate for sand filtration. After construction of a $10,000 testing plant and performance of 279 test borings, the advisers concluded that sand filtration was impractical due to the quality of the soil. Instead, they selected another site and recommended treatment in septic tanks, sprinkling filters, and sedimentation basins. They proved that 98 percent of the bacteria would be removed without the sand filters, making the effluent purer than the water of the Back River, into which it would be discharged ("Baltimore's Sewerage" 1907, 632–36).

The commission was successful in persuading the state legislature of the wisdom of their advisers' proposal. The slope of the plant's site on the Back River, east of the city, not only facilitated gravity flow, but also allowed the generation of hydroelectric power, which was used to run the plant ("Baltimore's Sewage" 1909, 769). Construction of the sewerage system began on October 24, 1906, and five years later, the first house was connected. About two-thirds of the city, whose population was then about 600,000, had sewers that flowed by gravity all the way to the plant on the Back River, about 6 miles east of center city. The sewage of the remaining third needed to be lifted at a pumping station before it joined the other sewage in the outfall sewer. In 1915, the system was completed, and the Sewerage Commission, having accomplished its mission over 22 years, disbanded. Approximately 500 miles of sewers had been laid, connecting more than 100,000 homes. Although Baltimore was the last large American city to get a sewer system, by the time it did, the city was able to profit from recent research and changing attitudes and build a state-of-the-art facility (Anderson 1977, 71).

The story of Baltimore's sewers reflects the shift toward viewing the hazards of sewage as residing in the bacteria it held. No longer was "the old bugaboo of sewer gas" the driving force in the design of sewer systems. Instead, bacteria were the items to be feared; as civil engineer George Whipple said, "The danger of sewage lies chiefly in the bacteria that it contains" (1911, 20). Airtight, fast-moving sewage disposal systems were no longer the goal. Instead, removal of the dangerous impurities became the focus. The previous concept that moving water purifies itself had given way to the theory of dilution, in that a large enough body of water could render sewage harmless. But research in the early 1890s, particularly at the laboratories of the Massachusetts State Board of Health, proved that typhoid bacilli could persist in sewage, bringing into question the idea of mere dilution and raising new interest in treatment. The necessity of treating sewage favored separate systems, as at Baltimore, because the sheer volume of combined systems meant that much more sewage would have to be treated (Tarr 1979, 331). Ironically, the design favored by the anticontagionists—separate systems—also proved to be the best one for science-based treatment. Americans adopted treatment slowly, though, due in part to its great cost. In 1909, 88 percent of the wastewater of sewers was discharged into waterways untreated, and it was not until the 1930s that less than half was untreated (Tarr 1984, 239, 245).

The changing understanding of sewage treatment reflected the shift from sanitarians to scientists. Laboratory testing of sewage began to inform various treatments, as the Baltimore example illustrates. Septic tanks, which relied on the decomposition of materials in anaerobic conditions, sand filtration, and other methods treated sewage. There was a limit, however, to the extent of municipalities' perceived responsibility.

One reason that cities were slow to treat their sewage was that they did not see it as within their purview. While municipal officials were content to treat sewage when it posed a hazard to the greater good—in Baltimore's case, the oyster industry, and then only when prodded by state legislators representing those interests—many engineers did not see it as a municipality's responsibility to ensure potable water for downstream communities. As George C. Whipple, a professor of sanitary engineering at Harvard, explained it, "It is unbusinesslike to compel the purification of the sewage of a large upstream city in order to protect the water supply of a small city lower down" (1911, 22). An article in the *Engineering Record* called it "more equitable" for the downstream city to treat its water than for the upstream city to treat its sewage ("Sewage Pollution" 1903, 117). Some even questioned whether it was in the purview of a municipality to spend its funds on something that would benefit another city (Melosi

2000, 165). Federal action reflected changed attitudes on this, with laws in 1948 and 1956 aiding cities in the treatment of their sewage, but it was not until the Clean Water Act of 1972 that pollutants in waterways were seen as something that could and should be entirely prevented (Melosi 2000, 334–35, 388).

In the early 20th century, the attention shifted to the treatment of water before a city used it, rather than after. If cities took their water from a river, they treated it with filtration, beginning in about 1897, and with disinfection by chlorination around 1910 (Tarr 1984, 242). Overlooked in the concern about sewage, though, were chemical pollutants discharged by industries. Initially, some felt that these chemicals would even help prevent organic material in the sewage from putrefying (Melosi 2000, 162). But water treatment had immediate results. Mortality rates often failed to improve significantly when cities installed sewers, because the resulting pollution of the water supply instead raised rates. It was the treatment of the water supply, along with other public health measures, that caused mortality rates to improve dramatically in the early 20th century (Tarr 1984, 239, 242).

The greater shift, though, was that water and sewage became regional problems, not confined to the city limits. Seeing sanitation as an environmental issue had meant, in the mid-19th century, removing sources of putrefaction from the home and yard. Municipal sewer systems helped achieve this end. Germ theory, though, identified the source of disease in specific bacilli, not in general filth. It also served to take the responsibility for sanitation out of the hands of generalist sanitarians and make it the responsibility of well-educated scientists and civil engineers. As the reach of the identified bacteria became known, the sanitation concern expanded to sewage disposal and water purity, stretching from the home to the city to the region.

Chapter 5

INEQUALITY: ACQUIRING
THE BATHROOM

In 1898, the Viennese architect Adolf Loos wrote enviously about the American bathroom, "A home without a room for bathing! Impossible in America" (46). Loos vastly overstated the case. While the installation of bathrooms was certainly on the rise at the turn of the 20th century, there were still multitudes of people without rooms with bathtubs or even any kind of indoor plumbing. Indeed, by 1940 only about 60 percent of Americans had a bathtub or a shower. Although the technology was available for bathroom fixtures, and the infrastructure was in place in most cities, less than half of Americans—and probably less than a quarter—had bathrooms with even one fixture by 1900.

The two large segments of the American population who lagged in the acquisition of bathrooms were rural dwellers and the urban poor. The latter faced an unequal distribution of services, with their neighborhoods less likely to be served by municipal water and sewer. Even if they had access to those services, bathroom fixtures presented a cost that working-class families or their landlords often could not bear. Rural dwellers confronted logistical problems of obtaining their own piped water supply and building their own cesspools, but they also had the advantage of space in which to locate and relocate privies, making the installation of toilets less urgent.

In urban areas, the provision of water and sewer was often a partnership between public and private interests. The public entity, or maybe a private water company, piped the water to the edge of a building lot, and private interests—the building owner—piped it into the house. This system functioned well except when it came to poor areas. There, the water was often left at the curb. Tenement landlords were unwilling to bear the expense of water hookups and water closets, and tenants were unable to pay the additional rent that an equipped apartment would require.

In Chicago, for instance, a majority of residents connected to the privately run water system by 1856, paying an annual fee based on the length of the street frontage of their lot. Public hydrants served those not connected to the water system, but the resentment of those who paid for water led to the phasing out of the public hydrants by 1865 (Keating 1988, 40). The municipal sewer system, on which construction began in the 1850s, was publicly funded, not based on assessments, until 1890. Even so, as late as 1893, 73 percent of Chicagoans had only outside privies. Despite laws requiring landlords and homeowners to connect to the sewer system where available, the added cost of providing pipes and fixtures created a burden for landlords, who passed the cost onto their tenants (Garb 2005, 97).

In newly laid-out areas, the same calculus was involved: would homeowners pay the extra expense of fully equipped dwellings? Generally, the financing of the extension of the water system, sewers, and streets was borne by both the city and the property owner, who paid an assessment for the improvement. While practicality had some role in determining where new services would be placed, property owners also had a say—either to request them or object to them (Simon 1996, 27). As one study of Chicago showed, developers of different subdivisions made different choices, providing an array of options, ranging from areas where the only improvements were street grading and tree planting to others where water and sewer mains, gas hookups, paved streets, streetlamps, sidewalks, parks, and a railroad station were provided, part of a pattern of subdivisions that were sorted by class (Keating 1988, 73–76). The lots in a neighborhood without amenities would be much cheaper, attracting poorer residents. A letter to the editor of a village in Michigan in 1897 explained the difficulties inherent in committing to a sewer system. In the working-class village of Laurium, the anonymous letter writer argued that for a population still paying off the mortgages on their houses, the added debt for the village, which would be passed on in the form of taxes, was too much. Secondly, because there was a water system and residents did not rely on wells, the danger to health from privy vaults was negligible. Finally, the writer maintained that few residents would be able to take advantage of the sewer system because they would be unable to afford the fixtures, which he estimated at $100 to $150 per house (Hoagland 2010, 139–40).

As this letter writer suggested, even if water and sewer were readily available in a neighborhood, fixtures were provided or obtained unequally. For homeowners, it was one more expense to be weighed against many others. For tenants, equipped houses and flats would cost more. For reformers, the lack of indoor flush toilets was a travesty. As Margaret Byington found in her 1908 study of Homestead, near Pittsburgh, indoor flush toilets were

Privies continued to be used in urban areas well into the 20th century, including this one in Hamilton County, Ohio. Photo by Carl Mydans, 1935. (Library of Congress)

absent, even though Homestead was fully equipped with sewers and had a law that required even outside vaults to be connected to them. But the common solution was that the vaults under privies were flushed only with wastewater from the yard. Not one of the 239 households she studied had an indoor water closet. In one block, a central privy, serving 20 families, had 10 compartments emptying into one vault, which was flushed with wastewater (Byington [1910] 1974, 136, 131).

Over time, landlords provided outdoor flush toilets for their tenants, rather than retrofit them into existing buildings. New York's Tenement House Act of 1901 required flush toilets, one for every two families, in new construction. For existing buildings, which mostly had privies in the yard, the law also mandated the replacement of group privies with individual water closets "of durable non-absorbable material" (Dolkart 2006, 85–88; Lubove 1962, 134). In Chicago, a 1902 tenement-house law required toilets within each housing unit in new construction, but a survey of selected housing units 30 years later found that 31 percent of them still lacked toilets within the units (Abbott 1936, 61, 213). For those units that did have their own toilets, two-thirds of them were entered through the kitchen or pantry, indicating that they had been put in found space, which the reformer termed "an arrangement that seems very objectionable" (Abbott 1936, 221).

While the lack of flush toilets for the urban poor was a public health issue, the lack of bathtubs became more of a moral one. The lingering association of dirt with disease caused some concern for the cleanliness of the poor in the late 19th century, and as late as 1905, one reformer asserted that New York's health commissioner said that "bathing reduces the liability to colds and throat trouble," thereby decreasing cases of pneumonia and tuberculosis (Smith 1905, 576). More importantly, though, cleanliness was identified with civilization itself; as Boston mayor Josiah Quincy said in 1898, "The advance of civilization is largely measured by the victories of mankind over its greatest enemy—dirt. One of the chief and most fundamental differences between the savage and the civilized man is that the former is dirty, while the latter is relatively clean" (142). He went on to identify cleanliness with morality: "Cleanliness of the body leads to self-respect and to an appreciation of the importance of cleanliness in the household; and, when physical dirt has been banished, a long step has been taken toward the elimination of moral dirt" (142). This link between clean body and clean soul was also identified by Albert Wilhelm in an article titled "Americanization by Bath," in which he argued that bathing led to cleaner homes, which led to self-respect (281). Or, as an editorialist for the *Ladies' Home Journal* put it, "A disregard of the body and disorder in dress soon grow into moral slovenliness" ("Morals" 1896, 14).

Immigrants who crowded into the poorer parts of cities posed a particular problem for reformers because their inability to bathe was interpreted as an unwillingness, perhaps due to cultural differences. One sign of this was the apocryphal misuse of bathtubs when provided. Reformer Bertha Smith found mixed evidence of this: "The tenement landlord contends that where baths are built they are not put to their proper use, and tenement-house inspectors bear out this statement to a certain extent, in spite of the declaration of the best-known settlement worker in New York, who is conceded to know her East Side as a good churchman knows his creed: 'In all my years of work here I have never come across the family which Jacob Riis says keeps its coal in the bath-tub' " (1905, 568–69). Smith's article was accompanied, though, by a photograph she took of a "tenement bathtub" used for storage. Nonetheless, the trope of an immigrant who stored his coal in a bathtub became a sign not only of ignorance—not knowing what a tub was for—but also unwillingness to bathe. It might better be interpreted as a sign that hot water was unavailable or that what landlords and reformers were providing immigrants was not what they needed or most wanted.

Bathtubs were scarce in tenements. An 1893 survey conducted by the U.S. Bureau of Labor of "the most congested slum districts" in four cities found that fewer than 3 percent of the families in Chicago and New York had tubs, while 7.35 percent of those in Baltimore and nearly 17 percent of those in Philadelphia did (Hanger 1904, 1249). One solution was to provide public bathhouses, funded either by charitable organizations or municipal governments. The early bathhouses, which operated seasonally, were float-ing structures on a river. In the 1890s, due to the interest of progressive reformers, bathhouses became substantial, heated buildings, located in the heart of the slum, and often included swimming pools, in order to entice children.

Bathhouses were a stopgap measure, though, until bathtubs could be provided in every tenement unit. Requiring landlords to retrofit bathtubs into existing tenements was not a tactic often employed, but some munici-palities required new construction to contain bathtubs. Baltimore, for instance, adopted an ordinance in 1888 that required every new dwelling of four or more rooms to include a bathroom with a bathtub ("Bathing in the Falls" 1888, 4; *Building Code of Baltimore* 1908, 326). Still, it was decades before most of the urban poor had bathtubs. Baltimore's last public bathhouse operated until 1959 ("City Is Throwing In the Towel" 1959, 44).

The ability to bathe was defined by class. Those who could afford houses or apartments with bathing facilities gladly took them, but many urban dwellers were faced with the choice between such facilities and other needs. As Anzia Yezierska explained in an impassioned article in the *New Republic* in 1919, she would have bathed if she could have. She was criticized for her appearance by a supervisor who said, "Soap and water are cheap. Anyone can be clean." Yezierska explained that while studying to be a teacher, she was also working in a laundry from 5:00 to 8:00 in the morning and from 6:00 to 11:00 at night. When she came home at night, she said, "I was so bathed in the sweat of exhaustion, that I could not think of a bath of soap and water. I had only strength to drag myself home, and fall down on the bed and sleep. Even if I had had the desire and the energy to take a bath, there were no such things as bathtubs in the house where I lived" (117).

Tenement reformers focused their attention on the provision of the fix-tures of a bathroom, which might be located separately, and not on the three-fixture bathroom as a whole. This approach was echoed in other working-class situations. The cost of a three-fixture bathroom, whether paid in rent or mortgage, was beyond the reach of most working-class peo-ple. Instead, people at the lower end of the economic scale acquired bath-room fixtures gradually, as their circumstances and available infrastructure permitted. Beyond the cost of the fixtures themselves, there was also a problem in finding a place to put them. For people building a new house, this was not an issue; it could simply be designed in. For people of means who were retrofitting fixtures into an existing house, a small addition could accommodate a bathroom, or existing surplus space, such as a small bedroom or large closet, could be adapted. But for those who had small, overcrowded houses, finding room for these new fixtures was a challenge.

In mild climates, such as the Deep South, flush toilets could be located where the privies had traditionally been: at the rear of the yard. At a steel-company town in Birmingham, Alabama, where more than 200 houses had been built between 1888 and 1900, the company put in water mains and sewer lines in 1917 and replaced privies at the rear of the yards with flush toilets in the same location. In 1949, the tenants acquired the houses and began to install three-fixture bathrooms inside (Shannon 1992, 6). In working-class areas of West Oakland and West Berkeley, California, toilets were added in enclosed back porches after 1920. Three-fixture bathrooms generally were not added until after 1960 (Groth 2004, 17). In cold climates, toilets were often placed in the basement. In company-owned housing in Calumet, Michigan, tenants requested that toilets be installed in their basements in the 1910s. If the company had installed a sewer on the applicant's street, it was happy to comply, but additions to company houses were not so readily granted. Often, the only access to the basement was through a trapdoor in the kitchen floor, but even this hard-to-reach toilet was seen as preferable to an outdoor privy (Hoagland 2010, 140–41). Similarly, in the coal-mining region of southwestern Pennsylvania, when two-story, four-room company houses were bought by their tenants in the 1940s, many of the families dug out a cellar and put the toilet there (Mulrooney 1989, 99).

Because bathtubs were much less of a priority than toilets, public or employer-run bathhouses continued to be an option for many. When three-fixture bathrooms were finally installed in small working-class dwellings, many of them after World War II, valuable space had to be carved out of existing rooms. In one half of a small double house in Calumet, Michigan, where basement toilets had been added (reached through trapdoors in the kitchen floors), tenants added bathrooms after they had bought their units from the company in 1939. In one unit, which had three rooms on the first floor and two on the second, the homeowners took a corner of the dining room and built a bathroom 7 feet 9 inches by 3 feet 4 inches, with toilet, sink, and stall shower. In the mirror-image unit, the homeowners put their slightly smaller bathroom in a corner of the kitchen, reached through a door in the dining room. In both cases, the new bathrooms made the already-small dining room and kitchen even smaller (Hoagland 2011, 33–35).

For many working-class residents, the three-fixture bathroom was a hard-won space. The expense placed it in the category of luxury, not necessity; it could be dispensed with until the homeowner or renter had the means to acquire it. The fixtures could be acquired incrementally, and space for them could be found. If water and sewer were provided, the decision was often a monetary one—was this something that the resident was willing and able to pay for? As such, the installation of bathroom fixtures was strategic, weighed against other expenses a family might have.

***

Rural America also lagged far behind the rest of the nation in the acquisition of indoor bathrooms. In 1960, 94 percent of urban Americans had indoor toilets, but only 62 percent of farm dwellers had them (U.S. Department of Commerce 1963, xliii). The lack of indoor bathrooms even became a sign of the cultural divide between urban and rural populations, with the stereotypical ignorant farmer's backward ways symbolized by his outhouse (Kline 2000, 206).

After World War I, a number of surveys quantified the farmhouse's modest modernization. A 1919 study of 10,000 farm women in the northern and western states found that only 32 percent of their houses had running water, and 85 percent of these households depended on an outdoor toilet (Ward 1920, 9). In 1926, the General Federation of Women's Clubs conducted a study of 40,000 farmhouses in 28 states, finding that 47.2 percent of them had water piped to the house, but only 16.6 percent had a flush toilet (General Federation [1926] 2001, 4:88). A 1929 study of 2,886 farmhouses in 11 states found that fewer than 6 percent of them had all the modern conveniences—defined as central heat, electric lights, and "running hot and cold water, including sewage disposal, for kitchen, bath and toilet uses" (Kirkpatrick 1929, 134). Wide disparities existed among regions; more than 8 percent of the New England and north-central states that were sampled had "completely modern" farmhouses, but only 1.7 percent of the southern ones did (Kirkpatrick 1929, 134).

Modernity was slow to arrive in the country before World War II, but the pace picked up afterward. The 1950 census showed that 58.2 percent of rural households had piped water, and 43.4 percent had flush toilets; this had risen to 79 percent of farm households with running water and 62 percent with flush toilets by 1960 (U.S. Department of Commerce 1963, xliii). A U.S. Department of Agriculture publication issued in 1965 gave detailed instructions on building and maintaining a privy, calling it a "satisfactory facility for the home without indoor plumbing," implying that houses without plumbing were a common condition (quoted in Kline 2000, 273).

In terms of sanitation, the early-20th-century farm was little changed from the 19th-century one. A well in the yard supplied water; a privy, if there was one, was located near the house or at a discreet distance; daily washing occurred with water in a bowl; and bathing took place in a tub brought out on Saturday nights, with water heated on the stove in the kitchen and emptied into the yard. Although a bathroom was possible to build without running water, a steady supply delivered automatically was seen by most to be a prerequisite. Water was needed for more than bathroom functions, of course; cooking, cleaning, and laundry all required water.

The burden of all this water procurement usually fell on the woman. Water is heavy—estimates were that a woman carried a ton of water on wash day—so the proximity of the well was critical (U.S. Department of Agriculture 1915a, 39; Strasser [1982] 2000, 105). The 1919 survey in the northern and western states found that in 61 percent of the farm households in which water had to be carried, women did that work; the average distance from the well was 39 feet, ranging from 23 feet in the East to 65 feet in the West (Ward 1920, 8). Farm women, whose opinions the U.S. Department of Agriculture solicited in a 1915 study, alleged that "the convenience of the stock instead of the housewife is consulted in locating the well and thereafter little effort is made to provide mechanical means for carrying the water into the house" (U.S. Department of Agriculture 1915a, 34). Mocking the idea of mechanical water delivery, a Mississippi farm woman wrote, "Our water power now is a mule and a barrel placed on a sled" (U.S. Department of Agriculture 1915a, 39). Or, as one Indiana farm woman claimed, "we had six rooms and a path" (quoted in Eleanor Arnold 1984, 44).

Although there were many reasons why indoor bathrooms were too expensive or difficult for farmers to acquire, it was also clear that in many cases bathrooms were simply a low priority. For urban dwellers, indoor bathrooms were critical for health and sanitation, but the expansiveness of the farm meant that privies could be moved when their vaults were full, a bathtub could be stored and brought out as needed, and a hand-operated pump would serve only the family. Away from the prying eyes of neighbors, visits to the privy would not be noticed, and more privacy concerning personal hygiene was ensured. In the first half of the 20th century, the technology for water delivery and bathroom fixtures was available, cultural pressures encouraged indoor bathrooms, and farm families themselves expressed a desire for them, yet bathrooms appeared only slowly in farmhouses. On the farm, bathrooms were treated as more of a luxury than a necessity.

The technology for bathrooms was available, if imperfect. A major difference between urban and rural areas was the ease of providing piped water to the former and the impracticality of building piped water and sewer systems to widely dispersed farmhouses. Instead, each farm had to provide its own water, but in most cases, it had to do this anyway for livestock and irrigation. A water source—stream, spring, or well—was essential for the establishment and viability of a farm. Without electricity, different kinds of pumps could move water, but even with electricity, bathrooms tended to be a low priority. And

A familiar sight across rural America, the privy was a practical solution for places where running water and septic tanks were unobtainable. Photo by Carl Mydans, West New Brunswick Township, New Jersey, 1936. (Library of Congress)

without large sewage systems, cesspools served as a suitable alternative.

The U.S. government, as well as commercial forces, encouraged the installation of indoor bathrooms. In 1908, President Theodore Roosevelt convened a Country Life Commission that explored ways to improve rural life, hoping to continue the nation's robust agricultural production and to discourage people from leaving farms for city life. Reflecting Progressive Era thinking, the Country Life Movement proposed efficient management and technological improvements, including mechanized equipment in the home (Jellison 1993, 2–3; Danbom 1979, 43–44). One result of the commission was the Smith-Lever Act of 1914, which provided matching funds for extension services overseen by the U.S. Department of Agriculture. Besides issuing publications and providing classes, the department supported extension agents who visited farms and made recommendations. Separate agents advised on farm and home, and the efficient and sanitary home included running water and indoor bathrooms. As a Department of Agriculture report said, one way of "reducing home drudgery" was "the introduction of modern labor-saving equipment in the home" (Ward 1920, 23). The goal of extension workers who concentrated on the farm homes was "to promote efficiency . . . as a means of stimulating a richer and more satisfying rural life" (Ward 1920, 24). In 1924, after 10 years of federally supported extension work, 52,823 farm families had installed water systems, and 15,454 had built sewage disposal systems in accord with Extension Service recommendations, but this still left the majority of farms without such facilities (Jellison 1993, 39; Danbom 1979, 72).

While sanitation was less of an issue than in urban areas, where overflowing privies flooded into neighbors' basements, pollution of the water supply was nevertheless a concern on the farms. A study of rural houses in 15 counties, conducted by the U.S. Public Health Service in 1914–1916, found that only 1.22 percent disposed of human excreta in a sanitary way and that 68 percent of drinking supplies were exposed to contamination from privy contents (Danbom 1979, 8). A significant number of those surveyed had no toilet or privy, including 31.98 percent of farmhouses in Dorchester County, Maryland; 28.71 percent in Tuscaloosa County, Alabama; and 10.69 percent in Wilson County, Kansas. Public health officials visited every farmhouse and recommended the construction of water closets and septic tanks for those who had the economic means; failing that, sanitary privies with watertight receptacles; and failing that, the "Mosaic method," as outlined in the Bible and explained by a U.S. Public Health Service official: "This method consists of voiding the matter directly into a shallow, freshly dug hole or ditch in the ground, at a suitable place, at least 200 feet from the dwelling or the water supply and not upslope from either, and immediately covering the matter with earth" (Lumsden 1918, 31). While in 1918 the Public Health Service found widespread ignorance about the causes of typhoid, a 1915 poll of the domestic needs of farm women revealed that many of them were familiar with the current knowledge about hygiene and desired to know more. The Department of Agriculture received 172 requests for government programs to "instruct the women on the farm how to care for the sick, prevent contagion, improve hygienic conditions, and introduce proper sanitary measures on the farm" (U.S. Department of Agriculture 1915a, 56).

Government programs had their limits, though. Unlike electricity, which could be collectively produced and distributed, water and sewers could not be centralized in rural areas. One New Jersey farm woman asked for help in a 1915 survey: "I suggest (and am indorsed by the neighboring farm women who are poor, like myself) that the Government help the farmers' wives by making their water supply easier. Oh, what a boon that would be. Our backs and arms ache, and we grow stooped and crippled from pumping water" (quoted in U.S. Department of Agriculture 1915a, 36). While government help enabled thousands of farms to receive electricity in the 1930s, there were no government programs to help farm families install running water in their houses. Although New Deal programs invested $424 million in water projects, with most of them benefitting small communities, they did not provide funds to rural areas or individuals (Melosi 2011, 64). As a result, more farmhouses had electricity in 1945 than had running water in 1940 (Neth 1995, 200).

Beyond the government encouraging the installation of bathrooms, farm families received pressure from other sources, such as advertising, which encouraged consumer spending on home comforts. Reaching farm families through magazines, catalogs, and the radio, advertisements increased awareness not only of what was available but of what other, more fortunate people presumably had. While effective in selling automobiles, radios, and washing machines, though, advertising was less directed at the indoor bathroom. The bathroom was, after all, a system, involving piped water, a water heater, fixtures, and accessories, and thus not a simple thing sold by one vendor. Instead, ads for bath soap might imply the desirability of an indoor bathroom, but they were not selling the concept. Still, farmers were exposed to the consumer culture and made aware of indoor bathrooms (Jellison 1993, 33).

Given available technology and external pressures, though, farm families resisted the installation of bathrooms. Because this was a personal decision, often not dependent on such outside systems as the provision of piped water and sewer, myriad explanations could be cited. Several national trends suggest why farm families might have been reluctant to undertake this improvement.

First, in the 1920s, when urban America was experiencing a boom and consumerist culture was thriving, the nation's farms were in a depression, which lasted through the 1920s and 1930s, lifting only with the United States' entry into World War II (Barre and Sammet 1950, 343). The installation of a bathroom was an expensive undertaking, especially for a family that was on the margin of profitability. And many families were making only small profits; even in 1945, a prosperous year, a quarter of American farms had a gross income of less than $600 (Barre and Sammet 1950, 342). At that time, a complete water system cost about $600—or as much as a secondhand car (Kline 2000, 56; Earl Arnold 1951, 4). The expense of indoor bathrooms also led farmers to install them incrementally, just as the urban poor did. The first step was to pump water to the kitchen sink and

Without running water, a washstand, like the one seen here in the house of Elmer Johnson, provided a way to clean the hands and face. Mr. Johnson was a farmhand in rural Indiana whose employer had a house with a modern bathroom. Photo by Lee Russell, 1937. (Library of Congress)

then install the bathroom in such a way as to spread out the cost over several years (Earl Arnold 1951, 4–5).

Secondly, tenant farmers were less likely to have indoor bathrooms. While an urban renter might pay more for indoor facilities, a rural tenant would be more concerned about the quality and size of the farmland; in other words, the installation of indoor bathrooms would be of no benefit to the landlord (Jellison 1993, 151; Bailey and Snyder 1921, 350). In the 1920s and 1930s, about 40 percent of American farms were rental, a figure that dropped to 30 percent by 1945 (Barre and Sammet 1950, 342). Tenant farms were concentrated in the South, where the climate also made indoor bathrooms less of a necessity. As late as 1960, only 41 percent of tenant farms had bathrooms, while 65 percent of owner-occupied ones did (U.S. Department of Commerce 1963, 1–41).

Thirdly, the lack of high-line electricity was a deterrent to the provision of running water in the house, although a number of ways to move water without electricity existed. Hydraulic rams used hydropower, force pumps could be operated by hand, windmills harnessed wind energy to pump, and water stored in cisterns could be moved by siphons and gravity. Individual farms could also generate electricity by gasoline-powered generators and batteries, but these were not powerful enough to run more than lighting and one appliance, and then the noisy generator had to run constantly (Barron 1997, 214). While many of these energy sources were suitable for pumping water for livestock, none of them provided the kind of steady, constant water supply desired for bathroom fixtures. The 1926 survey of 40,000 farmhouses found that 47 percent had "water at the house." To achieve this, 11.6 percent used gravity or a siphon, 10.5 percent a windmill, 10 percent a hand pump, 7.5 percent a stationary engine, 6.9 percent an electric motor, and less than 1 percent a public water system. Overall, only 16.6 percent of the 40,000 farm families opted to install flush toilets (Kirkpatrick 1929, 136; General Federation [1926] 2001, 4:88).

In the 1930s, two New Deal programs endeavored to provide electricity to farmers. The Tennessee Valley Authority, begun in 1933, operated in the southern states drained by the Tennessee River, while the Rural Electrification Administration (REA), established in 1935, eventually affected 46 states. The REA concentrated on getting transmission lines to the farms, purchasing electricity from local cooperatives and eventually helping cooperatives to build their own transmission lines (Nye 1990, 314–17). By 1941, the cooperatives had more than 900,000 customers, and the percentage of farms with electricity had grown from 13 percent in 1930 to 30 percent (Nye 1990, 318; Kline 2000, 215). After the war, between 1945 and 1949, the REA doubled the number of customers who were connected (Nye 1990, 321). Finally, a steady source of electricity, appropriate for water pumps that would enable indoor bathrooms, was available to thousands of farmers. Still, electricity and running water were not universal; in 1950, only 58.2 percent of farm households had piped water (U.S. Department of Commerce 1963, xliii).

The fourth reason bathrooms were slow to appear in farmhouses concerned priorities within each farm family. Unlike urban households, farms were a profit-making endeavor, and expenditures tended to go toward items that would increase profits. As one Iowa woman said in a 1923 study, "There's truth in the old saying: 'A barn can build a house sooner than a house can build a barn'" (quoted in Jellison 1993, 29). This was echoed by a New York State farm woman named Josie Sulich Kuzma, who married in 1932: "When we come here it was an old, tumble-down house, and my husband was gonna build a new one. But he says he'd better build a barn first . . . He said if we built the barn, the cows would build the house" (quoted in Osterud 2012, 30–31). Also, women's work was not usually monetized, so there was no perceivable profit in lessening the workload. A survey of farm women conducted by the U.S. Department of Agriculture in 1915 found that "any device which will lessen the labor in the fields is purchased without hesitation, but that no labor-saving devices are introduced into the house to lighten the woman's work is an almost universal grievance" (U.S. Department of Agriculture 1915a, 22).

Even when money was to be spent on the house, bathrooms were not always the first priority. Farm women in St. Joseph County, Michigan, surveyed in 1917, desired such modern improvements as running water, hot water, fixed bathtub, sewerage, gas and electric lights, and a furnace. Only 2 of the 91 farms surveyed had all of these. The priorities set by the others were "a good lighting system, next came a furnace, next a water system, next a bathtub, and last sewerage" (Bailey and Snyder 1921, 350). Also, when given the option for a purchase that did not go directly toward increasing profits, families often chose an item that would increase connections with the community: an automobile, for instance, that would enable isolated farm women to go to town more often; a telephone that would enable them to keep in touch with neighbors; or a radio, running on a battery, that would connect the farm to the larger world. In 1940, a greater percentage of farms had automobiles, radios, and telephones than had running water (Kline 2000, 5). As one farm woman replied, when asked why her family had purchased a Model T instead of installing indoor plumbing, "You can't go to town in a bathtub!" (quoted in Kline 2000, 97).

Neglecting the easing of women's work in the prioritization of purchases often caused deep resentment. A Kansas farm woman explained the situation in 1915: "In many homes, life on the farms is a somewhat one-sided affair. Many times the spare money above living expenses is expended on costly machinery and farm implements to make the farmer's work lighter; on more land where there is already a sufficiency; on expensive horses and cattle and new outbuildings; while little or nothing is done for home improvement and no provision made for the comfort and convenience of the women in the family" (U.S. Department of Agriculture 1915b, 15). A 1921 article titled "Feminism on the Farm" reported on a "Declaration of Independence" drawn up by Nebraska farm women. The document set forth a few quid pro quos, including, "A bath-tub in the house for every binder on the farm" and "Running water in the kitchen for every riding-plow for the fields" (440). As one Minnesota farm woman related in 1915: "This summer a neighbor dug a large cistern. The mother wanted the pump put in the kitchen; but the son (and he was a good boy) said, 'With the separator and everything in there this winter there would not be room for the pump,' so it was put outside and the mother has to run out and get the water, and it will freeze and be of no use during the winter. That boy should be educated to look at things differently and that mother should be educated to demand her rights" (U.S. Department of Agriculture 1915a, 37).

Women's lack of spending power rankled some. A New York State farm woman wrote in 1915 that "most farmers' wives have no share in anything on the farm but the labor. They are expected to do their own work and as much of the out-of-door work as they can, but none of the income is theirs. If it were, few of them would endure long the inconveniences which they now endure in regard to closets, water supply, cesspools, or proper drainage of some sort, etc." Once again, she saw the solution as a cultural shift: "This, I fear, will never be remedied by any law, but will have to wait for the mothers to raise up a better class of men, trained to regard women and women's work as it should be regarded" (U.S. Department of Agriculture 1915a, 45–46).

The provision of an indoor bathroom did not always dramatically decrease a woman's workload. Even running water, the greatest boon, did not always affect women's work. If a farm had already found some way of mechanically moving water, or if the burden fell on someone other than the woman, running water that operated more smoothly might not have been that much of an improvement. One woman reported in 1938 that their acquisition of an electric water pump lessened the work of her husband, in maintaining the gas engine they had used previously, and of her sons, who pumped the water for the house (Kline 2000, 266). An indoor bathroom also meant that there was another room to clean—one in which sanitation was key—and that burden usually fell to the woman. As Helen Musselman, an Indiana farm woman, related, "Grandmother always laughed when she would come to visit me, though, after we had our bathroom. She said, 'My goodness, you spend more time cleaning that bathroom, in spite of all the convenience . . .' She said she used to do her washing on Monday and she'd take the wash water out to the old-fashioned privy and scrub it out. It was done once a week, and that was the chore. And she said, 'You scrub your bathroom every day—sometimes twice a day'" (quoted in Eleanor Arnold 1984, 49).

Ultimately, indoor bathrooms would continue to be given a low priority as long as financial resources were scarce. Indoor bathrooms would not increase the productivity of the farm and might even occupy more of the farm woman's time than the lack of facilities had. The best that Florence E. Ward could argue in her 1920 report was that the indoor bathroom would provide an "untold release from drudgery" and "a sense of pride and ownership which is as important a factor in a woman's success in her daily round of work as is modern machinery in the success of the farmer" (9). Such a lack of tangible benefit meant that rural households would continue to lag in the acquisition of indoor bathrooms for many decades.

***

In the 1930s, New Deal housing programs both set the standard of three-fixture bathrooms and reflected the reality of their rarity among farmers and the working class. Including bathrooms in housing programs was not without controversy. Government officials, congressmen, and other critics never fully agreed whether these were relief programs, providing the minimum, or demonstration programs, worthy of emulation. One of the concrete expressions of the latter idea was the provision of an indoor bathroom.

One of the earliest housing programs, initiated in 1933, was through the Division of Subsistence Homesteads (first located in the Department of Interior, then in the Resettlement Administration, then in the Farm Security Administration), which built semirural communities for unemployed industrial workers that included garden plots for subsistence agriculture and small, single-family houses, all of which included a three-fixture bathroom. Because in 1933 most rural dwellings did not have indoor plumbing, some critics saw its provision as an extravagance (S. Baldwin 1968, 111). The fixtures also increased the cost of the dwellings, a burden for homeowners struggling to purchase their own houses. A government sociologist argued that the division should "build houses that provide a better standard of living than that to which the families are accustomed. If people are to be taken from slums where four or five families have used one toilet, either outside or inside, my position is that a sanitary outside toilet provided at a cost within the means of the homesteader is preferable to complete inside equipment but with the people so burdened by debt that they could not meet their obligations" (Melvin 1935, 9). Others, including Eleanor Roosevelt, who championed the poor and unemployed, visiting coal miners and relief efforts in West Virginia in August 1933, just as her husband was formulating this program, argued for the provision of facilities. And, as one advocate argued, providing bathrooms would create demand for fixtures, thus helping the sanitary-ware industry in the midst of the Depression. He noted that "if every family in the United States were to have one bathtub, all the bathtub factories in the United States would have to work eight hours a day for ten years to supply the demand" (Pickett 1934, 479). The 99 subsistence-homestead communities, consisting of more than 10,000 houses, all provided indoor bathrooms.

Another New Deal housing program established in 1933, the Public Works Administration, provided housing for the urban poor, building more than 20,000 units in 51 projects (G. Wright 1981, 225). The Public Works Administration housing program (which evolved into the United States Housing Authority in 1937) focused on slum clearance and rebuilding, offering one- and two-story row houses and three- and four-story apartment buildings (Schoenfeld 1940, 271). The Public Works Administration's Housing Division issued standards that included three-fixture bathrooms, so every unit in this program, whether directed at white or black populations, included bathrooms.

Besides subsistence homesteads, housing programs run by the Resettlement Administration included one to build low-cost housing in suburban areas near industrial centers. The three greenbelt towns of this program (Greenbelt, Maryland; Greenhills, Ohio; and Greendale, Wisconsin), lauded by planners, had three-fixture bathrooms in every unit. But the largest housing program of the Resettlement Administration (which became the Farm Security Administration in 1937) was the 17,000 units it built for rural dwellers. Although its ambition was for well-equipped houses, in an effort to reduce the per-unit cost from $3,000 to less than half that, officials reduced the number and size of rooms and omitted bathrooms (Schoenfeld 1940, 278). The impoverished farmers were accustomed to houses without bathrooms, but the government housing program failed to meet rising expectations.

The urban Public Works Administration and the rural Farm Security Administration both issued publications promoting their experiences with affordable housing as models, but neither of their booklets insisted on three-fixture bathrooms. In 1937, the Public Works Administration's Housing Division issued *Homes for Workers*, a booklet for adult-education classes. The standards it offered included running water, indoor water closet, and provision for bathing, but not a bathroom per se. Two years later, the Farm Security Administration issued a booklet called *Small Houses*, showcasing some of its designs for low-cost housing. In order to keep costs low, not all of the designs included indoor bathrooms. Finally, in 1945, the Federal Public Housing Authority (successor to the United States Housing Authority) issued standards that included not just bathrooms, but insisted that they be ventilated by a window or skylight (Vale 2005, 84).

Wartime accommodations introduced many Americans to indoor plumbing. In gearing up for war, the army constructed thousands of barracks to house troops for their initial training. In the three years prior to Pearl Harbor, the army built temporary facilities for more than 5 million soldiers (Wasch et al. 1988, 61). Because expectations had risen since World War I, where the stateside barracks had latrines in buildings separate from the barracks, the World War II barracks had indoor plumbing. In the most common army construction, the bathroom was located on the first floor of a two-story building, with urinal troughs and toilets without partitions, but it nonetheless set a standard for comfort in a minimal dwelling (Wasch et al. 1988, 55; Fine and Remington 1972, 116). The army of draftees and volunteers would return to civilian life after the war, perhaps with a new understanding of what was a necessity rather than a comfort.

In the quarter century after the war, three-fixture bathrooms became almost universal among the urban poor and increasingly common among

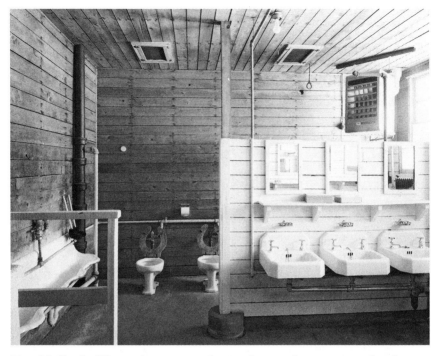

Fort McCoy in Wisconsin was one of several posts that accommodated army recruits in World War II, and indoor plumbing inside their barracks was probably their first introduction to this convenience. Photo by Martin Stupich, 1993. (Library of Congress)

rural dwellers. Roughly speaking, in 1870, the elites had begun to install three-fixture bathrooms; in 1920, the middle class began to obtain them; and in 1970, finally, the rest of the American population got them. Just as the development of the bathroom responded to political and cultural forces, so did its uneven acquisition.

Chapter 6

PRIVACY: LOCATING THE BATHROOM

The location of the bathroom in the house reflects ideas about privacy. The placement of the bathroom can guarantee its privacy from neighbors, guests, and even other family members, and as that placement changes, it demonstrates the rising expectations of the middle class through the 20th century. Where the bathroom is located—out of sight of guests, close to bedrooms, preferably upstairs—indicates a comfortable and genteel life. The introduction of the half-bath, or powder room, and multiple three-fixture bathrooms contributes to the exclusion of others from a bathroom shared only by spouses, siblings, or perhaps no one. And as much as Americans like their bathrooms private, there are also, conversely, other trends and past cultural traditions that take a different approach.

Privacy is often a function of wealth; the more money one has, the more one can afford separate, private spaces. A variety of dedicated spaces can be a sign of status, but there are other motivations as well for privacy in the bathroom, including modesty, guilt, shame, or simply a desire to be alone (Langford 1965, 15). Modesty about naked bodies and personal functions is taught as a virtue in many Western societies. Guilt, or self-censure for violating personal or societal norms, can also be related to activities performed in a bathroom or even the sight of one's own naked body. Shame is related to guilt but tends to focus on the reactions of others to one's behavior or appearance. These emotions push Americans to hide their nudity, bathing, and personal functions. The desire for privacy may also be unrelated to bathroom functions because the bathroom is the one room where it is acceptable to lock the door and escape from annoying siblings or demanding children. A bathroom that is not shared at all is a luxury most people could not afford in the mid-20th century, but the bathroom's placement in the house could at least provide some semblance of privacy.

The first significant move toward privacy was to bring bathroom functions indoors, which also changed the function of the yard. The privy in the yard exposed very personal functions to neighbors, and replacing the outdoor privy with the indoor water closet was a major change. No longer would each trip to the privy be seen by neighbors. Although this exposure was rarely mentioned in contemporary accounts, veiled references to women's modesty indicate that for some it was a concern. And when Thomas Jefferson occupied the White House in 1801, he had the very conspicuous privy in the yard demolished and ordered water closets, from a particular vendor in Philadelphia, to be installed to provide a more decorous privacy (Seale 1986, 1:90). Washing, too, became less public. Cleaning the face and hands, previously at an outdoor pump, moved indoors with the introduction of running water. Bathtubs replaced bathing in streams and lakes or visits to a public bathhouse. Before running water was available, the Saturday-night bath was performed in the kitchen, where water was heated for a portable tub, which was shared sequentially by family members. While not private from the family, this type of bathing was at least hidden from neighbors.

The introduction of running water and associated fixtures was only part of a great transformation of the yard from work space into a place of leisure in the early 20th century. Activities such as trips to the privy and washing at a hand pump no longer took place in the yard. Fruit trees, vegetable gardens, cows, and chickens disappeared from yards as stores or deliverymen increasingly provided food. The central furnace required deliveries of coal to the basement, not piles of firewood in the yard. Laundry was washed in machines, not in the yard, and later on dried in other machines, not on clotheslines. The introduction of various domestic technologies caused the yard to move indoors, in a way, but the most obvious of these changes was the disappearance of the privy.

Most bathrooms were retrofitted into preexisting houses. While there are no reliable statistics about the extent of this retrofitting, it is safe to assume that of the 16 million households in the United States in 1900, probably a quarter of them installed bathrooms over the next quarter century. Yet there was very little discussion of this significant remodeling in the professional or popular press (Hoagland 2011, 15–16). Retrofitting a bathroom into an existing house meant that there could be little choice about where to put it. Ideally, there would be a spare room adaptable for the purpose, but that might result in a bathroom far larger than it needed to be. The ends of hallways could also be turned into bathrooms ("Bathroom Layouts" 1948, 72). In smaller houses, the three fixtures might be put in different spaces, such as closets, with a bathtub in one former closet and a toilet in another. Wealthier homeowners could build an addition for the bathroom, but that might be on the first floor while the bedrooms were on the second. In this retrofitting, privacy might be sacrificed to convenience and availability because the bathroom's placement was usually dictated by factors other than preferred social relationships.

In new construction, bathrooms could be placed anywhere, theoretically. They also became consolidated into one three-fixture space, as urged by sanitarians of the late 19th century. A brief survey of late–19th-century pattern books, which compiled plans, elevations, details, and perspective views to serve as a sort of idea book for architects and their clients, yields insights into this development. In the early 1870s, before the sanitarians had successfully promoted the virtues of the three-fixture bathroom, the fixtures were located in various places and not necessarily together. In *Bicknell's Village Builder*, from 1872, 8 of the 29 plans did not indicate a bathroom at all, but 9 of them had a three-fixture bathroom on the second floor. Several plans had two-fixture (tub and toilet) bathrooms; a few indicated basins in the bedrooms, along with a two-fixture bathroom; and one had a water closet on the first floor at the rear of the house, along with a full bathroom on the second floor. In *Hussey's National Cottage Architecture,* a pattern book published in 1874, 19 of the 28 plans had no bathroom indicated, and the others had a variety of organizations: one with the water closet in a room separate from the tub and sink and another with a bathroom on the second floor and a privy on the first floor, reached from the yard. *Modern Architectural Designs and Details*, published by William T. Comstock in 1881, showed 7 of the 19 plans without a bathroom. The others included several with basins in the bedrooms, along with a three-fixture bathroom, and another with a two-fixture bath on the second floor and the water closet on the first.

By the 20th century, the three-fixture bathroom was becoming the norm. In 1909, the Radford Architectural Company of Chicago, which developed its own designs and then sold the working drawings and specifications to clients, issued a catalog of 200 plans in which about a quarter lacked a three-fixture bath, having either no bathroom at all or two fixtures: 37 had no bathroom at all, 11 had two fixtures in a variety of configurations— 4 with tub and toilet, 3 with tub and sink, and 3 with toilet and sink— and 1 with only a tub. While no reliable data exist as to where people actually put bathrooms, plan books such as this, marketed to a broad middle-class audience, reflect cultural norms about their acceptable placement.

The most desirable place for a bathroom was on the second floor, close to bedrooms and out of sight of guests, securing the family's privacy. About half (105) of Radford's designs placed the bathroom on the second floor, with the bathroom opening off the hall so that it was accessible to all family members without passing through someone else's bedroom. As long as houses were two stories, the second-floor bathroom was suitably private.

One-story designs proved to be the challenge. Keeping the bathroom out of sight of guests, close to the bedrooms, and not requiring passage through the public areas was not always easily achieved. And, as the bungalow gained popularity in the first few decades of the 20th century, there were more one-story houses. Previously associated with modest circumstances, one-story houses became a middle-class option, equipped with two or three bedrooms and of course a bathroom. Many factors accounted for the rise of this new building form. As other kinds of work for women competed with domestic service and servants became rarer, housewives preferred houses that were more compact and efficient, with more open space and fewer halls. One house catalog lauded "the passing of the pantry" as a move toward efficiency (*Aladdin* 1917, 69). Central heating permitted the opening up of rooms so that, rather than a parlor closed off from the hall, the living room could flow into the dining room. A desire for family togetherness, with the whole family congregating in one room, also arose at this time. Advice-givers urged fathers to participate in rearing their children by spending time with the whole family, just when Progressive reformers were focusing new attention on childhood (Marsh 1989, 514–15). And the higher cost of new construction, due to new technologies such as the bathroom, meant that houses had to be smaller (G. Wright 1980, 238). As a result of these and other factors, one-story houses became popular among middle-class homeowners.

By 1917, when the Aladdin Company issued a catalog of ready-built houses, for which the company would ship the precut materials for an entire house to be assembled onsite, half of the 62 house designs were one story. Among these one-story houses, 7 had no bathroom, and in 10 of them, the bathroom was awkwardly placed. For example, a common one-story plan had a bedroom opening off of the living room and the other two bedrooms, as well as the bathroom, opening off the dining room. Some plans created a small hall shared by the two bedrooms and the bathroom, effectively segregating the bathroom from public spaces, but this was difficult to do in three-bedroom plans. Similarly, in Sears, Roebuck's 1926 catalog of ready-built houses, about half of the 73 plans were for one-story houses with small hallways separating two bedrooms and a bathroom from more public spaces.

The preponderance of these plans through the 1920s had only one three-fixture bathroom, reflecting middle-class norms and what was acceptable

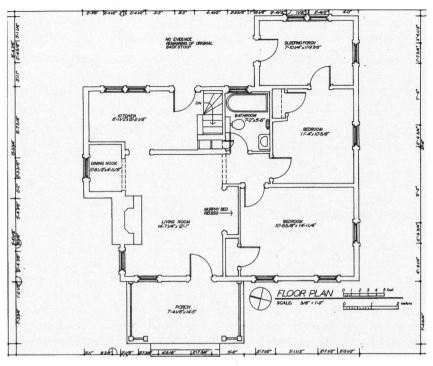

The plan of this one-story house in Garrett Park, Maryland, built in the 1920s, shows a three-fixture bathroom accessible to the two bedrooms and set apart from the more public rooms. (Library of Congress)

to a broad range of taste within a fairly narrow economic band. These plan books rarely pictured basements, though, and additional fixtures could be placed there. Also, given that these were plans and not recordings of existing structures, the bathroom fixtures were not necessarily installed in the indicated bathrooms, at least not initially. One example of these underutilized bathrooms occurred in northern Michigan, where the Quincy Mining Company ordered plans for 50 almost-identical units from Sears, Roebuck in 1917. The basic plan, prepared according to Quincy's requirements, was for a 28-by-28-foot two-story house in a foursquare plan. On the first floor, stair hall, living room, dining room, and kitchen each occupied a quadrant, while on the second floor were a three-fixture bathroom and four bedrooms, each with a closet. But as built, only about a quarter of the houses—those allocated to higher-ranking workers—received the three bathroom fixtures. In the rest of the houses, the plumbing was roughed in, and the houses rented for slightly less (Hoagland 2010, 152–61). Presumably, as tenants and owners installed bathroom fixtures over the years,

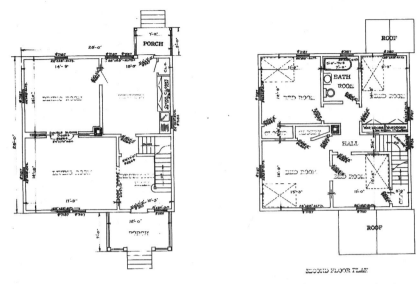

Sears, Roebuck and Company developed home plans for purchase in the early 20th century. These 1917 plans show a three-fixture bathroom on the second floor of a foursquare house. The Quincy Mining Company in Hancock, Michigan, used these plans for 50 houses, but installed bathroom fixtures in only a few of them. (Library of Congress)

they would have put them in the obvious place—the empty bathroom. It is likely that homeowners who purchased ready-built houses or just plans delayed installing bathroom fixtures as well but ultimately put them in the intended space.

The sizes of the bathrooms ranged widely. Bicknell's 1872 pattern book showed bathrooms that ranged from 7-and-a-half by 12 feet to less than 5 by 8 feet, although most were around 6 by 8 or 6 by 9 feet. The 1926 Sears catalog had bathrooms as large as 9 by 10 feet and as small as 5 by 5-and-a-half feet, but they averaged around 6 by 8 feet. The trend, though, was for smaller spaces, and the "compact bathroom" began to dominate in the 1920s. The compact bathroom was designed around the 5-foot-long tub, which, for example, accounted for three-quarters of the Crane Company's sales by 1944 (Giedion [1948] 2013, 704). The tub was oriented along the short wall, with the other two fixtures beside it on the long wall, so that plumbing was efficiently provided to only one wall. The compact bathroom, usually 5 by 7 feet, persisted into the 1960s, when one study noted that it was "still the rule" (Kira 1966, 5).

The compact bathroom's acceptability to Americans appears to have had its origins in the hotel. Providing a private bathroom to every room had long been a desire of hotel companies, accomplished in 1908 when Ellsworth M. Statler adopted a plan for his hotel in Buffalo that included a bathroom for every guest room. Two bathrooms were located between unconnected guest rooms, so that each guest room had direct access to its own bathroom. The plan paired bathrooms on either side of an interior ventilation shaft, the efficiency of space contributing to the frequent use of the "Statler plumbing shaft" (Davidson 2005, 87; Wagner 1917, 168). Statler's slogan, "A room and a bath for a dollar and a half," declared the availability of private bathrooms to the middle class; their small size was not an issue.

This small house in Columbus, Georgia, built in about 1930, had a compact bathroom with all the fixtures aligned efficiently on one wall. (Library of Congress)

The compact bathroom subsequently became an expectation in the middle-class home as well (Giedion [1948] 2013, 700). As the J. L. Mott Iron Works catalog proclaimed in 1914, "As in the modern hotel each guest is provided with a bathroom, so provision is made for guests in the residence. Thus, the modern residence instead of having only one bathroom now usually provides a bathroom in connection with every sleeping room or suite" (9). While the reference this catalog makes to standard hotel amenities is significant, in the interest of selling bathroom fixtures, it wildly overstates the number of bathrooms commonly provided in houses.

For decades, two-story houses had one three-fixture bathroom on the second floor, most efficiently placed over the kitchen, and that was deemed sufficient. In Radford's 1909 catalog, 105 of the 140 two-story dwellings had one—and only one—three-fixture bathroom. Similarly, 28 of the 31 two-story houses in Aladdin's 1917 catalog had only a three-fixture bathroom on the second floor, as did 32 of the 37 in Sears's 1926 catalog. Other options included a two-fixture bathroom on the second floor, a three-fixture

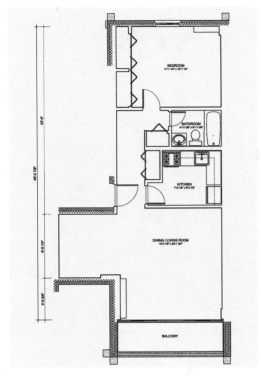

Apartments designed by Charles Goodman in McLean, Virginia, in the 1960s included a compact, 5-by-7-foot bathroom with the fixtures aligned along one wall. (Library of Congress)

bathroom on the first floor, or two bathrooms on the second floor. But increasingly, a half-bath on the first floor complemented the second-floor bathroom.

The powder room, or half-bath, with a sink and toilet, offered auxiliary services for families or guests. A half-bath on the first floor, placed close to the kitchen, could be intended for servants, but the increasingly servantless household placed the half-bath off of the main hall on the first floor. Jonathan K. Allen mentioned it in his 1907 book, *Sanitation in the Modern Home*, where he noted, "A lavatory and closet [i.e., sink and toilet] are now often provided on the first floor of an ordinary dwelling. This arrangement is found to be very desirable, saving many steps and much stair-climbing for members of the household. It is especially convenient for the use of guests who are in the house for a short time only." He advised placing it near the coat closet. While often placed under the stairs, Allen called this unwise because of "the probable lack of light and ventilation" (235). A 1933 article, "The Modern Bathroom," in *Parents Magazine*, also urged the addition of a second bathroom. While one option was to adapt hall space on the second floor for this purpose, downstairs, the author asserted, "perhaps in that closet under the stairs, a toilet and lavatory will save many steps for the mother with young children, to say nothing of enhancing the general convenience of the whole family" (Sprackling 1933, 51).

Through the Depression and World War II, however, bathrooms were acquired at a slow pace, and it is worth a reminder that in 1940 barely half of Americans had bathrooms in their houses. The sale after the war of small houses with one compact bathroom found willing buyers because these houses were far more luxurious than urban apartments with shared facilities or rural farmhouses with no facilities. The developer William Levitt is a case in point. In his Levittown on Long Island, he built 17,500 houses between 1947 and 1951 and then built additional communities on the East Coast. In the original Levittown, the one-story, gable-roofed houses in two basic plans had two bedrooms and one bathroom, adjacent to the bedrooms. There was room for expansion in the attic, but one study showed that while many people added bedrooms there, few installed bathrooms, in the attic or elsewhere (Kelly 1993, 115). One bathroom seemed sufficient. By 1950, 92 percent of new houses nationwide had just one bathroom, due to postwar material restrictions and the lowering of expectations during wartime (J. Jacobs 2015, 117).

As Americans flocked to new houses in the suburbs in the decade after World War II, one-story houses proved popular. Often loosely called "ranch houses," which before the war had been larger, sprawling, western dwellings, these one-story houses might be in the colonial revival style with steep gable roofs, a more modernist flat-roofed variety, or any other exterior design. Generally, though, they were compact houses with most of the living taking place on one floor and, like Levitt's houses, equipped with two bedrooms and one bathroom. The bedrooms and bathroom were located together in one half of the house, forming a private zone separate from areas likely to be visited by guests. In the 1950s, with increased prosperity nationwide, houses more often were built with three bedrooms and a dining room. Still, the one-story house persisted, offering a relaxed, casual family life. To increase space without the formality of a second floor, developers offered split-level designs, in which a utility-and-recreation floor, a living-dining-kitchen floor, and a bedroom-and-bathroom floor were staggered, half a story apart. By the 1960s, raised ranches, which contained the living and sleeping areas on the top floor with a recreation room and utilities on the ground floor, gained popularity. Casual living gave way to more separated portions of the house as privacy gained ascendancy over togetherness (J. Jacobs 2015, 123, 154, 172).

A single bathroom, while a great improvement for many families, had its drawbacks and began to receive negative press as contemporary observers noted a "traffic bottleneck" ("It Takes More Than Plumbing" 1950, 144). There were several solutions to this crowded situation: a powder room, a compartmentalized bathroom, or a second bathroom. A 1950 survey of developer-built houses found that only 8 percent of them built that year had a second bathroom or powder room, although a survey of custom-built houses from the year before found that 32 percent of them had powder rooms ("How to Plan" 1955, 86; Paxton 1955, 46). By 1955, according to one account, a powder room on the main floor of a split-level or two-story house was "standard planning" ("How to Plan" 1955, 87).

The compartmentalized bathroom began to appear in the early 1950s. The drawback to the three-fixture bathroom was that only one person could use it at a time, and that person was using only one fixture at a time. By compartmentalizing the fixtures into separate rooms, more than one person could use the facility. Thus the consolidated bathroom, so beloved by sanitarians, was divided into separate, usually adjacent, rooms. As one 1953 article advised, "Without adding any fixtures at all, you can break up your present bath into a two-passenger bath by putting the toilet in a separate 3' x 5' compartment." Or, "You can break your present one-passenger bath up into a three-passenger bath, i.e., you can put tub, basin and toilet each in a separate compartment" ("39 Ways" 1953, 99).

The compartmentalized bathroom was a smart option but not as popular as it might have been, because another solution presented itself: more bathrooms. As the desire for privacy began to overtake the yen for togetherness, the master suite, which had a bathroom opening off of the master bedroom, became popular. And the gender implied in the title "master" was not accidental; equipped with a shower, not a bathtub, the master bathroom was designed for the male head of the household to perform his morning ablutions unimpeded, before he left the house for work (J. Jacobs 2015, 175). Joseph Eichler, a California developer of modernist houses targeted at the middle class, claimed to be the first to include a second bathroom (Busch 2008, 4:102). In 1953, in his Fairmeadow project in Palo Alto, the houses featured master bathrooms off of the master bedrooms. The other bathroom was located between the children's bedrooms (Adamson and Arbunich 2002, 65). The 8 percent of developer-built houses in 1950 that had second bathrooms had grown to 12 percent by 1955 ("How to Plan" 1955, 86). At Belair, near Bowie, Maryland, developed by Levitt and Sons in 1961–1962, all of the five designs of houses had at least two bathrooms; four of them had en suite master bathrooms. In at least one model, the master bathroom had blue fixtures, while the second bathroom was pink, implying a gendered use. By the 1960s, two bathrooms were the expectation in middle-class homes (Langford 1965, 11).

Other efforts at increasing the functionality of the bathroom included two sinks, which enabled two people to use the room at the same time, without infringing on truly private functions. As one magazine described it, "If yours is a large family, you can cut the time between the alarm clock's ring and the first bite of breakfast by installing two washbasins side

Double sinks became popular for mid-20th-century bathrooms, as seen in this one, designed by architect Walter Gropius for his own home. The house was built in Lincoln, Massachusetts, in 1938. (Library of Congress)

by side. Then two can wash or shave at the same time" (Brooks 1948, 212). Another option was to place basins in bedrooms: "You can put an extra wash basin in the master bedroom, preferably screened off in some kind of closet. Since this basin will be for adults *only*, you can get extra dividends by setting it in 6 [inches] higher" ("39 Ways" 1953, 99). A practice frowned on by sanitarians in the 19th century, sinks in bedrooms gained new attention as an option for alleviating the bottleneck. While the multiple-sink option remained popular, the preferred alternative, if affordable, was additional bathrooms.

The most efficient place for a second bathroom was to place it against the first bathroom so that they shared a plumbed wall. More often, though, convenience to bedrooms, and therefore recognition of privacy concerns, determined the placement. Location was also dictated by the requirement for an exterior window, which posed a problem in the compact bathroom. With the bathtub across the short end of the bathroom, opposite the doorway, the window was often placed over the bathtub. This made the window difficult to operate, introduced drafts above the tub, and discouraged the installation of a shower over the tub. One article advised that windows should be placed "where you can reach to open them, and where you won't be in a draft when bathing" ("Will It Be a Dream House?" 1949, 207). Mechanical ventilation of the bathroom was introduced in the 1930s, and by 1955, the Federal Housing Administration, which issued standards for houses whose mortgages it insured, dropped its requirement for bathroom ventilation by exterior windows ("How to Plan" 1955, 86). The sanitarian belief in ventilation as necessary to counter the deleterious sewer gas, which resulted in the insistence on windows in bathrooms, was finally overruled. Now bathrooms could be located in the interior of houses, and they were. Particularly in townhouses and apartments, the compact bathroom nestled near bedrooms in a compact floor plan.

Privacy for bathrooms takes many forms. One is privacy of sight, and concerns continued to be expressed that bathrooms be placed not only out of living rooms, but out of sight of living rooms. A survey of homebuyers in 1949–1950 found that many were dissatisfied with the location of the bathroom, citing the desire for "privacy and convenience." The survey report noted, "The placement of the bathroom drew fire when it was within unobstructed view from the livingroom, when it could be reached from the kitchen or other parts of the house only by passing through the livingroom, and when occupants of one bedroom had to go through another bedroom to reach it, thus destroying the privacy of the second bedroom" (Paxton 1955, 48). Another kind of privacy related to odors, and the preference for windows to ventilate bathrooms, even after mechanical ventilation had made them unnecessary, shows how important the perception of ventilation was. A third kind of privacy was that of sound, and contemporary articles encouraged soundproofing. One article advised building "ordinary mattress-type insulation into the walls of your bathroom"; using a massive wall, such as a fireplace wall, to insulate one side of the room; or placing the bathroom between such dead spaces as closets and utility rooms ("It Takes More Than Plumbing" 1950, 146).

Privacy also entails not just getting away from others—from guests and other family members, through sight, smell, and sound—but also getting private time with oneself. As the only room in the house where it was acceptable to lock the door and be alone, the bathroom attracted family members who wanted privacy for themselves. Reading was a popular activity in the bathroom. In one survey, 15 percent of the respondents read in the bathtub, and 40 percent read while on the toilet, but many others sought the bathroom just as a place to read (Langford 1965, 62). Young women retreated to water closets to read novels in the 1880s, much to the dismay of one observer, who fumed, "A great many people, especially young women, pass much more time than is necessary in the usually unwholesome atmosphere of these places [water closets], taking books and newspapers with them. This is a vicious habit which entails more than one evil consequence upon those who practice it; but it is nevertheless very common. [A water closet] certainly is not a place in which to pass an idle hour reading novels" (Bayles 1884, 97). Americans have continued to resort to bathrooms for activities they wish to perform alone.

The bath is one of these activities that can serve as a retreat, and women were disproportionately drawn to the bath. As one observer noted, "The tub bath may be said to be generally considered more relaxing, more luxurious, and more feminine than the shower," while the shower had a number of masculine qualities: "it is fast, efficient, Spartan," with a "general businesslike, no-nonsense character" (Kira 1966, 8–9). In a survey of 1,000 middle-class households published in 1965, four out of five men showered and four out of five women bathed, when they had a choice. And they often did: at that time, all of the houses in the survey built since 1955 had both a shower and a tub (Langford 1965, 33). That women were using the bath as a retreat was crystalized by an TV advertisement for a Calgon bath product in the late 1970s. The ad featured an overstressed woman on the edge of losing it, declaring: " 'The traffic! [Shot of traffic.] The boss! [Shot of bald man yelling into a telephone.] The baby! [Shot of crying infant.] The dog! [Shot of barking sheepdog.] That does it! Calgon, take me away!'" she beseeches. The woman is then shown in a bubble bath, and a male voiceover encourages the viewer to "love yourself in luxury" (Klein 2016, 36). While the advertisement was obviously overdrawn, it is hard to imagine a shower offering the same kind of retreat. The bathtub remained associated with relaxation and restoration, while the shower was more often a place of rejuvenation and stimulation.

Privacy may have been a driving force for many Americans when considering their bathrooms, but some immigrants brought cultural traditions that viewed bathing differently. The Finns—300,000 of whom immigrated in the half century before World War I, mostly to the Upper Great Lakes region—brought with them the sauna. The basic construction was a *savusauna*, or "smoke sauna," which was a small building, usually built of logs, with a chimneyless stove built of dry-laid stones. Because of the inherent danger from fire, saunas were usually located at a considerable distance from the house. Saunas often had two rooms, one in which to disrobe and one in which to bask in the heat in the nude. Built without a chimney, the savusauna filled with smoke, which was vented, but the vent was sealed before the bathers entered. Providing intense heat, probably 194 to 212 degrees near the ceiling, the savusauna

Finnish immigrants introduced the sauna, a type of steam bath, to the United States. Bathers could sit on a higher or lower bench, depending on how warm they liked to be; the heat rose to the top of the room. (Sergey Nazarov/Dreamstime.com)

caused the bathers to sweat, cleaning their pores. After a time, bathers might throw water on the stones, creating steam, which would intensify the heat. Benches at different heights provided options for experiencing more intense or lesser heat. Bathers might also whisk their bodies with bath whisks, or switches, usually made of leafy birch branches (Kaups 1976, 16). Bathers would then rinse in cold water and cool off either in the dressing room or outside, even rolling in the snow or jumping in near-frozen lakes (Lockwood 1977, 76). Bathers could then reenter the sauna and begin the process again. Washing with soap could be part of the sauna experience but was not essential for a sauna, occurring more infrequently (Kaups 1976, 16).

By the early 20th century, saunas incorporated chimneys to reduce the risk of fire. Other improvements, introduced as the century went on, included concrete floors, running water, and electric stoves (Nordskog 2010, 3). The tradition of a sauna endured; in 1962, 77 percent of Finns in Minnesota and 88 percent of those in Michigan had saunas (Lockwood 1977, 72). In the 1990s, one Finnish American in northern Michigan nearly rejected thousands of dollars of home improvement assistance because the state agency insisted on putting a bathtub in his house. He had a sauna and felt that was sufficient (Hoagland 2010, 152).

Taking a sauna was inherently a social activity because more than one person did it at a time and, given the leisurely pace, conversation was a part of it. Depending on the size of the sauna and of the family, they might all take a sauna together, or the men would go first, followed by the women and children. In the summer, families might take saunas daily or every other day, as opposed to weekly or fortnightly during the winter (Kaups 1976, 15). For large families, a sauna was an easy and efficient way to clean

The Japanese *furo*, normally situated indoors, is a large tub used for soaking. (Dmitri Maruta/Dreamstime.com)

multiple children (Sando 2014, 15). Neighbors and guests were also invited to share the sauna, which became an important social institution and place for the exchange of news and gossip. In some areas, farm families would rotate hosting "sauna night" each week among a group of friends (Kaups 1976, 19). When more than one family was using the sauna, the sexes were usually not mixed (Lockwood 1977, 79). Through the sauna, young Finnish Americans learned traditional customs, as well as the meaning of being truly clean, as only a sauna could clean (Lockwood 1977, 80–81).

Japanese Americans also had a different approach to bathing, one that, while not explicitly communal, was rooted in the family and in tradition. The heart of the process was the *furo*, a hot tub in which the user soaked. When the Japanese came to the United States in the late 19th century, they brought their bathing habits with them. If they were situated on farms, they built a separate building for a furo. As described in 1933, the bathhouse was "about 6 by 10 feet in size, containing a large metal tub about 4 feet deep and 5 feet square, oval or round. This is so placed that the water can be heated in it by an outside wood fire. To prevent burning of the feet, a wooden grill is placed in the bottom of the tub. Bathing takes place just before retiring every night, and of course, all use the same bath water" (Dubrow 2002, 326).

The tub was explicitly for soaking, not for cleaning. Bathers were expected to wash themselves outside of the tub, with water and cloths provided for the purpose, before getting into the tub. Family members would bathe individually, with the male head of the household going first and proceeding through the family according to status. Bathers were not meant to linger, taking 10 or 15 minutes to soak. The housewife had the task of preparing the bath, an onerous chore in places without running water. Rather than physical cleanliness being the goal of the bath, the furo served more as a ritual of purification. Internment during World War II, when the government removed virtually all the Japanese from the West Coast, disrupted this custom, though, and after the war, few returned to their furos, although some rare examples of the buildings remain (Dubrow 2002, 326; Bell 2017; Dubrow and Graves 2002, 36, 101).

Bathing could also be done in public facilities. While outside the scope of this book, public bathing is worth acknowledging in the context of privacy. In cities and industrial communities, public bathhouses that included showers, bathtubs, and maybe even a swimming pool provided facilities for thousands of people who did not have them at home. While bathtubs were usually placed in cubicles, providing privacy to the bather, showers were seen as a more communal activity, as well as more often male. Men's supposed lack of modesty made the shower an efficient mechanism for bathing en masse. And public baths could also serve a specialized clientele. A Japanese public bath, a *sento*, survived in Seattle, in the basement of a hotel, and was used until the 1960s (Dubrow and Graves 2002, 83). Saunas were also available commercially for Finnish populations, such as one that survived in Calumet, Michigan, into the 1990s.

The Japanese hot soaking tub and the Finnish sauna also survived in other forms. Transformed into the hot tub and sauna, which found their ways into houses beginning in the 1960s, both hot tubs and saunas are found in non-Japanese, non-Finnish houses in the United States today. Both of them allow, if not encourage, communal bathing, casting aside the hard-won privacy of the bathroom in mid-20th-century America.

Most Americans, though, clung to their private time in the bathroom. With more bathrooms in a house, there was a greater likelihood of a family member finding some private time in one. The multiplication of bathrooms also reflected increased use; Americans were spending more time in their bathrooms. Persuaded by commercial interests after World War I that suggested personal hygiene was vital to social acceptance, they cleaned and shaved, fixed hair and nails, primped and preened in the bathroom. As a 1948 article observed, "The importance of personal hygiene has been nurtured by soap manufacturers and physicians alike. Not only is cleanliness a social must, but a health measure as well. As a result, the Saturday night bath has become a daily occurrence and social America the most fragrant society in the world" ("Bathroom Layouts" 1948, 72). The next chapter will examine the factors that affected bathroom usage and furnishing in more detail.

Chapter 7

CONSUMERISM: EQUIPPING THE BATHROOM

George Babbitt, the fictional creation of Sinclair Lewis, was proud of his house in Zenith, Ohio. "Though the house was not large it had, like all houses on Floral Heights, an altogether royal bathroom of porcelain and glazed tile and metal sleek as silver. The towel-rack was a rod of clear glass set in nickel. The tub was long enough for a Prussian Guard, and above the set bowl was a sensational exhibit of tooth-brush holder, shaving-brush holder, soap-dish, sponge-dish, and medicine-cabinet, so glittering and so ingenious that they resembled an electrical instrument-board." But this morning in 1920, Babbitt was not pleased. Other family members had gotten there first. The floor was wet; the smell of a "heathen toothpaste," not his usual brand, was in the air; and all of the towels were soaked, forcing him to use the embroidered guest towel after his daily shave (Lewis [1922] 1950, 5–6).

Babbitt, that archetypal middle-American conformist, provides a good introduction to the consumerism—or the relationship of humans to consumer goods—of the bathroom of the 1920s (Martin 1993, 142). His bathroom contained fixtures and walls of shiny materials (porcelain, tile, metal), as well as a number of accessories, mostly containers and towels. Babbitt's achievement of the bathroom—the space, fixtures, and finishes—reflected larger currents in society that, in the 1920s, encouraged the consumption of goods to a degree that had not been seen before. How and why a Babbitt would have acquired these furnishings are the subject of this chapter.

After World War I, mass production provided goods for a national market, and Americans' expenditures soared. The New Public Health (or New Hygiene) movement promoted an interest in personal cleanliness, which

Sinclair Lewis (1885–1951) wrote evocatively about George Babbitt's bathroom of 1920. This late–19th-century bathroom in the house where Lewis grew up in Sauk Centre, Minnesota, had a roll-rim tub, a toilet with a raised tank, and a wall-hung sink with two faucets. (Library of Congress)

sanitary-ware manufacturers were happy to serve. This interest in personal hygiene, pushed by advertising, resulted in new ways of envisioning the bathroom, which became a place of style, color, and self-expression.

In the first few decades of the 20th century, the New Public Health gained ascendancy, convincing Americans that, because germs caused illness, their personal behavior could play a part in fending off disease. No longer were such environmental factors as sewer gas and stagnant pipes seen as a cause of illness; instead, the transmission of disease occurred through personal contact with contaminated bodily fluids. Spitting on sidewalks was discouraged. Common drinking cups at public fountains and common roller towels in public bathrooms were frowned on. And personal behavior, such as washing hands, played a large part in public health.

Charles V. Chapin—the superintendent of health for Providence, Rhode Island, and one of the key proponents of the New Public Health—crystallized the new field in a slim volume called *How to Avoid Infection*, published in 1917. In it, he once again discarded the "filth theory" of disease and pointed to germs. While transmission by germs had to be fairly direct, carriers of disease who did not appear to be ill could be the transmitters, so broad cautions against contact were warranted. Common drinking cups, shared pencils that users unconsciously put in their mouths, and the string that a clerk used to tie a package could all be carriers. Coughing, spitting, and sneezing could all transmit disease. Besides avoiding these and other dangers, Chapin also encouraged some active steps, including, "Wash the hands well before eating and always after the use of the toilet." The simple actions of avoidance and cleanliness were inexpensive, easy, and effective: "Personal cleanliness is the cheapest insurance against infection" (61, 62).

Spreading the gospel of the New Hygiene involved influencing people to change their personal behaviors. While a book such as *How to Avoid Infection* sold widely to adults, an easier target was schoolchildren. As early as 1901, Chapin headed the Committee on Diphtheria Bacilli in Well Persons, which concluded that schoolteachers should instruct their students about personal cleanliness. Chapin's committee offered some fundamental health rules, which included, "Do not spit," "Do not put the fingers in the mouth," "Do not put anything in the mouth but food and drink," "Never cough or sneeze in a person's face," and "Keep your face and hands clean; wash the hands with soap and water before each meal" (cited in Cassedy 1962a, 112). Similarly, the National Tuberculosis Association devised a "Modern Health Crusade" for schoolchildren in 1915. Adherents pledged to abide by health rules that included "Keep windows open," "Play and exercise every day in the open air," and, as Chapin had also admonished, "Wash your hands always before eating or handling food," but the Tuberculosis Association went even further: "Wash your ears and neck as well as your face and clean your finger-nails every day. Bathe your whole body twice a week at least and shampoo often. Brush your teeth and rinse your mouth thoroughly every day, after breakfast and supper. Use dental floss." By 1919, more than 3 million children joined the "crusade" (Shryock [1957] 1977, 171).

While the New Public Health had many public policy aspects, including an important role for local government in securing a clean water supply and a sanitary sewer system, the focus on personal hygiene meant that Americans generally paid more attention to cleanliness and their bodies. Sanitary-ware manufacturers took advantage of this new interest in the bathroom, at the same time that production efficiencies were making fixtures more affordable. The manufacturers began the post–World War I period by emphasizing sanitation and cleanliness but shifted in the 1920s to take advantage of the spending promoted by the consumption economy. The offerings of sanitary-ware manufacturers, as evidenced by their catalogs and advertisements, illustrate a fundamental shift in perceptions of bathrooms in the 1920s, from a place of utility to one of style.

In the early 20th century, manufacturers began to target their sales of bathroom fixtures toward homeowners, not just plumbers, thus changing consumption patterns and making their catalogs an interesting barometer of changing intentions. Earlier, manufacturers marketed to plumbers or builders, while selling through jobbers or wholesalers. Standard Manufacturing Company's 1888 catalog, which began with eight pages of cast-iron soil pipes and fittings, was clearly directed at plumbers. In 1901, after Standard Manufacturing's merger into Standard Sanitary Manufacturing Company, the firm's catalog was entitled *Modern Bath Rooms and Appliances: A Few Suggestions about Plumbing Valuable to Home Builders or Those about to Remodel Their Present Dwellings*, indicating that the market now went beyond plumbers. The catalog began with nine designs of bathrooms, perspective drawings showing fixtures in place, and a price list on the facing page. The illustrations were intended to help homeowners visualize how their new bathroom fixtures would appear, while the price list could be handed to a plumber or builder to obtain the fixtures. The 1904 catalog introduced photography, also showing prototypical bathrooms, but with the added realism of photographs. Standard even had a pocket-sized version, complete with photographs and price lists, for plumbers and builders to carry with them.

In the 1910s, as discussed above, concerns for hygiene and sanitation still governed the bathroom. Sewer gas and amorphous threats were no longer thought to be the cause of disease; instead, germs were. Because germs could be removed by cleaning, the bathroom became a place of hard surfaces and whiteness, to better expose the dirt. Such wooden fixture settings as paneling around bathtubs and enclosures around toilets were removed for a more open look. Beginning in 1911, the smooth-fronted double wall enabled bathtubs, once elevated on legs, to be dropped again to the floor. Vitreous-china toilets, once elaborately molded, became simpler for easier cleaning. The catalogs depicted colorful rooms, with tiled walls and floors, paint in a contrasting color, and maybe even a stained-glass window, but the fixtures themselves were white and plain.

Standard frequently invoked the word "modern" in its early-20th-century catalogs. What was modern about its offerings was apparently understood—what could be more up-to-date than the latest domestic technology? The catalog assured its reader of "health, cleanliness, happiness," implying that one flowed from the other (9). J. L. Mott Iron Works titled its 1914 catalog *Modern Plumbing* and heralded "the utility, the convenience, the sanitary and economic advantages of a well-planned, well-equipped bathroom" (9). Both of these companies associated modernity with cleanliness, reflecting the New Hygiene. Mott also emphasized efficiency, a Progressive Era sentiment.

In the mid-1920s, however, a noticeable shift occurred, illustrated by Crane's 1920 and 1926 catalogs. Both carried the same color image on the front, a large house seen obliquely through gateposts. Crane's 1920 catalog, titled *Plumbing*, contained just two perspective drawings showing entire bathrooms, followed by 14 pages of unadorned vitreous-china

pedestal sinks, 6 pages of
vitreous-china wall-hung
sinks, and 4 pages of
enameled cast-iron sinks,
before moving on to tubs.
By 1926, the strategy had
changed completely. The
catalog was now titled
Homes of Comfort, and it
promised to explain "how
Crane fixtures help make
them possible." In a sec-
tion titled "The Bathroom
Beautiful," the catalog
assured readers that "it
need not be a ready made
room, in a cold monotony
of white, reminiscent of
the hospital," but it could
"express your personal
taste, your individuality"
(3). This could be achieved
through "such simple aids
as color and line." While

**The Crane Company depicted an ideal
bathroom in this sketch, ca. 1927:
double-walled tub with shower, pedestal
sink, low-tank toilet, medicine cabinet,
towel rack, soap dishes, and toilet-paper
holder. (Library of Congress)**

mentioning "luxury and elegance" and "distinction without extravagance,"
the catalog also maintained that "the daily bath is your birthright" (2). The
catalog included four perspective drawings of bathrooms, each with a plan
and hyperbolic text on the facing page. The sinks, again receiving their
own pages, were pictured with mirrors, lights, and shelves. The catalog
embodied the new interest in the bathroom as a place of style.

The smoother lines of the bathroom of the late 1920s and 1930s dem-
onstrated this aesthetic. Bathtubs could be set in recesses, surrounded by
walls on three sides, now that pipes no longer had to be exposed to guard
against the buildup of sewer gas. Showers, too, gained in popularity, with
the development of mixing valves to provide a more even temperature.
Showers could be set in their own recesses or over the tub. Crane's 1926
catalog depicted six tubs, all walled on at least two sides, sometimes three;
all of these tubs had showers, and none of them had exposed pipes or hoses.
Pedestal sinks, with substantial vitreous-china center legs, gave way to
sinks perched on slender metal or glass legs. Crane advertised one of these
on "crystal glass legs" in 1926, Standard showed sinks on legs of metal

and glass in 1927, and Kohler the same in 1929. With the less-obtrusive sink supports and concealed pipes, the bathroom of the late 1920s had smoother lines and more coherent forms.

Some efforts at rethinking the tub also emphasized a streamlined quality. Standard introduced a new shape of tub in the early 1930s. The "Neo-Angle" tub was about four feet square, with the well set diagonally across it, achieving the full five-and-a-half-foot length. The Neo-Angle easily fit in a recess and provided room on the edge for sitting, either for washing the feet or showering. The catalog copy advised, "What a boon . . . to elderly bathers, to invalids or tired bathers of any age," but the images promoted it as sleek and modern (89). Kohler countered in 1936 with a "three-way tub" that allowed users to bathe in the tub, shower while standing in the tub, or sit on a seat built into the back of the tub.

The greatest change in the late 1920s, driving the discussion of the new emphasis on style, was the introduction of color. Until the mid-1920s, many elements of the average American home were monochromatic— white bathroom fixtures and kitchen sink, black stove, black automobile. Suddenly, that changed. Such colored items as alarm clocks, trash cans, and typewriters began to appear. As one observer wrote in 1930, "During the past few years a great pail has up-ended itself over the American scene, has splashed our household goods and gods with a rich, warm stream of flat, bright color" ("Color in Industry" 1930, 85). Responding to the prosperity and consumerism of the 1920s, manufacturers sought a way to differentiate their products, and color—whose application was aided by technological advancements in paints and manufacturing—helped do that. *Vogue* magazine argued in 1927 that "gay colours and good taste bring chic into the bathroom." The article proclaimed of bathrooms that "even the whitest and most 'sanitary-looking' need not be given up as quite hopeless." Instead, tiles, plaster walls, wallpaper, window shades, shower curtains, and towels could all be colored. "Cerulean-blue, Italian-pink, a delicate mauve, or a jade-green are all delightful colours" and could even be mixed together ("New Orders" 1927, 19).

Soon thereafter, colored bathroom fixtures hit the market. Once the technology of color consistency across two materials—vitreous china and enameled cast iron—was developed, initially by Universal Sanitary in 1926, other manufacturers quickly offered colored fixtures as well. Kohler's 1928 catalog, *Color Charm Enters the Bathroom*, offered fixtures in six pastel colors: Autumn Brown, Lavender, Spring Green, Old Ivory, West Point Grey, and Horizon Blue. The catalog, just 16 pages, showed the colored fixtures in a perspective view with tiled walls and floors in a contrasting color; on the facing page, a slightly smaller image showed the same colored fixtures with similarly colored floors and walls. In 1929, Kohler offered toilet seats in a variety of colors in a "bright pleasing wavy Pearl finish," designed to harmonize with, but not necessarily match, the flat colors of the fixtures (46).

Also that year, for an exhibit at the Metropolitan Museum of Art, architect Ely Jacques Kahn created a bathroom that utilized jet-black Kohler fixtures. Consistent with the modernist esthetic, Kahn claimed that the room was "without decoration as a basis," but its rich materials gave it a busy appearance. Glass and tile walls, metal radiator grills, rubberized floor "that should obviate the need of bathmats or warm floor covering," and a plush chaise longue offered a variety of textures. Kahn set the black bathtub in an alcove, and at the focal point of the room placed a wide but thin black sink, perched on chrome legs (Metropolitan Museum 1929, 62–65). Not only was color fashionable, but the most extreme color of all—black—was celebrated.

By 1930, Standard offered fixtures in nine colors and for each one suggested complementary colors for floors, walls, and draperies. Perspective views in its catalog that year showed such combinations as bright pink fixtures with green walls and yellow draperies, bright blue fixtures with off-white walls and green tiled floor, and purple fixtures with yellow walls and dark blue tiled floor. Standard balanced the innovation of colored fixtures with historic and familiar, albeit exotic, names—the Rose du Barry bathroom with pink fixtures, the Ming Green, the Ionian Black. The National Bureau of Standards published colors for sanitary ware in 1931, setting parameters for six colors: green, orchid, ivory, blue, light brown, and black. Kohler initially resisted this standardization, wanting its colors to be a distinctive marketing tool (Blaszczyk 2000, 201–2).

The introduction of color into bathroom fixtures meant that consumers had to be taught about harmony and compatibility. Manufacturers and consumers were united in the belief that all of the fixtures had to be the same color, which meant that color helped sell additional fixtures. Consumers would be inclined to buy all the fixtures at the same time and from the same manufacturer, which was good for business. But how to set the fixtures off against the appropriate walls and floors required implied coaching in the form of colored perspective views and color charts, which the catalogs were happy to provide. This new emphasis on proper selection was also seen in the promotion of fixtures in terms of ensembles—a ready-made selection that took the guesswork out of compatibility.

Viewing bathroom fixtures as an ensemble was not entirely new—when catalogs grouped fixtures into a perspective view of a prototypical bathroom, they were suggesting that certain fixtures were compatible with each other.

They did not name their fixtures across type, however; the Mott catalog in 1914 showed a Valcour bathroom, but it had a Plaza tub, a Langham toilet, and a Valcour lavatory. These fixtures could be put in other arrangements. The introduction of color forced manufacturers to conceive of the bathroom as an ensemble. When Kohler introduced color in 1928, it announced, "We had color in the bathroom; now we have *the bathroom in color*—a complete color *ensemble*, a new color charm" (2). In 1931, Kohler introduced "Matched Beauty in Plumbing Fixtures," two sets of fixtures with the same design motifs. As the catalog explained, through these sets "discriminating women can now carry out in bathroom composition, the unity of feeling and harmony of style they strive to express in other home rooms" (18-D). Standard featured a Chateau Group, Neo-Mode Group, Villa Group, and so on, in its catalog from about 1935. The Manor Group offered "complete harmony of fixture line" (10). Crane also offered groups of fixtures in 1936; the Corwith Group offered "a widely approved ensemble of related designs" (3). In 1940, the company offered "Crane ensembles to suit every taste and pocketbook" (5). Kohler also noted the advantages of ensembles to salesmen: "Where old merchandising methods sold a single piece, this new Kohler suggestion promotes the sale of *an entire bathroom*" (1931, 18-D).

In the late 1920s and 1930s, sanitary-ware manufacturers gave "modern" a new meaning. Bathroom fixtures were not just a sign of contemporary, advanced technology; they were also an expression of artistic taste. The popular style at the time was a modernism influenced by art deco that favored streamlined appearances, new materials, and color—perfect for the ahistorical space of the bathroom. When Standard offered a line it called Neo-Classic, in about 1930, it called its products "Fixtures of Modern Design" and noted that while "all plumbing fixtures are modern in the sense that they are recent," these fixtures "have that unstudied simplicity and beauty of line which make them adaptable for the present form of interior decoration" (32A). One article recommended such antimodernist decor as flowery wallpapers and chintz curtains to offset the sleek fixtures, and the same article argued that "the last notes of white can be eliminated," celebrating beauty's victory over "utilitarian plainness" (Sprackling 1928, 730). The challenge, as expressed by Kohler in 1929, was to sell "modern beauty and usefulness," turning the utilitarian space of the bathroom into a place that expressed style and taste. As one writer observed in 1930, "For a long time the plumber had been selling mere sinks. Now he was selling Beauty." The bathroom had become a "show place" ("Color in Industry" 1930, 90, 92).

Although sanitary-ware manufacturers did not sell directly to consumers, they did advertise to them, encouraging them either explicitly to visit a showroom or, implicitly, to demand their product from plumbers and architects. Differing subtly from their catalogs, the manufacturers' advertisements were more likely to show people in the illustrations, suggesting who should use the new fixtures and how. Kohler's advertising campaign in 1916 included six national magazines (such as the *Saturday Evening Post*) that together had a circulation of 2 million, as well as seven professional journals (such as *American Architect* and *Plumbers' Trade Journal*) (Moskowitz 2004, 94). Initially, the sanitary-ware manufacturers emphasized the sanitary effects of new bathroom fixtures, as might be expected. A 1905 Standard ad showed a maid bathing a child in a bathtub and promised that its products would "guarantee the comfort and sanitation of your home." In 1926, Standard was selling "a frank little book on home sanitation" written by a Mrs. Ann Richards. Without ever mentioning the word "toilet" but depicting one in the background behind two elegantly dressed women, the ad suggested that toilets differed in important ways: some were easier to keep clean, some were more sanitary, and some were "commended by feminine hygiene." And the consumer should know the difference and, presumably, select one made by Standard.

The use of people in advertisements aimed to catch the reader's attention. Men were rarely shown; instead, women, often wearing demure robes, were pictured. Children, too, were popular subjects, especially in Kohler ads. Children could be depicted naked, being safely sexless, and evoked the idea of home. A Kohler ad from 1923 showed two children at the bathroom sink and was titled "The Shrine of Cleanliness." The next year, Kohler's ad called "The Pride of Cleanliness" declared, "The modern bathroom is one of Youth's great teachers." The ad evoked the New Public Health movement and its focus on training children in sanitary habits.

By the mid-1920s, though, even before the introduction of colored fixtures, the manufacturers' ads also reflected a new interest in style. Advertisements could be in color, even if the products were not. The *Saturday Evening Post* first included a four-page insert of color advertisements in 1924, and other popular magazines followed suit ("Color in Industry" 1930, 87). Sanitary-ware manufacturers showed their products, still white, in vividly colored surroundings. With the introduction of colored fixtures in 1928, though, they declared a revolution. "The great change has come in plumbing fixtures," said a Standard ad, and declared "the enchanting transformation of the bathroom from plainness to beauty." Early in 1928, Standard ads depicted white fixtures while the accompanying text assured consumers that these fixtures would soon be available in a range of colors, and by July, Standard was able to include colored fixtures in its ad; for *Better Homes and Gardens*, it selected pink. The next year, Standard encouraged readers to send away for its catalog, *Color and Style in Bathroom Furnishing and Decoration.* To achieve the right combinations of color, consumers had to be advised by professionals. "What colors would you use with plumbing fixtures of Ming Green?" one ad queried. "If you believe that the enchanting beauty of color is due as much to the correct and harmonious use of it as to the color itself," then the reader was advised to send for the catalog.

The bathrooms that Standard depicted in its ads were opulent, often with the bathtub and toilet in separate recesses covered discreetly by curtains, the sink perched on thin metal legs, and occasionally the tub sunken into the floor. In one ad, dark blue fixtures were set against a blue and yellow floor and accented with red curtains. Standard pushed its Neo-Classic line, hoping not to alienate consumers by being *too* modern. It showed a yellow tub and pedestal sink "in a *Directoire* setting," with red walls and a blue floor. A Directoire-style stool and towel rack provided the historicist clues. Crane apparently had no compunction about being modern, showing white marbled fixtures against black walls and floor with some gold decoration in an art deco design. Kohler, in contrast, remained conservative, describing the introduction of colored fixtures as "charm" and showing wholesome family scenes in its ads.

The introduction of style to the bathroom was a convenient way to suggest that the consumer should replace fixtures in already existing bathrooms. This had been a strong argument even before the concern about esthetics, given that manufacturers were pitching their products to an upper-class clientele who could afford to install bathrooms before World War I. As a Standard Sanitary ad said in 1921, "Is your bathroom ten years old? If so, it is possible that the fixtures should be replaced." The implication that they might be faulty and unsanitary was corrected in the next sentence, when the ad copy pointed out that "they may not be up to date." But the introduction of colored fixtures meant that they were horribly, visibly out-of-date. A 1929 ad said, "Bathrooms have aged more in the past year than in all the twenty gone before. The coming of color, freeing bathroom decoration from the dominance of white, has 'dated' the bathrooms of many fine homes."

The promotion of style also led the advertisers to invoke architects. Associated Tile Manufacturers, promoting its Keramic Tiles, showed an octagonal bathroom designed by the architect Frederick G. Frost. The view of the bathroom with a pink tub and walls, a brownish-yellow floor and vaulted ceiling, and dark gray trim was accompanied by a small floor plan. The accompanying text assured the reader that "today architects everywhere—not satisfied with designing the bathroom as a mere utility—are making it one of the architectural jewels of the house." To encourage this trend, Standard sponsored a competition among architects and then distributed a collection of their designs at a cost of $2. The architect Richard Haviland Smythe proffered a bathroom that had a sunken tub and sink on metal legs set in a room with black glass walls ornamented with gold seaweed and fish. Salvatore Grillo, of the prestigious architectural firm of McKim, Mead and White, designed a bathroom in which the "Pompeiian motif is worked out in Verona marble with inlays of black terrazzo."

Another influence on the elevation of the bathroom to a place of style was Hollywood movies, which depicted opulent bathrooms (Sivulka 2001, 164–65). Reflecting a cultural shift toward loosening sexual mores and an interest in luxurious surroundings, *Male and Female*, a 1919 film starring Gloria Swanson and directed by Cecil B. DeMille, was one of the first of these (L. Jacobs 1939, 338, 399–400). To establish the heroine as a spoiled noblewoman living a life of luxury, the film showed her taking her morning bath, assisted by two maids who carefully screened her with towels and robes while she got in and out of the tub. An animal-skin rug lay on the black-and-white tiled floor, and rich materials and fabrics decorated the bathroom. A mirrored wall, discreetly covered with a curtain when needed, helped frame the sunken tub. Swanson's bath, enhanced by bath salts, was followed by a shower of rose water. The Hollywood movies of the post–World War I era instructed viewers in new behaviors, evidenced particularly by an intertitle in *Male and Female* that pondered the status of the bathroom: "Humanity is assuredly growing *cleaner*—but is it growing more artistic? Women bathe more often, but not as beautifully as did their ancient Sisters. Why shouldn't the Bath Room express as much Art and Beauty as the Drawing Room?" Advertising copywriters could not have said it better.

As *Male and Female* suggested by a lingering shot of a shelf of decorative glass containers, accessories were critical to the achievement of the styled bathroom. A 1921 article titled "The Well-Equipped Bathroom" recommended the purchase of a stool, laundry hamper, scale, rug, guest towels, and a bowl of potpourri (58–59). By the end of the 1920s, color had taken over, at least in advertisers' copy. As one magazine article noted, "Even the bath sponge takes on color; and for the punctilious they come in rose, lavender, green, and blue." Bathroom sets, in color of course, included a mat, "a rather large-sized rug," a stool, and a lid cover. But it was glass that the author thought lent the greatest beauty: "Bottles of all sizes, shapes, and colors come in sets of assorted sizes just to hold and surround with colorful glamour such mundane contents as eye lotion, hand lotion, boric acid, and many others" (Sprackling 1928, 797). Sinclair Lewis likened the "sensational exhibit" of medicine cabinet and containers in

Babbitt's bathroom to "an electrical instrument-board," identifying it with modernity (Lewis [1922] 1950, 6).

Sanitary-ware manufacturers provided many of the built-in accessories, such as towel rods, shelves, toothbrush holders, and so on. Mott's 1914 catalog included eight pages of soap dishes, tumbler holders, towel racks and hooks, shelves, toilet-paper dispensers for either sheets or rolls, mirrors, a chair, and a stool. By the late 1920s, the previously nickel-plated items were now produced in chrome or even in vitreous china. With the accessories colored to harmonize or contrast with the surrounding wall, one style maven celebrated "an amazing choice of about thirty-six colors" to "satisfy the most exacting taste" (Sprackling 1928, 751, 793). Even the lowly sponge holder had become an object for which discernment was required.

The guest towel particularly raised the ire of Sinclair Lewis's Babbitt, who apparently had only one bathroom in his house, because he had to share it with potential guests. Reaching for a dry towel after shaving, he found none but the towel reserved for guests: "Then George F. Babbitt did a dismaying thing. He wiped his face on the guest-towel! It was a pansy-embroidered trifle which always hung there to indicate that the Babbitts were in the best Floral Heights society. No one had ever used it. No guest had ever dared to. Guests secretively took a corner of the nearest regular towel" (Lewis [1922] 1950, 5). Lewis's identification of the guest towel as a status symbol was complemented by his skewering of its fussiness, which seems to have been justified. A contemporary advice article promoted guest towels with mosaic embroidery, Madeira cut work, cross-stitch border, or filet insertions ("Well-Equipped Bathroom" 1921, 59).

Wall coverings, another opportunity to add style to the bathroom, had provided color while the fixtures were still white. The introduction of colored fixtures meant that "color has inundated the floors, crept up to the walls, and spilled over into the bathtub" (Sprackling 1928, 750). Tiled walls were preferable, available in a wealth of color, finish, and size, so that "it would seem that no one could ever again use plain white tile, so glaring, so deadly uninteresting" (Sprackling 1928, 793). Tile might form only a wainscot, though, which provided opportunity on the upper wall for "paneled wood, tile board, colored cement, or merely painted plaster," on which could be hung "canvas, chintz, or innumerable colorful papers, purchased already glazed, or to be covered with a waterproof finish" (Sprackling 1928, 794). Or an artist could produce a mural "with frescoes in colour and with contrasts of silver, gold, and black" for "a gay and sophisticated effect" ("New Orders" 1927, 91). Another author heralded a "rather elaborate" bathroom in which "no white tiling shows, except inside the bathtub." "The floor, baseboard, washstand, and tub are all marbleized black," and "the wall tiling is covered with aluminum leaf," which unlike silver leaf did not tarnish ("New Orders 1927, 138). This art deco fondness for metallic colors could also be achieved with mirrors applied to an entire wall surface. As outrageous as these suggestions were, and as unlikely as it is that they were followed to any great degree, the consideration of the bathroom for such effects or even for far more modest decoration reflects the elevation of the bathroom to a place that was "as much an embodiment of the taste and personality of the owner as his own living-room," as one *House Beautiful* writer insisted (Sprackling 1928, 750).

The desire for a bathroom of luxury and style that flourished in the 1920s dissipated as the Great

Water is meaningful in Death Valley, California, so the shrine created for this bathtub in 1922 is understandable. Elaborate tilework runs throughout the house at Death Valley Ranch. Photo by Jack E. Boucher, 1987. (Library of Congress)

Depression took hold, causing consumers to seek cheaper options. Plumbing-industry sales dropped by 90 percent between 1929 and 1932, before rising again slowly (Blodgett 2003, 87). Sanitary-ware catalogs recognized the need for economy and began to downplay colored fixtures. Kohler's 1936 catalog discussed "an attractive economy" in bathroom design, offering fixtures for "modest homes," and acknowledged that "there is much to be said in favor of white," which was cheaper than colored fixtures (5, 7, 9). Three years later, the catalog called white "gay and inexpensive." One proposed ensemble showed a white tub and toilet and a red enameled cast-iron sink and labeled it a "rouge-accented budget bath." The text assured readers that "the cost of one colored fixture is negligible" (6). Crane's 1939 catalog admitted that "most people prefer white fixtures," although the company offered fixtures in eight other colors. On two pages of color options, white fixtures were set in blue, green, red, yellow, orchid, or brown bathrooms, achieved through colored walls, floors, and shower curtains (6, 11, 12). Besides their greater initial expense, colored fixtures had faced some resistance from landlords as well as homeowners concerned about resale value (Blaszczyk 2000, 205). Style could be expensive, which was also the point. Colored fixtures and other expensive materials expressed not only taste but also wealth—the means to afford costlier furnishings.

Unfamiliar to the previous generation, the hard-surfaced bathroom of the 1910s and 1920s, with its gleaming fixtures and tiled walls and floors, was unhindered by tradition. Sanitary-ware manufacturers and the advertising industry developed the idea of the bathroom as a place of self-expression, where a family's status would be on display. The chic bathroom appealed to only a narrow slice of the population—far fewer than one-half of Americans had indoor bathrooms in the 1920s—but like Hollywood movies, they suggested a life of wealth and material accumulation that was to be aspired to. Lost in the shift to glamor in the late 1920s was the white sanitary bathroom of the early 20th century, promoted by the New Hygiene. Cleanliness was assumed by the upper class; it did not need to be proven by white fixtures and tiles. Whether consumers actually installed colored fixtures in proportion to the ads for them is doubtful, but the push to remake the bathroom as a place of style and therefore status reflected changed attitudes toward a utilitarian, hygienic place.

Chapter 8

PERSONAL CARE: SELLING THE BATHROOM

The enhancement of the bathroom as a place of style was accompanied by an interest in personal care to make the body equally stylish. A scent that appealed, soft skin that was a pleasure to touch, hair that shone, teeth that gleamed—all were part of an interest in personal care that blossomed after World War I. As American manufacturers, aided by increased mechanization, produced more goods in the 1920s, the economy shifted from one of production, or providing enough goods to satisfy demand, to one of consumption, or focusing on consumers and creating demand (Potter 1954, 173). Product differentiation was necessary to attract consumers, and advertising achieved this. In the 1910s and 1920s, advertising for perfumes, makeup, and toiletries increased tenfold and production tripled (Sivulka 2001, 181; Vinikas 1992, 55). Advertising not only helped sell products, but it also instructed consumers on what to do in the bathroom—how to apply shampoo, how often to bathe, why mouthwash was essential (Potter 1954, 169).

Several factors contributed to the interest in personal care, including the New Public Health movement that stressed personal cleanliness as a means of disease prevention. Also, the United States was increasingly an urban nation, which meant that more people crowded into cities, living and traveling in close proximity to one another. They also spent more time indoors, at work and play, so that body odors were more noticeable. The bathroom mirror illuminated by electric light exposed flaws that had not concerned Americans before. All of these influences led people to be more anxious about their appearance and odor, concerns that were amplified and assuaged by advertising and a thriving toiletry market and that were addressed largely in the bathroom.

In 1920, the journal *Domestic Engineering* inaugurated a campaign called "Take a Bath Every Day" in order to increase the business of its readership, which was mostly plumbers and contractors. In the next two years, the journal distributed 5 million stickers, as well as window signs, buttons, posters, brochures, and articles to reprint in local newspapers, encouraging the daily bath ("What the 'Take a Bath Every Day' Campaign Means" 1920, 399–400; "Two Years Old" 1922, 369). By the end of the decade, though, manufacturers of products for use in the bathroom had completely usurped the plumbers' role of encouraging Americans to bathe, and print advertising was their medium.

Employing a variety of approaches in the early 20th century, advertising helped introduce new bathroom products and position old products for new uses. It also instructed consumers in the use of these products and promoted their frequent use, in order to enhance sales. The development of ensembles and selling the idea of style, as the sanitary-ware manufacturers were doing, were also effective sales strategies. But the most important element was to develop a brand, and soaps led the way with this in the 19th century.

In the mid-19th century, soap manufacturers faced a challenge. Their product was not particularly branded, in that they sold long slabs of soap to grocers, who cut off pieces on demand and sold it by weight. Consumers did not usually choose between multiple soaps. Consumers also did not necessarily use soap for bathing. The common soap was yellow in color, harsh in feel, and mostly employed for laundry. Consumers could make yellow soap at home, combining ashes with water to make potash or lye and then mixing that with animal fats to make soap. Achieving consistency with homemade soaps was difficult, though. Perfumed toilet soaps imported from Paris were individually wrapped and too expensive for everyday use. Toilet soap was marketed for beauty enhancement, not cleanliness (Bushman and Bushman 1988, 1233). The English government even taxed soap as a luxury item until 1863 (Gibbs 1939, 187).

Procter & Gamble, a Cincinnati firm established in 1837 when William Procter, a candlemaker, and James Gamble, a soap maker, combined forces to make soap. Eventually, they developed a white soap that was suitable for both bath and laundry. Trademarked in 1879, Ivory's name emphasized its whiteness. The company employed university chemists to determine that it was "99 and 44/100% pure." Its other virtue, that it floated, was achieved by a serendipitous mixing error, but Procter & Gamble realized that consumers liked its floatability because it was less likely to get lost in a laundry tub or in a soap-sudsy bathtub. The manufacturers sold a large bar of Ivory, appropriate for the laundry, with notches in the middle, so that the consumer could use a string to divide it in half, creating two bath-sized bars.

Procter & Gamble's next task was to sell this new product. One marketing strategy was for manufacturers to put their own name on a product, implying a personal guarantee of quality. Benjamin Talbot Babbitt began producing individually wrapped all-purpose soap in 1836 and named it "Babbitt's Best Soap." As a promotion later in the century, the wrappers themselves became collectibles, and consumers could exchange 25 of them for an item such as a harmonica. Similarly, druggist John H. Woodbury put a picture of his face in every advertisement

IVORY SOAP

99 ⁴⁴⁄₁₀₀% PURE
IT FLOATS

Procter & Gamble revolutionized bathing when it introduced Ivory soap in 1879. Ivory's whiteness contrasted with the all-purpose yellow soap that had been the norm. The notches in the bar enabled the user to cut it in half for the bath, or use it whole for the laundry. (Jay Paull/Getty Images)

for his Woodbury's Facial Soap (Sivulka 2001, 52–53, 75). But Procter & Gamble chose another approach, which was to give their product a name that implied something about its quality—hence, Ivory and its association with whiteness.

In an effort to inspire brand loyalty, soap became one of the first nationally advertised products in America. In the 1880s, four companies pioneered national advertising on a grand scale, and three of them were soap manufacturers—Sapolio, Pears', and Procter & Gamble (Potter 1954, 170). (Royal Baking Powder was the fourth.) In 1889, Pears', a British competitor that marketed a translucent soap, pioneered the celebrity endorsement when it quoted Rev. Henry Ward Beecher likening cleanliness to godliness, splashing it across the front page of the *New York Herald*. By 1900, Babbitt spent $400,000 annually on advertising, and by 1905, Procter & Gamble did the same (Sivulka 2001, 93, 84).

Advertising strategies varied among the soap producers. For Ivory, Procter & Gamble often chose images of children and babies, to emphasize the purity of its product. Palmolive, a toilet soap made from palm oil and olive oil, in 1909 set out to capture the market that was interested in beauty. Lifebuoy, made by a subsidiary of the British firm Lever Brothers, played off of its name that implied it was a life-saving product, linking the soap to the then-current interest in hygiene.

Woodbury was the first to use sex to sell its soap. Having been acquired by the Andrew Jergens Company in 1900, Woodbury's soap was advertised beginning in 1911 with the tag line, "A skin you love to touch," with implications of woman's sexuality (Sivulka 2001, 149–52; Scott 2015). A 1916 full-page ad showed an elegantly dressed woman being nuzzled by a handsome man, along with the tag line. A picture of the Dr. Woodbury–faced bar of soap appeared in one corner, along with text instructing the consumer how to use the product: "Just before retiring, lather your wash cloth well with Woodbury's Facial Soap and warm water. Apply it to your face," and so on. A few years later, the "skin you love to touch" campaign was heralded as a triumph of advertising: "What a monument of argument! What a poetic figure! Could anything be more alluring! The phrase sings itself into your memory. It even scans" ("Words That Sing" 1919, 575).

Woodbury's introduced a new advertising strategy, which would become popular after World War I. Rather than simply describe what the product could do (clean a body, achieve soft skin), ads increasingly described the effect (e.g., gain the attentions of an attractive man). Advertisers identified problems, such as self-consciousness about one's appearance, and argued that their products could solve this failing. Using melodramatic stories, the ads appealed to desires, either to achieve a certain end or to avoid social ignominy. As an advertising executive noted in 1930, the inferiority complex had become "a valuable thing in advertising" (quoted in Marchand 1985, 13). The industry also increasingly directed its ads to a female audience, recognizing that women did the majority of purchasing items for the home. One advertising man remarked sarcastically about his profession, "All women need nowadays is the right soap and the right toothpaste, and the world is theirs . . . in a cellophane wrapper" (Edwards 1937, 12).

A second strategic shift addressed the appearance of ads. Text-heavy ads before the war shifted to sparer ads with more white space and one main image, usually of people, not the product itself. The marketing of color in all products was aided by the introduction of color printing in national magazines in the mid-1920s (Marchand 1985, 7). Advertisers hired prominent illustrators to produce memorable color images, which were also sold to consumers as prints. Clarence Underwood illustrated some of Woodbury's "A Skin You Love to Touch" ads. Readers could send away for a print of the image, along with a small bar of soap, for 10 cents. The 1930s saw a shift away from color to black-and-white photography, appreciated for its realism. Renowned photographers, such as Edward Steichen, produced images for ads, like the tastefully nude women used to sell Cannon towels and Woodbury soap (Sivulka 2001, 204–5). A 1938 ad for Marelle Bath Foam, which was sold in an art deco–style container, showed a naked woman sitting on the edge of a sudsy tub, only her feet and hands covered by foam. The nudity was attention-grabbing, but the ads were deliberately discreet.

A third strategic shift in advertising involved reflecting the tenets of the New Public Health. Advertisers promoted not only cleanliness but also antiseptic, germ-free, and sanitary results. A 1911 ad for Lifebuoy soap urged the use of "this pure and wholesome antiseptic toilet soap with your bath and shampoo" and promised, "Its use is fatal to disease germs." Consistent with the Progressive Era reliance on experts, advertisers often pictured doctors or druggists recommending a particular product (Lears 1994, 174–75). Especially for biological issues, advertisers were willing to offer advice that even one's best friend was reluctant to proffer. Advertising took on such intimate matters as menstruation, body odor, bad breath, and constipation. During the 1920s, though, cleanliness became less of an objective, while personal presentation grew in importance. By the end of the decade, hygiene was rarely mentioned.

In preying on personal insecurities, advertisers promoted a body image that was untainted by natural smells, hair, fat, or imperfection. To some degree, it was a denial of biological realities. The ideal promoted in advertisements was white and Anglo-Saxon, reflecting anti-immigrant concern among middle-class whites in the 1920s (Fox [1984] 1997, 101). The ideal was also free from body odors, which went beyond the cleanliness demanded of the New Hygiene and into personal preference. Middle-class women did not generally use perfume in the 1910s, but by the mid-1920s, nearly three-quarters of American women did (Vinikas 1992, 43). The perfect body promoted in advertisements was sweet-smelling, modern, sleek, white, and most of all clean (Lears 1994, 171). This ideal could be achieved with specific products, most of them used in the bathroom.

One strategy for profiting from the new interest in personal hygiene was to reposition existing products for new uses. The classic example is Listerine. Developed by Joseph Lawrence and licensed to Jordan Lambert in 1881, Listerine was an antiseptic solution intended for use in surgery, to replace the harsher carbolic acid then in use. Lambert even traveled to England to seek the imprimatur of the greatest proponent of antiseptic surgery, Joseph Lister, and to obtain his permission to use his name. Sales were steady for several decades, providing a tidy income for the family.

Aside from surgical use, the Lambert Pharmacal Company promoted Listerine for colds and sore throats, dandruff, and teeth cleaning. In 1922, Lambert's son Gerard, deeply in debt, decided to enter the family business in St. Louis. After streamlining production and cutting costs by a third, Gerard Lambert turned his attention to the product's advertising. Seeking an acceptable way to discuss bad breath, Lambert appropriated a term used in an obscure article in the British medical journal the *Lancet*: halitosis. Lambert seized on this word for his advertising, effectively repositioning his product for greater usage and inventing a disease in the process. His ads suggested that consumers suffered from bad breath unknowingly, using such headlines as "Even Your Best Friend Won't Tell You" and "Often a Bridesmaid but Never a Bride." These minidramas were described by the copywriter's eulogist as "advertising dramas rather than business announcements—dramas so common to everyday experience that every reader could easily fit himself into the plot as the hero or culprit of its action! He directed his appeal mainly to human hopes and vanities with the advertiser's commodity always subordinated to the human color of his story" (Lennen 1926, 28).

Lambert increased the advertising budget from $100,000 in 1922 to more than $5 million in 1928; the business grew exponentially as well. There were, admittedly, other reasons that mouthwash grew in popularity at this time. Increased smoking and decreased acceptability of drinking, due to Prohibition, also contributed to the perceived need for mouthwash (Vinikas 1992, 36). Lambert promoted Listerine as an aftershave tonic, a deodorant, a scalp treatment, and a cure for colds and sore throats, as well as a mouthwash, and brought out a Listerine toothpaste too. After a year in St. Louis, Lambert moved to New York City and founded an advertising firm, realizing that pushing a product was even more lucrative than making it. In the fall of 1928, Lambert sold his interests both in the family company, Lambert Pharmacal, and his advertising agency, realizing a profit of $25 million (Fox [1984] 1997, 97–98; Marchand 1985, 18).

Lambert's identification of a disease that people did not know they had was complemented by efforts to give popular names to obscure diseases. *Tinea trichophyton*, a skin condition caused by a ringworm fungus, was repositioned as "athlete's foot" when it began appearing at a greater rate in gymnasiums and locker rooms in the early 20th century. An adman proposed a campaign to the makers of the liniment Absorbine Jr. using this term. Consequently, "athlete's foot" entered the lexicon, and an old liniment had a new use (Fox [1984] 1997, 98).

Even identifying a new problem without giving it a new name could be effective. When the makers of Pepsodent toothpaste asked Claude

Hopkins to devise an advertising campaign, he identified a "film" on teeth that he decided needed to be removed in order to enhance beauty. "They keep teeth white in a new way now—by removing film," read one 1919 ad. Or, 10 years later, "FILM: A dangerous coating that robs teeth of their whiteness." Hopkins observed that, while toothpaste's best use was as a preventive, consumers were more interested in treating troubles than in preventing them. He also rejected a strategy of depicting the negative results if someone did not use Pepsodent, noting, "People do not want to read of the penalties. They want to be told of rewards" (Hopkins 1927, 152). Pepsodent's campaign as "the special film-removing dentifrice" was hugely successful,

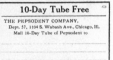

The Price You Pay

For dingy film on teeth

Let us show you by a ten-day test how combating film in this new way beautifies the teeth.

Now your teeth are coated with a viscous film. You can feel it with your tongue. It clings to teeth, enters crevices and stays. It forms the basis of fixed cloudy coats.

Keeps teeth dingy

Film absorbs stains, making the teeth look dingy. Film is the basis of tartar. It holds

food substance which ferments and forms acids. It holds the acids in contact with the teeth to cause decay.

Millions of germs breed in it. They, with tartar, are the chief cause of pyorrhea. Thus most tooth troubles are now traced to film. And, despite the tooth brush, they have constantly increased.

Attack it daily

Careful people have this film removed twice yearly by

their dentists. But the need is for a daily film combatant.

Now dental science, after long research, has found two ways to fight film. Able authorities have proved their efficiency. A new-type tooth paste has been perfected to comply with modern requirements. The name is Pepsodent. These two film combatants are embodied in it, to fight the film twice daily.

Two other effects

Pepsodent also multiplies the starch digestant in saliva. That is there to digest starch deposits which otherwise may cling and form acids. It multiplies the alkalinity of the saliva. That is Nature's neutralizer for acids which cause decay.

Millions employ it

Millions of people now use Pepsodent, largely by dental advice. The results are seen everywhere — in glistening teeth.

Once see its effects and you will adopt it too. You will always want the whiter, cleaner, safer teeth you see. Make this test and watch the changes that it brings. Cut out the coupon now.

Pepsodent
REG. U.S. PAT. OFF.

The New-Day Dentifrice

Endorsed by modern authorities and now advised by leading dentists nearly all the world over. All druggists supply the large tubes.

10-Day Tube Free

THE PEPSODENT COMPANY,
Dept. 57, 1104 S. Wabash Ave., Chicago, Ill.
Mail 10-Day Tube of Pepsodent to

Only one tube to a family

Toothpaste manufacturing was a highly competitive industry that relied on advertising for sales. In this 1922 ad, Pepsodent used several ploys: it mentioned a new problem, film on teeth; it cited experts; and it offered a free ten-day supply—which was also a way to gauge the effectiveness of its ads. (Smith Collection/Gado/Getty Images)

making it one of the most popular brands by the late 1920s and earning Hopkins $1 million. Dentifrices—toothpastes, powders, and liquids—served as a textbook example of the effectiveness of advertising. A dozen heavily advertised brands took 90 percent of the market, even though they cost significantly more than their less-advertised competitors (Borden 1942, 294).

Another strategy for filling consumers' desires for things they did not know they wanted was to develop a new product, such as deodorant. To address the delicate subject of underarm odor and perspiration, Odorono, developed in 1912, used an ad campaign that was both elegant and scary. Its 1919 full-page ad, showing a picture of a woman gracefully reaching out to a man, was captioned "Within the Curve of a Woman's Arm." But its subhead, "A frank discussion of a subject too often avoided," suggested that the consumer might be unaware of her social transgression. As was necessary for new products, the consumer was advised how to use it: "Put it on the underarms with a bit of absorbent cotton, only two or three times a week." Previously, women had used rubberized dress shields to guard against a display of underarm perspiration (Sivulka [1998] 2012, 152).

Odorono's main competitor, Mum, which had been patented in 1898, suggested discretion in its very name. It originally used unobtrusive, word-heavy ads in the back of magazines. But in 1924, Mum came out with a full-page color ad picturing a woman with a finger on her lips, with the headline, "Even more than beauty, 'Mum' is the word!" Also in the mid-1920s, deodorants started marketing to men. But the real breakthrough came in 1928 when Lifebuoy soap was advertised as a cure for body odor, or B.O. (Fox [1984] 1997, 97). Once the condition had a name, like a disease, everyone was susceptible. Body odor was vilified, and the norm for men and women was not to display, or smell of, sweat.

VIGILANCE IS THE PRICE OF BEAUTY

"Mum" is the word!

Deodorants were a new concept in the early 20th century. By the 1920s, the makers of Mum deodorant used full-page ads of beautiful people and the slogan "'Mum' is the word," while also cautioning "vigilance" in the fight against "body odors." (Fotosearch/Getty Images)

Shampoo was another new product. Until the early 20th century, people used bath soap for washing their hair, if they used any cleanser at all. As late as 1925, bars of Lifebuoy soap were advertised for shampooing "bobs," the latest hairstyle. By 1910, though, Canthrox Shampoo was on the market, promising "a pleasure and a delight." It was not ready-made, however; the consumer was instructed to dissolve a teaspoonful of Canthrox in a cup of hot water and then use it to wash hair. By 1920, fully prepared shampoo was available, so that the consumer could "avoid the harsh effect of ordinary soap." The advertisements of this product, Watkins Mulsified Cocoanut Oil Shampoo, used photographs of movie stars, showing off their "soft, fresh, and luxuriant" hair, along with their testimonials.

Another newly invented product was Kotex sanitary pads, which hit the market in 1920. According to their early advertising copy, army nurses during World War I noticed the extra-absorbent quality of cellulose bandages and adapted them for personal use. Kimberly-Clark, faced with a surplus of cellulose after the war, set up the Cellucotton Company to market it as sanitary pads. Previously, women had used rags that they washed and reused. As the ads noted, Kotex was cheap enough to be disposable. The product was instantly successful, but advertising such an intimate product was key. Advertising copy called them "sanitary pads," without ever mentioning menstruation, and the term "sanitary pad" did not even appear on the box, just "Kotex." The company urged women to request the product by name, Kotex, to avoid embarrassment and, not coincidentally, promote an identity that was synonymous with the product. By 1923, Cellucotton advertised that it provided vending machines in ladies' rooms in theaters, hotels, and restaurants so that women could access Kotex directly. The company also offered to send Kotex, wrapped in unmarked brown paper, directly to the consumer. By 1924, "Ellen J. Buckland, Graduate Nurse" provided the text for the ads, but she wrote somewhat cryptically, "It protects you against embarrassment in two all-important ways. What these ways are, their overwhelming importance, can best be learned by trial" (Marchand 1985, 21–22; Brumberg 1997, 37–47). Cellucotton managed to advertise an embarrassing product by promoting the name more than the function, by providing ways to acquire the product without asking a salesclerk, and by offering the expertise of a medical professional.

Toilet paper also gained prominence in the 1920s through advertising. Americans who used the privy had employed a variety of materials to wipe their private parts, including leaves and corncobs. The pages of mail-order catalogs, prevalent in rural areas, also served. But sewage disposal systems, especially those using the small-diameter pipes recommended by sanitarians, could not handle many of these materials, and a soluble paper was required. At Fort D. A. Russell, in Wyoming, when the post built a sewer system in 1890, the post quartermaster immediately issued a requisition for 333,000 sheets of toilet paper, which was "deemed essential to guard against the choking and damage of the new sewerage by the use of newspapers" (Hoagland 2004, 193). In 1905, Scott Paper Company produced Balsam Sanitissue, which was "new, soft, balsam-treated parchment covered toilet paper," but by 1924, it had changed the name of its product and its approach. The company hoped to identify ScotTissue with toilet paper generically, so the ad encouraged the consumer to "just say 'Scot-Tissue.' Saves conversation." In 1928, Scott launched a scare campaign, warning consumers of rectal infections if they did not use the proper toilet paper. One ad showed a close-up photograph of a masked doctor and nurse, looking down at a patient. The copy opened with, ". . . and the trouble began with harsh toilet tissue."

Other new products concerned the washing of the bathroom itself, not the body in it. Developed in 1911, the toilet cleanser Sani-Flush advertised by 1915 that "you won't need a brush with Sani-Flush." The ad explained it "keeps the bowl spotless, and bathroom free from odors" and that "you won't have to dip out the water." Odor and appearance were the offenders here, not the possible hazard of sewer gas emanating from dirty traps. Bathtubs needed their own cleanser. Bon Ami was developed in 1886 and, to address the concern that a cleanser would scratch the vitreous china and enameled cast iron of the bathroom, used a chick as its emblem, with the slogan "Hasn't scratched yet," counting on consumers' knowing that newborn chicks do not scratch until they are three days old. By 1920, Bon Ami had added a powdered option to its original cake form and took out a full-page ad in the *Saturday Evening Post*, claiming, "Bon Ami powder makes the tub so clean and white that I just like to stand and look at it!" Bon Ami also claimed to be appropriate for nickel faucets. A third bathroom product was a clog remover, Drano, developed in 1923. Drano had the disadvantage that it was cleaning a place that was not visible—the insides of pipes. It advertised that it "scours like a scrub-brush—where a scrub-brush won't reach." It claimed that it would clean drains and "give them a thorough scrubbing—purify them—sterilize them," allying itself with the antiseptic bent of the New Public Health, not the dangers of dirty pipes dreaded by sanitarians.

Toiletry manufacturers encouraged the frequent use of their products as a means of increasing sales. Consumers were used to obtaining information on how to use a product from its ad, and informing the consumer how often to use a product was an extension of this counsel. The modern-day instruction to wash one's hair twice was first used in the 1920s. Watkins

Mulsified Cocoanut Oil Shampoo instructed consumers to wash their hair and then "rinse the hair and scalp thoroughly using clear, fresh water. Then use another application of Mulsified." The shampoo may have been hamstrung, though, because it conceded that women were washing their hair only once a week: "make it a rule to set a certain day each week for a Mulsified Cocoanut Oil Shampoo." Far more profitable were products that were designed to be used every day, such as Listerine. As one observer wrote about its adman: "He amplified the morning habits of our nicer citizenry—by making the morning mouth-wash as important as the morning shower or the morning shave" (Lennen 1926, 25).

Bon Ami, a cleansing powder for bathtubs, was advertised widely, as seen in this issue of *Ladies' Home Journal* from 1934. The ad includes a chick and the slogan "hasn't scratched yet," along with a picture of a fashionable Art Deco container. (Bettmann/ Getty Images)

Whether people were actually showering or bathing daily is disputable, but they were certainly encouraged to do so.

Cannon towels, which did not promote its brand to the general consumer until 1924, became the largest American maker and distributor of towels by 1927. The company then worked to "get the American public into the habit of using towels with greater frequency. Hence the idea of selling more baths." A contemporary observer applauded the 1928 ad campaign: "It does not advise a bath a day, but presumes that everyone who reads it follows such a habit. It compliments them on their wisdom and then advises on more than one bath a day" (Haase 1928, 86). The ads also included this advice: "Because the first towel absorbs impurities from the skin it must never (under any circumstances) be used again before washing." The repeated use of products was one of the easiest ways to increase their consumption.

As with ensembles of bathroom fixtures, in the 1920s, producers pushed ensembles of clothing, tinted glassware, cutlery, and even pen and mechanical pencil sets. In the bathroom, towel manufacturers also adopted this strategy. Previously, towels had been a sanitary white, perhaps with some colored decoration at the hem. In the late 1920s, towel producers began offering them in color, to complement the newly colorful bathroom fixtures. In 1930, Cannon began selling them as ensembles, in packages wrapped in a new product, Cellophane, that included two bath towels, two face towels, two washcloths, and a bath mat (Webster 1930, 95; Dickinson 1931, 34). Martex offered a "Towel Color Guide," pairing the 16 most common bathroom colors with the appropriate towel colors. Now that the bathroom was awash in color, the peril of clashing colors had to be avoided. Manufacturers feared that if women bought the wrong colors, "they would inevitably turn away from color in towels and think of towels purely as a convenience item and not at all as a style item" ("Color Harmony" 1931, 108). As the bathroom became a place of color and choices, it was also a place of style, and that had to be taught. Fortunately, not only would advertisers helpfully advise the consumer, manufacturers provided more products. The cleanser Bon Ami even came out in stylish new packaging with an art deco design: "Keep the handsome black and gold DeLuxe Package of Bon Ami right on the tub. It looks so smart and saves so many steps!"

The flourishing of the toiletries market in the 1920s shifted Americans' attention away from the cleanliness that could be obtained with soap and toward multiple products for different parts of the body. Bath soaps competed furiously with each other, and, as sales began to slip in the late 1920s, they introduced new products and new approaches (Vinikas 1992, 82). Procter & Gamble had insisted for decades that Ivory was a bath soap appropriate for feminine complexions, but in 1926, it introduced Camay to appeal to women in particular (Lief 1958, 152–55). Its main competitor was Lux, introduced in 1925 by the British firm Lever Brothers. Lux's advertising emphasized connections to fine French soaps and used art deco designs and exotic imagery to suggest its stylishness (Sivulka 2001, 192–94). In 1927, Lever used endorsements by Hollywood stars, posing them in sumptuous bathrooms. Lever built 25 bathrooms, some even with running water, in movie studios for this campaign. Consistent with bathrooms depicted in motion pictures, these sets showed bathrooms as places of luxury and style, appropriate for a soap named Lux (Sivulka 2001, 195–96). Clara Bow was photographed at her bathroom sink, which was set on thin legs before a mirrored wall, saying, "a beautifully smooth skin means even more to a star than to other women." Not only did "9 out of 10 screen stars use Lux Toilet Soap for smooth skin," the ad claimed, " 'Without smooth skin no girl can be really fascinating,' say 39 leading Hollywood directors." By 1930, the leading toilet soap in America was Lux (Scott 2015).

Aside from competing with each other, the soap manufacturers banded together to push soap as an idea. The Association of American Soap and Glycerine Producers formed in 1926 and the next year established the Cleanliness Institute to promote personal hygiene, especially to children. The institute produced books, such as Grace Hallock's *A Tale of Soap and Water: The Historical Progress of Cleanliness*, in order to teach schoolchildren the virtues of soap. But the association also realized that Americans were turning away from the belief in cleanliness promoted by the New Public Hygiene. One 1930 ad, which urged readers to send for the free publication *The Book about Baths*, advocated baths to give energy, to provide a "quick, sound sleep," to avoid sore muscles, and to head off a cold—everything, it seems, but to get clean. The ad claimed the Cleanliness Institute was "established to promote public welfare by teaching the value of cleanliness," but it was also interested in promoting more reasons to take baths.

Soap manufacturers developed another innovation to promote their products—the soap opera. In 1932, Procter & Gamble's advertising agency produced *Ma Perkins*, a 15-minute radio program that related a family's melodrama in a serial fashion. The program, which pushed Oxydol, a laundry detergent, was wildly popular, running for more than 20 years. Procter & Gamble soon launched additional programs: *O'Neills* sponsored by Ivory, *Pepper Young's Family* and *Forever Young* for Camay, and *The Guiding Light* for White Naphtha. By 1939, Procter & Gamble had 21 programs on the air, spending more than $8 million on them, compared to about $5 million for print advertising (Lief 1958, 176–80). After the war, soap operas made a successful transition to television. In 1950, Procter & Gamble introduced *Search for Tomorrow* and adapted *The Guiding Light* from radio (Lief 1958, 271–72).

The target audience for this plethora of bathroom products and advertisements was the minority of Americans who had bathrooms. Ads in the 1910s with uniformed maids working in the bathroom were supplanted by those in the 1920s that showed mothers tending to children in the bathroom, indicating that as bathrooms became more widespread, the advertisers targeted more middle-class consumers. The preferred customer was undeniably white, though. Ads employed racist images of blacks, associating them either with their traditional role as domestic servants or "humorously" suggesting that the use of a certain soap would turn their skin white. In 1892, a series of ads for Dreydoppel Soap depicted a cartoon character of an African American boy along with a poem: "A mite of queer humanity, / As dark as a cloudy night / Was displeased with his complexion, / And wished to change from black to white." After trying other strategies, he lights upon Dreydoppel Soap, which does the trick. When given dialogue, these characters spoke in dialect.

African American entrepreneurs responded to the lack of regard for, if not outright discrimination against, the African American market by developing their own products. Madame C. J. Walker produced and marketed shampoos and soaps nationally, founding a company that was one of the most successful black-owned businesses by the time of her death in 1919. Her company's advertisements appealed to cleanliness and beautification as forms of racial pride. By the 1920s, other black-owned toiletry manufacturers injected sex appeal and modernity into their advertising. While some white toiletry manufacturers began to advertise in black magazines and newspapers, it was not until the 1970s that white businesses appealed directly to the African American market (Sivulka 2001, 273, 274, 280, 287, 290).

Advertisers' relationship with ethnic groups was more complicated. Chinese people often appeared in ads because of their long association with laundries. Speaking in accented English and depicted with pigtails flying, these characters were often mocked. Other cultures of the world— at least those that were dark-skinned—were sometimes depicted as gratefully receiving the enlightenment of soap. Babbitt's proclaimed itself "Soap for all Nations," depicting groups of people in the four corners of the ad, implying the four corners of the world. "Cleanliness is the scale of Civilization," it asserted. But the 1910s and 1920s were also a time when other cultures were evoked for their exoticism, which contributed to the sense of style that toiletry manufacturers were trying to imply. Armour and Company, which offered a "Fine Art Toilet Soap," which had "Exquisite Quality, Flower-Like Fragrance," showed a half-clad red-haired woman bathing at a fountain. The columns, mosaic tile floor, and marble walls suggested an ancient Greek scene. In 1915, Palmolive Soap set one of its ads in front of the Sphinx and a pyramid, saying, "If the Sphinx could whisper the story of Ancient Egypt's queens it would tell of the use of Palm and Olive Oils." In the 1920s, Palmolive showed two women in vaguely Byzantine clothing, Chinese junks floating in the background, with no explanation other than "Have a beautiful skin."

Exotic cultures helped sell soap, but it was another story when these people were in the United States. Faced with an unprecedented influx of immigrants, the United States in the early 20th century also expressed an unprecedented hostility toward them, culminating in a series of laws passed in the 1920s that severely restricted immigration. One mark of the supposed inferiority of immigrants was their lack of cleanliness and offensive odor, deriving from their crowded urban living conditions and lack of basic services. For many Americans, though, cleanliness became a marker of class and acceptability. Soap and toiletry ads set a standard of personal care that few could meet but that many could aspire to, denigrating those who could not achieve basic cleanliness.

Production, marketing, and purchasing of bathroom-related goods dropped in the Depression, as might be expected, and was restrained by the issues of materials availability during World War II. But the surge of advertising in the 1920s had succeeded in normalizing the bathroom for the vast American public. Even though most Americans did not have a bathroom in the 1920s, the ubiquity of bathrooms and products in magazines implied that one should have one, and, as soon as they were able—which for many Americans was not until after World War II—they would get one. Negotiating this new space required subtle coaching from ads—how to match colors, how to wash hair, how to clean a toilet. Advice was offered directly by health professionals or indirectly by showing healthy, happy, beautiful, and clean middle-class families enjoying the new space of the modern bathroom. The use of nearly every product also required more time spent in the bathroom, as consumers were instructed to bathe daily, wash hair frequently, brush teeth twice a day, use mouthwash, and so on. Finally, with each family member spending more time in the bathroom, one bathroom in the house would no longer suffice. Although such a luxury was beyond the reach of most Americans in the 1930s and during the war, greater prosperity after the war would bring with it a demand for multiple bathrooms in the house.

Chapter 9

BEYOND CLEANLINESS: EXPANDING THE BATHROOM

In the late 20th century, two books, published nearly 30 years apart, crystallized the changing attitudes toward the bathroom. In 1966, Alexander Kira's *The Bathroom* examined the usage of the various fixtures and questioned their design in terms of ergonomics and efficiency. In 1993, Diane von Furstenberg's *The Bath* lauded the bathroom as a place of luxury and sensuality. While both of these books promoted an ideal bathroom, they also discussed real trends. The bathroom went from Kira's vision of a laboratory accommodating necessary functions to von Furstenberg's view of it as an extension of the bedroom, with an emphasis on comfort and pleasure. To enable this shift, by the end of the century the bathroom expanded in two ways: it grew in size to accommodate a number of activities, and it grew in numbers, or bathrooms per house, as the two-bathroom household became increasingly common.

This chapter examines the bathroom of the late 20th century, beginning with Kira's scientific study. As a problem to be solved, the bathroom has always attracted those interested in building cheaper, more efficient, and more beneficial units, with the sanitarian emphasis on health evolving into Kira's emphasis on ergonomics. New materials, especially fiberglass and plastics, challenged the domination of enameled cast iron. But by the end of the century, the growing prosperity of the country had taken the bathroom in a different direction than one foreseen by Kira, toward spaciousness and luxury materials.

The publication of Alexander Kira's *The Bathroom* in 1966 attracted articles in *Time*, *Life*, *Newsweek*, and *Business Week*, as well as on the front page of the *New York Times*. The idea of studying such a mundane place was shocking, but the press coverage focused on the critique: "American

Bathroom Rated Low in Study," "What's Wrong with Bathrooms?" and "The Outmoded U.S. Bathroom." In his study funded by the American Radiator and Standard Sanitary Corporation (soon to be renamed American Standard) and Cornell University's Agricultural Experiment Station, Kira used a field survey of 1,000 Los Angeles housewives to ascertain users' opinions, laboratory experiments to examine how the bathroom actually functioned, and related literature to conclude that the American bathroom poorly suited its users. Kira charged that bathroom fixtures had been designed more for the convenience of the plumbing industry than to address the "underlying problems of human accommodation, comfort, and safety" (iii).

Two aspects of Kira's approach were innovative. His ergonomic study, measuring people's usage of fixtures, such as how far they had to bend over to wash their face at a sink at the usual height, recalled efficiency studies of the early 20th century, but those had not been done for the bathroom. Kira's study included photographs of people using each bathroom fixture, along with careful measurements. But he was equally intrigued with the psychological aspects of the bathroom, particularly the societal taboos that have "built up into a culture-wide embarrassment" (iii). He paid particular attention to people's need for privacy in the bathroom, even as he deliberately used graphic language and revealing illustrations to challenge that privacy.

Kira focused on suggestions for individual fixtures rather than the bathroom as a whole. For the sink, for instance, he proposed a fountain-type water source so that the spout was not in the way; a pressure-regulating device, to bring the water closer or farther away from the user; throttle-type controls, off to the side, so that they were reachable; and a rounded basin that was deeper in the front and convex in the center, preventing the water from splashing toward the user and also creating a swirling action (17–22). For the bath, Kira proposed a longer tub that was contoured to fit the reclining body (27). The shower should have a built-in seat, an illuminated recessed shelf, grab bars, water controls near the entry, and a hand shower (48).

The toilet received much attention. For ease of defecation, Kira recommended a low fixture, 9 to 11 inches high, which put the internal organs in the most favorable position (63). For male urination, he analyzed splash diagrams and advised a pull-down urinal over the toilet, with a funnel-shaped container (80). For cleaning private parts, Kira clearly favored a bidet but recognized that Americans' association of the bidet with sex made it unlikely to be adopted. Instead, he suggested that the toilet be equipped with two streams of water to enable direct cleaning of the genitals, or at least one stream of water to wet a tissue for better cleaning (51).

Kira recognized that the bathroom was used for much more than bathing, washing hands and face, and relieving oneself. He included lists of other activities, including oral hygiene (such as brushing teeth and gargling), miscellaneous hygiene (such as vomiting and cleaning ears), quasi-medical uses (such as taking medicines, applying bandages), grooming and body care (shaving, fixing hair, weighing oneself), related activities (hand laundry, cleaning), and nonhygienic activities (smoking, reading, listening to the radio, using the telephone). He noted that about 40 percent of survey respondents said that their children played in the bathroom (84). To accommodate some of these uses, Kira recommended more storage ("the single greatest shortcoming in present-day bathrooms"), space for hanging towels, and a place to hang clothes that have been removed (87). He also noted that 75 percent of the women surveyed wanted a built-in vanity (83). As *Newsweek* described it, "In addition to its traditional functions, the contemporary American bathroom also serves as powder room, laundry room, phone booth, library, gymnasium, storage closet and, for the affluent at least, a place of sybaritic luxury" ("Bathroomology" 1965, 69).

Plumbing-fixture manufacturers had been aware of these multiple uses even without commissioning studies. In 1961, Kohler ran a couple of ads that illustrated this. In one, two boys play with toy boats in a partially filled blue bathtub, while their mother enters the bathroom with a younger sister who clearly needs a bath. The tagline reads, "Is your bathroom *a family room?*" In another ad, a teenaged girl sitting on a stool between a green sink and a green tub talks on the phone. The message is that the consumer needs "enough bathrooms in the home for everybody's comfort, all the time." Overlooking these activities and desires, Kira maintained a focus on the fixtures, not the design of the bathroom as a whole, and did not include any diagrams of bathrooms. He ignored issues concerning materials, building codes, and engineering, concentrating on the *what*, not the *how* (iii).

Despite his claims, Kira was not the first to rethink the American bathroom, but most earlier ideas resulted in proposals that were too expensive for wide adoption. Although prefabrication provided a tantalizing opportunity for cost reduction, the bathroom generally resisted prefabrication efforts because plumbing codes varied according to locality. One of the more intriguing efforts was Buckminster Fuller's Dymaxion Bathroom. In 1929, Fuller, an engineer who developed several widely publicized innovations for living, designed a Dymaxion house, in which the entire hexagonal house was suspended from a central mast. After the war, he built a prototype of the redesigned Dymaxion house, which was circular in plan. In the 1950s, Fuller developed a geodesic dome for living (Auer 1991, 83–99).

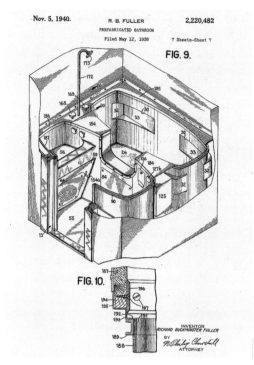

FIG. 9.

FIG. 10.

INVENTOR

RICHARD BUCKMINSTER FULLER

BY

ATTORNEY

Buckminster Fuller's Dymaxion bathroom, patented in 1938, was a prefabricated, copper construction in four pieces, designed to fit into a 5-by-5-foot space. In one half, the toilet faced the sink, while the tub and shower filled the other half. (U.S Patent and Trademark Office)

He also designed a stand-alone Dymaxion Bathroom, which was prefabricated, die-stamped in copper, and designed to fit into a five-by-five-foot space. In order to be able to get it through doorways and up the stair-case of a preexisting house, it was divided into four parts: one with the sink and toilet facing each other, one with the shower and tub, and two lids for them. The pieces would bolt together, the fixtures were prep-lumbed, and the whole unit weighed only 250 pounds. The bathroom included sev-eral practical features: all of the corners were rounded for easy cleaning; the floor of the tub was raised, so bending over to clean it was easier; the nozzle of the sink was closer to the user so that it would splash away; and the faucet handles were to one side of the sink. The toilet did not flush with water but, rather, packaged the disposal to be collected later and used for compost or fuel. The shower used only a cup of water, converting it into a mist that Fuller insisted was cleaner than water (J. Baldwin 1997, 30–33). Fuller succeeded in getting several prototypes built and entered into an agreement with Phelps-Dodge to produce the "Five by Five," as it would be known, in 1937. But the prefab-ricated bathroom never went into production ("Integrated Bathroom" 1937, 40–41; "Design Decade" 1940, 270).

Other efforts at reducing the price of bathrooms focused more on materials that would permit cheaper installation. While ceramic tile had always been preferred for floors and walls, less costly alternatives existed. Early in the 20th century, advisers suggested oilcloth or enameled paint on the walls. In the 1930s, advertisers promoted Masonite and other wood fiberboards. One was stamped with pseudomortar joints so that, as described in one advertisement, "the gleaming tile-like wainscoting and shower walls are . . . black with white lines and canary-yellow trim." Linoleum was widely promoted for bathroom floors. After the war, metal tiles were offered, such as Hastings Alumitile, "the modern wall covering of aircraft aluminum." The "inside story for 1950" was the "Formica Vanitory": "Never in home building history has a new idea so quickly and completely captured the hearts of American home owners. The color, the beauty, the ruggedness of Formica have made it a long time number one choice for kitchen cabinet tops. These same qualities, plus the common sense desire for usable space around the lavatory, have made the Formica Vanitory idea an instant success." Formica, a plastic laminate, was a popular material for kitchen counters, adapted to bathroom counters.

The biggest innovation in materials, though, was the use of fiberglass, beginning in the 1960s. Some observers credited Kira's study with pushing this development. An article in *Business Week* noted that when Kira's book came out, only one plumbing-fixture manufacturer was using fiberglass, and that was Universal-Rundle Corporation (previously Universal Sanitary). Just two years later, Owens-Corning, Crane, American Standard, and a host of smaller companies were marketing fiberglass-reinforced plastic bathtub-showers, and Crane was even marketing a factory-assembled bathroom in which the only non-fiberglass component was the toilet. New apartments were the primary customers for these fiberglass-reinforced plastic fixtures because the size of the bathtub-shower unit made it difficult to maneuver into preexisting spaces. Even though the new fiberglass tub cost nearly three times as much as a cast-iron one, the labor involved in installation was much less ("U.S. Builders" 1968, 100). Other advantages included surfaces that were not cold to the touch, easy cleaning, light weight, and malleability. The "seamless bathroom" promised sleek lines and low maintenance ("Seamless Bathrooms" 1968, 162).

Safety was another concern reflected in these new materials. The fiberglass-reinforced plastic showers and tubs came equipped with grab bars and nonskid bottoms (H. Brown 1970, 101). A nonskid bottom in enameled cast-iron tubs was pioneered by American Standard, which, just before Kira's book came out and probably with advance knowledge of it, produced a no-slip surface for the bottom of the tub, called "Stan-sure," that is still in production today (Penner 2013b, 9; Mok 1966, 84D). Despite the success of reinforced-fiberglass plastic fixtures, the prefabricated bathroom never succeeded. By 1974, one observer claimed that "increased manufacturing and shipping costs are closing the seamless route," but that manufacturers continued to concentrate on separate units, including the one-piece tub and shower enclosures (Lees 1974, 144). Fiberglass fixtures failed to capture the high-end market, though. As an article in the *New Yorker* observed in 1972, the new tub-shower combinations "are at least as attractive as the bulk of today's plastic furniture," but their "surface can be effectively dulled and marred within five years" (Malcolm 1972, 112).

While technological approaches to the bathroom might have been one result of Kira's study, fixture design was of less interest to the American public than the bathroom as a whole. Kira's reshaped fixtures resulted from his "user-centered" approach, but what users actually wanted was more space for all of the activities that took place in the bathroom. Kira recognized this when he revised his book for reissue 10 years after the original. In an article written while he was working on the new edition, he called it "the live-in bathroom." He declared that the bathroom had become acceptable and fashionable, attributing the change in attitude toward "a feeling of relaxation on the part of many people, more discussion about sex and body" (quoted in "The Case for the Live-in Bathroom" 1972, 108). Essentially, the sexual revolution of the late 1960s and early 1970s had affected people's attitudes about the body. The 1976 edition of Kira's book had new illustrations that showed naked users, whereas the first edition had discreetly clothed them in bathing suits and obscured their faces. It also included chapters on public restrooms, as well as facilities for the elderly and disabled.

Several aspects of Kira's book pointed to larger bathrooms and more of them. The new freedom about the body meant that people were more likely to share bathrooms, while the multitude of functions that occurred there meant that there should be more of them. In 1940, 45 percent of American households lacked complete plumbing facilities. This number had dropped to just under 17 percent by 1960 and to a negligible 1 percent by 1990 (U.S. Department of Commerce 2011). As soon as bathrooms became widely adopted, it seemed there were not enough of them. Even as early as 1964, focus groups of homeowners in six cities agreed that two bathrooms were "indispensable" (National Association of Home Builders 1964, 30). A 1978 survey about homeowners' preferences found that 25 percent of them would like another bathroom, and 54 percent of them thought the average-size bathroom, defined as five by eight feet, was too small (Tarshis 1979, 173). Reflecting that desire for more bathrooms, a survey of thousands of representative households found that in 1975 about 20 percent of them had two or more bathrooms. That increased to 38 percent by 1997 and 51 percent by 2013. New construction overwhelmingly includes multiple bathrooms: 80 percent of the houses built between 2009 and 2013 had two or more (U.S. Department of Commerce 2013).

There are few statistics on the size of bathrooms, but the increasing number of fixtures that went into them indicates their expansion. The vanity—a cabinet into which the sink is set—grew in popularity in the postwar period, answering in part consumers' demand for more storage space. By the 1960s, the trend was toward two basins set in a long counter. As *Time* magazine observed in 1963, "Double sinks are sprouting everywhere, enabling tooth-brushing, face splashing and shaving to take place side by side without strain on a marriage" ("Modern Laving" 1963, 56). By 1970, *Sunset* magazine declared, "The long lavatory counter with two wash basins seemed a bit startling 10 or 15 years ago. Today, however, it's quite commonplace in the West in both custom and merchant-built houses" ("It Began" 1970, 78). The single-handled faucet also changed the appearance of the bathroom sink. Developed by Alfred Moen before the war, the faucet, which mixed hot and cold water with one movement, went into production in 1947.

Bathtubs underwent many permutations in the late 20th century. The first was the sunken tub, realistically possible only in new construction. The tub was more onerous to clean, though, and, while easier to get into, it was also more difficult to get out of, especially since grab bars tended to ruin the elegance implied by a sunken tub. Nonetheless, it was popular in the 1960s. "Progress in redesigning the tub," as seen in 1960, "has meant going back to the ancient concept of an ornamental pool sunk into the floor" (Kellogg 1960, 66). The next year, *House Beautiful* heralded "the big swing to the sunken tub," identifying it with leisure: "The sunken bathtub is a thing of beauty. Tailored to your measure, it offers unrestricted space to luxuriate in as you bathe, with water buoyantly pampering every part of your body." Sunken tubs were easy to install, the magazine assured readers, so "little wonder, the trend to them is growing" (1961, 74). A few years later, *Time* magazine connected the new sunken tubs to the 1963 movie *Cleopatra*, in which Elizabeth Taylor in the title role luxuriated in a large tub attended by handmaidens. "The Crane Co. has taken the plunge with a line of sunken tubs, dubbed the Marc Antony, the Caesar, and the Centurion," emphasizing the Roman bathing experience. Luxury was a constant refrain through the latter decades of the 20th century, as shelter magazines and their advertisers tried to persuade the American public to pamper themselves by spending more money on large, well-equipped bathrooms.

The next development for the tub, for those who could afford it, involved making it suitable for more than one bather. Shelter magazines ran articles about double bathtubs, or his-and-hers tubs next to one another, but to lure one's neighbors into the tub, whirlpools, hot tubs, and outdoor settings were recommended. The American insistence on privacy and retreat afforded by the bathtub gave way during the sexual revolution to the bathtub as a party place—at least by reputation if not in actuality. The 1959 movie *Pillow Talk*, starring Doris Day and Rock Hudson, played off of the sexuality of bathing by showing the two characters in a split screen, each in his or her own bathtub, talking to each other on the phone. Even without sharing a tub, the characters suggested the sociability that the bathing experience could provide.

Two cultural traditions, discussed in chapter 6, that had seen bathing as a less than private undertaking provided some basis for the new facilities. *Life* magazine declared the sauna the "hot fad from Finland" in 1963, noting that prefab saunas designed for the home were on the market. These redwood-paneled rooms incorporated an electric stove, which heated a small pile of stones. Measuring at least seven by seven feet, these rooms were not necessarily placed in the bathroom, although the desire for a cooling shower or bath afterward meant that they may have been placed nearby ("Hot Fad" 1963, 94). When Hollywood celebrities made the news as having saunas (dry heat) and steam baths (wet heat) in their houses, heat baths were "in." As one observer noted drily, "A short while before, private heat baths had been popular in this country only with homesick Finns. Now it was clearly just a matter of months before the mania became nationwide, and not owning a poach-yourself outfit would be counted a social error" (Skow 1965, 87.). One salesman said, "This has gone beyond the status symbol. We are changing the American way of life" (Skow 1965, 87). Although heat baths could be used alone, they also indicated a new willingness among Americans to share the cleansing experience. As the *Saturday Evening Post* noted in 1965, "sauna parties are becoming popular" (Skow 1965, 87).

The hot tub also drew people into a communal experience. In its simplest form, it was a wooden, circular, straight-sided tub designed to hold four or more people. Derived loosely from the Japanese furo, the hot tub began appearing as a vehicle for multiple users in the late 1960s. In 1972, *Life* magazine featured a "modest but authentic Japanese bath" that accommodated six to eight people. "The party-sized living tub, while not yet a serious threat to the coffee tables of America, is making its wet, sociable mark" ("Party-Time Tubs" 1972, 40–41). Spoofed by *Saturday Night Live* in 1983, with Eddie Murphy doing an impression of James Brown testing the water in his hot tub, the hot tub soon became a symbol of sybaritic excess.

In 1968, Roy Jacuzzi began marketing a whirlpool bath for relaxation, not only therapeutic, reasons. With pumps, jets, water heater, and filter, the modern "home spa" (or Jacuzzi)—built not of wood of but of an

The Jacuzzi, a whirlpool bath designed for pleasure, not merely rehabilitation, gained popularity in the 1970s. (Luna Vandoorne Vallejo/Dreamstime.com)

easily cleaned, fiberglass-reinforced plastic—became popular. One user described the experience in 1977: "Whirlpool bath. Let the words swirl into your imagination. Think of tired muscles massaged by wavering fingers of water flowing from jets; your skin soothed by pain-banishing heated water and buoyed by clouds of tingling air bubbles. If it sounds pleasurable, relaxing, even slightly sensual, your thoughts are moving in the right direction. It is all of that" (Ingersoll 1977, 12).

Home spas could be installed indoors and for solo use. One *Sunset* article illustrated the installation of a 42-by-60-inch whirlpool tub in a home ("He Grabbed Space" 1983, 131). Often, especially in warmer climates, home spas were placed outdoors or in a glass-enclosed space that seemed like the outdoors. Hot tubs were meant to see and be seen, used by multiple people and winning the envy of neighbors. How they were actually used may not have always reflected their designs. In a focus group of women pulled together by the National Association of Home Builders in 1964, one upper-class woman from Texas said, "I think bathrooms have become the new status symbols. The bigger and more window space the better. And our friends love our master bathroom . . . We have a built-in sunken bathtub that must be about 5 × 9 in size. Now and then I let the boys fill it up, and take a real boy's bath, you might call it." But then she admitted to not using it herself, "because, heavens, I would never fill a huge bathtub to take a bath myself. But it has heat coils under this tile with a switch that turns it on and even a thermostat that controls how warm you want the bottom of your tub to be. So our friends really enjoy it" (quoted in National Association of Home Builders 1964, 109).

Not just the party tub but the whole bathroom opened up to the outdoors. Numerous articles depicted bathrooms with glass walls that faced walled, private patios or else distant views. The glass-walled bathroom was not designed for voyeurism, but, even so, it is unclear how popular they were. In 1964, an upper-class woman from Los Angeles expressed reservations about her neighbor's sunken tub with adjacent solarium: "It's just beautiful, but I couldn't bathe in it. I like privacy. I don't even like clear shower doors. When I bathe or take a shower I don't want to feel that the eyes of the world are on me. I like a private bathroom" (quoted in National Association of Home Builders 1964, 108). A woman from Texas of more limited means spun out a fantasy: "I would like to have a private walled-in patio outside of the master bedroom and the bath that connects with the master bedroom, so that if you were so brave, you could leave the curtains open while you were in the bathroom because it is thoroughly enclosed and you can use this private patio for sitting, for talking, sunbathing in complete privacy and yet it would be outside and it would be landscaped with growing plants" (quoted in National Association of Home Builders 1964, 110).

The bathroom also became more free-form, even bleeding into other rooms in the house. A 1980 *New York Times Magazine* article contrasted the modern bathroom to that of the 1970s, which it called the "Epoch of the Palazzo Bath," explaining, "During that so-called me-generation decade, scrubbing among the swells was commonly performed in surroundings that rivaled for unbridled opulence a flamboyant Hollywood set designer's meditations on Imperial Rome." By contrast, the current trend was "simple, straightforward, clean-cut. . . . The new bathroom is meant to blend seamlessly with adjacent rooms—so seamlessly in fact, that it may not even attempt to gain full status as a separate space." Instead, "these bathrooms open onto bedrooms which, themselves, may be open to the rest of the house. The bathroom, that last bastion of total privacy, has fallen prey to togetherness" (Bethany 1980, 60). It is likely that this "trend" remained so only among high-end designers. While open-plan bathrooms and bathrooms illuminated by large floor-to-ceiling windows might have gained attention in the media, the windowless interior bathroom, which made good use of artificial ventilation, was a popular option, especially for apartments and small houses.

This 1980s bathroom expressed luxury through its bathtub in a bay window, suggesting that the bather had views of the landscape, but also enough property that privacy was insured. (Photographs in the Carol M. Highsmith Archive, Library of Congress, Prints and Photographs Division)

By the 1980s, justifications for mental well-being emerged in defense of more than one bathroom. A professor of interior design at Purdue University studied 200 families and concluded that families in one-bathroom houses perceived their houses to be "more confining, crowded, and lacking privacy," while those with more than one bathroom thought their houses were "more pleasing, spacious, well-designed, comfortable, and organized," regardless of the actual size of the house. One bathroom was seen as far more stressful (Inman 1988, 88, 89). Similarly, Dr. Avodah K. Offit, a psychiatrist and sex therapist, found that "small bathrooms are hard on marital equanimity." For Dr. Offit, though, the desire was not for more privacy but rather for "a bigger room in which one could not only bathe but also make love in comfort, without having to change rooms." Her ideal bathroom had "large showers, a tub for two, a whirlpool bath, maybe a Japanese soaking tub—and also a matted surface, possibly covered with toweling where people could powder, oil, or massage each other and then, perhaps, make love" (Offit 1981, 85).

By 1990, the expansive bathroom had taken hold. Only 11 percent of American bathrooms were less than the formerly standard 5 by 7 feet, or 35 square feet, while 8 percent were bigger than 150 square feet, or 10 by 15 (Kanner 1989, 12). Generally, new bathrooms were twice the size they had been in 1970, or 7 by 10 rather than 5 by 7 ("Comfortable Stations" 1991, 79). While the newsworthy, over-the-top bathroom was far from ordinary, the sheer size of most new bathrooms indicates that the bathroom was being designed for more than one person at a time, symbolized by double sinks, and used for new functions, such as hairstyling, facilitated by handheld blow-dryers. The grander bathrooms received snide attention in the press, such as this from *Newsweek*: "Welcome to the Bathstyles of the Rich and Famous—where there's much more to going to the bathroom than going to the bathroom. Step into the brave new loo. As you can see, it comes in exciting new designer colors: taxicab yellow, Dresden blue and honeydew whisper. And isn't it spacious—enough room for a party-size whirlpool and a cute little bidet in there with the standard equipment." The new high-end bathroom served as private getaway, health spa, and party place. A new school of interior designers concentrated on bathrooms alone, and one of them insisted that most of her business came from the middle and upper-middle classes, not the superrich (Givens 1986, 80). Although more than 70 percent of fixtures were still white, the designers tended to select such vivid shades as black, teal, red, and navy (Kanner 1989, 13).

The fixture manufacturers were not slow to pick up on the new trends. In 1967, Kohler introduced its "Bold Look of Kohler" marketing campaign. Intended as a short-lived sales-conference theme, the slogan became a memorable advertising hook that has persisted to the present. In 1967, Kohler's "bold look" featured "plumbing fixtures in avocado, Kohler's new 'go-with-everything' color" ("National Marketing Meeting" 1967, 1; Blodgett 2003, 15). In the mid-1970s, Kohler upped the ante, with its "Edge of Imagination" campaign. Surrealistic scenes of Kohler fixtures in outdoor settings—two cowboys playing poker in a red whirlpool bath in the middle of the desert, an orange toilet in the center of a two-lane blacktop with a woman in an evening gown walking on the side of the road—caught the eye and provided name recognition. Intended to appeal directly to consumers rather than plumbing contractors, the ads had little text but memorable images. The colors of the fixtures became bolder as well: Antique Red, Blueberry, Jade, and Tiger Lily, bright colors that overshadowed the pastels of the 1960s. By 1990, Kohler was outselling American Standard in the domestic market (Kanner 1989, 12).

In 1993, Diane von Furstenberg crystallized the recent interest in the bathroom with the publication of her book *The Bath*. Von Furstenberg was a fashion designer, most famous for the wrap dress she introduced in 1974. Following the 1991 publication of her book *Beds, The Bath* was a coffee-table book with sumptuous color photographs of bathrooms, most of them owned by her wealthy friends on the East Coast and in Paris. Her take on the bathroom, unlike the trends in the 1960s and 1970s, emphasized solitude and privacy. As she wrote, "One bathes for cleanliness and purification, but also for serenity, isolation, and pleasure" (11). That these were the bathrooms of the upper classes is evident from this description: "Not only has space expanded, but so has décor. The basic trilogy of tub, sink and toilet has been elevated to high design. These functional fixtures are in harmony with the overall look of the room. Tubs are sunken and fitted with ornate, sculptural handles and spouts. Basins are inlaid with semiprecious stones, and toilets are so integrated in the design and décor of the room that they all but disappear. Classical shapes soothe the senses, streamlined designs promote calm at the end of a complicated day, and fireplaces add warmth and an elegant decorative detail." And, lest you forget where you are, "Even a simple window can add a touch of luxury to the bathroom suffusing the room with light while affording the bather a view of an English country garden, the canals of Venice, or the Manhattan skyline" (113). It was unlikely that readers would attempt to replicate any of these bathrooms, but the book served as an indiscreet look into the lifestyles of the rich and famous. Von Furstenberg insisted that the reader, too, could benefit from an elegant bath. "The bath is one of the few places where you can be totally alone and completely self-indulgent. You can easily create a bathing experience as elegant and beautiful as you wish" (147). Rather than end the book with an appendix of plumbing-fixture dealers or even bathroom decorators, she concluded with aromatherapy "recipes" that would help the bather achieve the following states in her bathtub: contemplation, enchantment, renewal, exuberance, and vitality.

Through the prosperous 1990s, Americans continued to install large and expensive bathrooms. As one observer noted, bathroom expenditures were not driven by better fixtures, necessarily, but rather by "fashion, ego and self-indulgence" (Adler 1998, 66). In 1998, the architect Philippe Starck offered a line of sanitary ware that he introduced at an event at a monastery in Germany, where "sculptural seventy-five-hundred-dollar tubs and toilets were set against rough-hewn planks of raw cypress, creating the effect of a well-appointed outhouse" (Adler 1998, 66; "Rub a Dub Dub" 1998, 27). Generally the decor relied on marble, chintz, and tile, as shown in von Furstenberg's book, but by the end of the decade, a trend toward historic bathrooms of the 1920s and 1930s emerged, with claw-foot tubs, two-handled bathroom faucets, and white fixtures (Adler 1998, 66).

The soaking tub, a dramatically shaped freestanding bathtub, appeared at the turn of the 21st century as a mark of luxury. In this bathroom, double above-counter sinks add to the stylishness. (Epstock/Dreamstime.com)

The signature fixture at the turn of the 21st century was the soaking tub. Slightly deeper than the normal tub, the soaking tub was designed to be freestanding, unaccompanied by shower or whirlpool jets. In 1998, one designer observed the turn away from whirlpool baths— "too much fuss"—and toward "what their grandparents may have had: a tub that is freestanding and in which they can take long, hot soaks" (Abramovitch 1998, 66). Reflecting the trends identified by von Furstenberg, the soaking tub was quiet, elegant, and designed for one person. And because it stood alone, it could be placed anywhere, like a piece of sculpture. The center of the room, in front of a large window, or even in the bedroom—all were likely places for bathtubs, according to designers.

As beautiful as the soaking tub could be, it was undoubtedly the walk-in shower that got more use. By the end of the century, a majority of Americans took a shower every day (American Standard 2016). Showers had increasingly developed as spaces apart from the tub in the late 20th century. Acrylic doors complemented metal and fiberglass stalls. Later, glass-enclosed showers reflected a new esthetic known, appropriately, as "Naked"—unadorned, uncolorful, and very exposed (Jennings 2011, 308).

The clear-glass shower enclosure implies, perhaps, that the user has the entire bathroom to himself or herself.

The growth in both the number of bathrooms and the size of them took place in a context of overwhelming growth in the size of the single-family American house. The average size of an American house grew from 1,660 square feet in 1973 (the first year that the U.S. Census collected the data) to 2,687 in 2015, while the average household size fell from 3.01 to 2.54 persons. Undoubtedly, the number and size of bathrooms reflect a rising standard of living, but it is significant that this new wealth was expressed in the attainment of bathrooms. The two-bathroom house reflected more functions deemed appropriate for the bathroom and more time needed to perform them. Privacy may be valued by some, but the two-sink bathroom indicates a willingness to share the space (Murphy 2006, F1). The expanding bathroom is less a function of cleanliness than it is an accommodation of the multiplicity of activities that now take place there.

Chapter 10

CURRENT ISSUES: USING THE BATHROOM

"Using the bathroom" may serve as a euphemism for functions too graphic to mention, but Americans also use the bathroom as an embodiment of political issues and social trends. Social status, available technology, public investment, the power of advertising, attitudes toward cleanliness, and physical pleasure are just some of the influences on the form and appearance of the bathroom discussed in this book. This final chapter explores three current issues that shape the bathroom of today. While the desire for ever-larger bathrooms continues, some checks on consumption have arisen in recent decades. The need for water conservation, while more urgent in some parts of the country than in others, has produced federal and state mandates for low-flow toilets and shower heads. Legislation to accommodate disabled persons in public facilities has translated into a desire for universal access in bathrooms, particularly as baby boomers consider aging in their homes rather than moving to institutions. And a resurgent fear of bacteria, similar to the germ awareness of the early 20th century, has generated the development of touchless toilets and sinks among other new technological innovations. Altogether, as a reflection of political and medical trends, the private bathroom remains an expression of public concerns.

Water shortages, wastewater treatment limitations, and the energy crisis sparked interest in household water conservation in the 1970s. Since then, federal and state legislation and encouragement have spurred the development of toilets and shower heads that are increasingly less water-consumptive. With toilets consuming more water than any other fixture and with showers the second-largest consumer of indoor residential water, conservation has naturally focused on toilets and shower heads. Low-flow toilets offered a solution, but the federal requirement for low-flow toilets in the early 1990s was not well received because of poor design. Subsequent generations of low-flow toilets, now more efficient than ever, have had to overcome the prejudice against them caused by the premature insistence on technology that lagged behind efficiency.

In the first half of the 20th century, toilets usually consumed 7 or 8 gallons per flush (gpf), reflecting sanitarians' concerns that harmful substances be diluted and moved far away from the house as fast as possible. By the 1950s, consumption had been reduced to 5 or 6 gpf. In the 1970s, a new environmental awareness intensified a concern for both water and energy consumption. Some of the first actions occurred at the local level. The Washington Suburban Sanitary Commission, which served two fast-developing counties in Maryland, foresaw a water shortage and lack of sewage treatment capacity. A budding conservation movement worked to prevent the expansion of the wastewater treatment system to accommodate the new construction. It also made lavish water use suddenly seem excessive. As one official noted, likening the situation to the energy crisis, "Luxurious bath facilities, lawn irrigation systems, and car washes were the water utility equivalents of gas-guzzling cars and total electric homes" (Brusnighan 1981, 428). The commission decided to curtail water consumption in an effort to ease demand for sewage facilities. Beyond publicity and education programs, as well as a revised rate structure, the commission also oversaw a new plumbing code in 1972 that required toilets to consume no more than 3.5 gpf and shower heads to restrict flow to 3.5 gallons per minute or less. In 1979, Maryland adopted these standards for the whole state (Brusnighan 1981, 429).

Meanwhile, drought conditions in California in 1976–1977 had provoked statewide action. Most water use there—nearly 85 percent—was agricultural. Of urban water use, 65 percent was residential, and just over half of the residential use was interior, as opposed to lawn and garden use. Of the interior residential use at that time, 43 percent of the water went to the toilet and 30 percent to the bath and shower (Griffin and Soehren 1984, 5–6). For the toilet, the most popular low-flow version was the shallow trap, with which the bowl kept less water, and the flush required less as well. These low-flow models became the standard when state law, effective January 1, 1978, prohibited construction of new houses and apartment buildings with toilets that consumed more than 3.5 gpf and shower heads more than 2.75 gallons per minute (Griffin and Soehren 1984, 5–6). Voluntary conservation methods for older toilets that consumed more than 3.5 gpf were also encouraged, with one of the simplest ways being to displace some of the water in the tank. The state distributed plastic bags to be filled with water and hung inside the toilet tank, along with flow restrictors for shower heads (Butterfield 1981, 451).

The requirement for 3.5 gpf toilets caught on more widely in the late 1970s and early 1980s. With many states and municipalities concerned with water consumption and wastewater treatment capacity, reductions in consumption were welcomed by many government officials and environmentalists. Energy savings also resulted from the reduction in water and wastewater to be pumped and treated. Flow restrictors in shower heads further contributed to energy savings due to a decrease in water that needed to be heated.

Continued concern on the part of environmentalists resulted in further reductions. Massachusetts became the first state to call for ultra-low-flow toilets when its plumbing code, effective March 2, 1989, required that toilets installed either new or as replacements consume no more than 1.6 gpf. The state had experienced several years of drought and foresaw savings in water consumption, household water expenses, and wastewater treatment costs (Vickers 1989, 48–51). By the time the federal government got involved, 17 states had mandated ultra-low-flow toilets (Murdoch 1994, 2). Sweden had led the way with ultra-low-flow toilets, requiring them in 1972 due to concern about the pollution of estuaries with wastewater (Sullivan 2008). The Swedish requirement of 6 liters per flush translated to the 1.6 gallons per flush mandated in the United States. Despite European experience and technology, American manufacturers were slow to adopt designs that would provide an effective flush using only 1.6 gallons of water.

The federal requirement for low-flow toilets and shower heads was a small part of a much larger bill, the Energy Policy Act of 1992, in a section titled "Energy Conservation Requirements for Certain Lamps and Plumbing Fixtures" (Title 1, Subtitle C, Section 123). Unlike states and localities, which can regulate through plumbing codes, the federal government could regulate only what was sold, so it prevented the sale of toilets that exceeded 1.6 gpf or shower heads that exceeded 2.5 gallons per minute. The bill provided separate standards for commercial buildings and required adherence to the residential standard after January 1, 1994.

Problems appeared even before the act was passed. An article in a trade-industry magazine reporting on the Massachusetts law in 1989 identified three issues with the performance of the ultra-low-flow toilets: double flushing, or the necessity of flushing twice to remove the contents of the toilet bowl; bowl streaking, or the need to clean the bowl more often because the new designs provided less water surface area; and sewer stoppages, because the reduced amount of water meant that flow could be hampered farther down the line (Vickers 1989, 50). After the federal law passed, most U.S. manufacturers made such modest adjustments to their 3.5 gpf models as "early close" flush-valve flappers or a toilet dam in the tank, both of which were designed to reduce the amount of water consumed (Tobin 2001, 16). Neither of these fixes worked well in the long term. A more expensive solution, on the market by 1994 but costing up to four times as much as the other models, was a pressurized tank that used air to push the water into the bowl with additional force. This was more effective but also noisier (Murdoch 1994, 2).

Due to poorly performing ultra-low-flow toilets, opposition to the federal law was immediate and vehement. Unable to buy a higher-volume toilet in the United States, homeowners sought them at yard sales and across the border in Canada (Gorman and Grace 1996, 59). The shower head requirement could be subverted by simply installing more than one shower head in a shower or altered by the consumer after installation. Rep. Joe Knollenberg, a Republican from Michigan, introduced legislation to roll back the changes in 1997 and again in 2001, but neither bill got out of committee. In 2011, Sen. Rand Paul, a Republican from Kentucky, objected strenuously in a House hearing to the intrusive nature of a federal law that restricted his right to choose what kind of toilet he could put in his house (Good 2011).

By the time these objections gained traction, however, the industry had already developed better-performing ultra-low-flow toilets. By 1997, *Consumer's Digest* declared, "Manufacturers of today's low-flush units have solved most of the problems of earlier models" (Geary 1997, 52). By the early 21st century, consumers had a variety of ultra-low-flow toilets to choose from. Besides the pressure-assist type available in the mid-1990s, there is also a power-assist one, in which electricity helps pressurize the water in the tank, as well as a vacuum-assist type, in which a pressurized air pocket between the bowl and the exit to the sewage line helps pull the contents of the bowl (Hauenstein, Quinn, and Osann 2013, 6–8; Blodgett 2003, 274–75). In 1999, the Australian firm Caroma introduced the dual-flush toilet to the U.S. market. Dual flush gives the user the option of selecting either a 1.6-gallon flush or a 0.8 one.

The efforts at indoor water conservation have been successful. In California, by 2003, toilets consumed 32 percent of the indoor water and showers 22 percent (Gleick et al. 2003, 38). But continued concern about water supply, especially in drought-prone California, has prompted the development of toilets that are even more water sparing. In 2007, California adopted a law that went into effect in 2014 that restricted toilets to no more than 1.28 gpf (Hauenstein, Quinn, and Osann 2013, 4). These toilets, known as high-efficiency, went on the market in the United States in 1999. In 2007, the federal government developed a program to encourage the use of these high-efficiency toilets. The Environmental Protection Agency offers a WaterSense label to verify that a toilet consumes 20 percent less than the ultra-low-flow toilets, or 1.28 gpf. Comparable to the Energy Star program for appliances, WaterSense is a voluntary program that identifies toilets with exceptionally low water consumption, and manufacturers proudly advertise their WaterSense labels. Even in 2007, though, the program had to contend with prejudice against low-flow toilets stemming from the poor quality of the first generation. "Not your father's low-flow . . . ," one brochure assured the reader. "Many tend to associate lower flow with lower flushing power. Not true. New technology and design advancements, such as pressure-assisted flushers and modifications to bowl contours allow high-efficiency toilets to flush better than first-generation low-flow toilets" (Flush Fact vs. Flush Fiction 2008).

One concern about the high-efficiency toilets was that they did not provide enough water to move waste through the wastewater collection system. Problems with clogging, odors, and pipe corrosion in systems that were designed for much higher flow remain a concern if water consumption drops dramatically. Generally, toilets, while the largest consumer of water within the house, provide only a minor amount of the water in the collection system (Hauenstein, Quinn, and Osann 2013, 35–36). Yet the concern about flow through the system echoes that of George Waring 140 years ago, although the danger of sewer gas is no longer the reason.

Rather than seek ever more parsimonious water-consumptive toilets, a few people have turned to fixtures that consume no water at all. Reminiscent of the earth closets of the 1860s, these are marketed today as composting toilets. Rikard Lindstrom of Sweden developed a composting toilet in 1939, founded a company to develop it in 1962, and incorporated in the United States in 1973. Called the Clivus Multrum, the toilet separates urine and feces and then uses microorganisms to decompose the feces in an aerobic environment to produce a compost material similar to topsoil, while also reducing its volume by more than 90 percent. The waste is mixed with wood chips, sawdust, or straw to absorb moisture and achieve the proper ratio of carbon to nitrogen. After about a year, the product is safe to use in gardens.

Other manufacturers also produce composting toilets, which can be significantly more expensive than a water-based one, but composting toilets can also be made by homeowners. In 1995, a roofing contractor named Joseph Jenkins published *The Humanure Handbook*, which went into three editions and has been translated into 12 languages (Fisher 2009, 74). Jenkins explains how to build your own "$25 humanure toilet." Composting toilets are suitable not only for water-scarce areas, but also such places as shorelines where septic tanks are not suitable. The production of compost is both the toilet's advantage, in that it provides a usable material, and its disadvantage, in that it requires handling and maintenance. Globally, the need for waterless, sanitary toilets has sparked new interest in composting toilets, making this one of the frontiers of innovation.

The history of low-flow toilets in the United States demonstrates the power of political action resulting in a significant change in the residential bathroom. Environmental activism, expressed through concern for water and energy conservation, has resulted in laws that mandate the universal use of low-flow toilets, however unpopular initially. Today's bathroom contains a toilet whose design has been altered to accede to users' political demands. The once-outrageous—a toilet whose water consumption is regulated by the government—has become so acceptable that it is unexceptional.

A second trend in bathroom design was influenced by laws that did not directly affect private, residential bathrooms. The Americans with Disabilities Act of 1990 introduced handicapped-accessible fixtures and design to many Americans. As American baby boomers age, they have begun to incorporate these fixtures into their bathrooms voluntarily, foreseeing the day when they might become explicitly useful. At the same time, manufacturers see a market for well-designed accessible fixtures and are not only producing them, but are also making some features standard.

In the United States, accessibility for the disabled has been framed as a matter of civil rights and the necessity to provide equal access for all. It also reflected a social policy of moving people with disabilities out of institutions and into the community. The first piece of relevant legislation was the Architectural Barriers Act of 1968, which required federal facilities to be accessible to people with disabilities. The Fair Housing Act of 1988 required new multifamily housing to have such accessible features as wide doorways to accommodate wheelchairs, reinforcements in bathroom walls to enable the installation of grab bars in the future, and bathrooms large enough to accommodate a wheelchair. The Americans with Disabilities Act of 1990 imposed more rigorous standards and greatly expanded the number of buildings required to be accessible, applying to the private sector as well as state and local governments. It did not, however, affect private homes (U.S. Access Board 2017; Lawlor and Thomas 2008, 25–26; Institute for Human Centered Design 2016).

The effect of these laws, particularly the 1990 one, was to make accessible design familiar to all. Restaurants, schools, stores, museums, and virtually everywhere that someone was likely to visit provided accessible bathrooms, introducing Americans to grab bars, entries without steps, lever faucets, and larger toilet stalls. As the disability community began to organize, it resented the "us versus them" dichotomy of minimum design standards that created separate facilities for the disabled. "Universal design" gained favor as a term, repositioning the concern as design that would work for the broadest range of people and products that would be more universally usable (Institute for Human Centered Design 2016). A related concept is that of visitability, which champions inclusive environments so that a disabled person would find it possible to visit such a house. Following DeKalb and Fulton Counties, Georgia, several municipalities have adopted ordinances that require single-family homes to have a basic level of accessibility. A walkway without steps, doorways with a minimal width of 32 inches, and a main-floor bathroom that can accommodate a wheelchair are the primary requirements for houses meeting the visitability standard (Lawlor and Thomas 2008, 27–29).

The greater concern for many Americans is "aging in place," the desire to remain in their current dwellings for as long as they can. With the population bulge known as the baby boomers reaching older age, by 2060, the number of people aged 65 and over is projected to double, forming nearly a quarter of the U.S. population. According to AARP, nearly 90 percent of these people want to stay in their homes as they age (Askar 2016, 44; Bayer and Harper 2000, 4). The improved economic status of older people has given them more options, and in-home services supported by government programs have become more available (Lanspery et al. 1997, 9). As a result, making accommodations for aging has received the attention of policy makers and manufacturers. As one book on the subject explains it, "Properly applied, aging-in-place principles allow an individual to remain in an environment that he or she chooses, often in a house that he or she owns and has lived in for many years in a familiar neighborhood with which he or she has established a connection" (Lawlor and Thomas 2008, 5). To be able to live independently, aging Americans turn to the plans and fixtures advocated by universal design and codified by the Americans with Disabilities Act.

Much of the attention of universal design and aging in place focuses on the bathroom because of the private nature of activities that take place there. As people contemplate losing their independence due to illness or age, requiring assistance to use the toilet or to bathe is a line that many do not want to cross (Zola 1997, 30). Therefore, recommended designs offer arrangements that allow wheelchair users to transfer to toilets unaided or to bathe themselves. Another reason for the focus on the bathroom is that it is perceived to be a particularly hazardous place. The Centers for Disease Control and Prevention found that in one year, 2008, 234,000 people were treated in emergency rooms for bathroom-related injuries, 80 percent of them slips and falls due to the hazardous combination of hard surfaces and water found in bathrooms (Conley 2011). A closer look at the requirements and recommendations concerning bathrooms reveals accommodations, both simple and complex, that can benefit the daily life of a disabled person while not impeding, and in some cases aiding, the daily life of the able-bodied.

One important accommodation is to have a bathroom on the first floor. Adding one can be expensive, but it provides access not only for people in wheelchairs, but for anyone who finds stairs difficult. The National Association of Home Builders reports that more than a third of the aging-in-place modifications made by their members are to add an entry-level bathroom (National Association of Home Builders 2016, exhibit 10). Ideally, bathrooms should be planned so that they have a five-foot turning radius for a wheelchair. Doors should also be wide enough for wheelchairs—at least 32 inches, preferably 34 or 36 inches.

A simple change to the toilet—raising the height of the seat—has become widespread. While Alexander Kira argued for a low height—9 or 10 inches—for optimal intestinal functioning, the move has been in the opposite direction, toward higher seats to accommodate people with impaired mobility. Disability advocates advise raising the seat to 17 to 19 inches from the floor, as opposed to the 14 or 15 that is customary. Manufacturers have advertised the new height as "comfort height," normalizing the new configuration. Kohler's catalog lists the features of Comfort Height, which it has trademarked: "Sit at chair height—approximately two inches higher than standard-height toilets. Makes standing and sitting easier. Many are ADA-compliant" (Kohler Company 2016, 129). Comfort Height toilets now dominate Kohler's sales (M. Smith 2017).

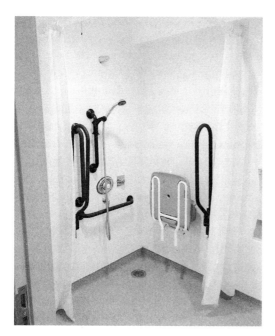

This curbless shower includes grab bars, a fold-down seat, and a handheld showerhead. Initially designed for the disabled, many of these features are now found in bathrooms whose owners are planning for old age. (Coloradonative/Dreamstime.com)

For the shower, curbless entry has gained new favor, responding to the inconvenience, if not danger, of climbing over a tub wall or a tall threshold. Applying only to stand-alone showers, the curbless entry, also known as zero entry, relies on good drainage and a curtain or door to keep the water in the shower area. If the shower is large enough to accommodate a wheelchair, then it is even less likely that water will spill into the bathroom. Seats or benches provide respite for those not in wheelchairs. Water controls located near the entry to the shower, rather than on the far wall, provide a measure of safety and utility, as do preset water-temperature controls, preventing overly hot temperatures that might scald a bather.

Bathtubs with doors, which the bather enters before it is filled, also accommodate the disabled but have found less favor among the general public. A wide bench or deck on at least one side of the tub, which enables a user to sit while sliding legs into the tub, can be useful for many other situations as well. Both showers and tubs are increasingly equipped with hand showers—detachable handheld shower heads that serve people in a sitting position.

Grab bars to assist people getting on or off the toilet or in or out of the shower or tub have also found new favor. While the ADA standards are fairly explicit—grab bars must be rounded so that there are no sharp corners, must be 1-and-a-quarter to 1-and-a-half inches in diameter, and must be 1-and-a-half inches from the wall so that if someone leaned on it their arm could not slip down behind it—the most important aspect is that it be anchored to the wall (Rodriguez 2017). Towel bars and soap holders are not usually attached firmly enough to bear someone's weight, so the screws for grab bars should be placed in wall studs or into walls that have been reinforced with three-quarter-inch plywood behind Sheetrock. While functional, grab bars can be both stylish and dual-purpose, serving as towel rods or drying racks.

At the sink, lever-type faucets are easier to operate, especially for sufferers of arthritis. Sink height is more complicated. While 30 inches used to be the standard, in recent decades, Americans have preferred higher sinks, even as high as 36 inches. People in wheelchairs need a sink that is much lower. Some advocates recommend the installation of two heights of sinks, although this is an expensive adaptation (Lawlor and Thomas 2008, 134–35). Better lighting throughout the bathroom, including night lighting, and nonskid floors, both in the shower and in the bathroom itself, are also recommended.

Many of these accommodations, initially promoted for the use of the disabled, have through the concept of universal design become standard in home bathrooms. A 2016 survey of home builders who did remodeling found that, in the previous year, 80 percent of them had undertaken modification work related to aging in place. The top three projects were grab bars (94 percent), higher toilets (82 percent), and curbless showers (79 percent) (National Association of Home Builders 2016, exhibit 10). Manufacturers have embraced the trend, advertising the comfort and utility of some of these adjustments. They downplay their applicability for the disabled and elderly, fearing negative associations, but the normalization of some of these fixtures has changed the appearance and functionality of the bathroom. Renaming some of the items also helps make them acceptable: not only are higher toilet seats "comfort height," but grab bars are called "shower rails," and lever-style faucets are "ergonomic." And as *Consumer Reports* noted, "The very things that make your bathroom safer and easier to navigate—large, walk-in showers; higher toilets; natural lighting—are also some of the latest design trends" ("A Bathroom for the Ages" 2015).

The voluntary adoption of accessible fixtures and designs provides an interesting contrast to low-flow toilets, which were mandated over vehement objections from users. By emphasizing utility and ease, accessible fixtures have been welcomed into homes. Comfort and convenience in the form of comfort-height toilets and sturdy grab bars enhance the user's experience while remaining, for the most part, a voluntary adaptation.

Germophobia—the excessive fear of bacteria and viruses—is the third trend that has affected the bathroom. Arising in the 1990s, the fear of germs continues today, with advice articles answering such questions as "what diseases can you really get from toilet seats?" (Answer: realistically, very few.) The new awareness of germs spawned hundreds of products. Antimicrobial cleansers and such items as hand soap, disinfectants, sponges, socks, cutting boards, pencils, and facial tissues are joined by such larger objects as redesigned fixtures for the bathroom. Although the efficacy of some of these products has been called into question, the fear of germs continues, and the new offerings for bathrooms are just beginning to catch on.

By the mid-20th century, the concern about infectious diseases so prevalent earlier in the century had subsided. In 1969, the U.S. surgeon general declared that "it was time to close the book on infectious diseases" because they were no longer a serious threat (Tomes 1998, 254). Antibiotics and general hygienic practices seemed to have conquered germs, and the public's attention turned to heart disease and cancer, both killers of more Americans, as more valid concerns. But the appearance of AIDS in the 1980s raised alarms. This initially mysterious disease, contagious but in unknown ways and without a known cure, scared the public. Tales of contagion through drinking glasses, toilets, and swimming pools echoed contagion stories of the early 20th century. Although the parameters of the disease were soon identified, and direct transfer of bodily fluids through sexual interaction or shared needles was identified as the method of contagion, a wariness persisted. Subsequent outbreaks of *E. coli* and *Norovirus* kept infectious diseases in the public eye. The ease of transportation around the world means that infectious diseases travel just as easily, as witnessed by the Ebola epidemic in 2014 and the Zika epidemic of 2015–2016. In addition, the appearance of "superbugs"—bacteria that are resistant to common antibiotics—further undermines Americans' confidence that they have conquered infectious diseases.

Reflecting this new concern about germs, the market for home hygiene products grew by 80 percent from the late 1980s to the early 1990s (Tomes 2000, 194). By the 1990s, the introduction of numerous products responded to Americans' new germ awareness. The 36 new antibacterial products on the market in 1992 increased to 140 by 1997 (Rosin 1997, 24). These included not only antimicrobial soaps, but also such items as cutting boards and mattresses. The efficacy of these antimicrobial products has not been proven; while an antibacterial sponge might kill germs in the sponge, it does not necessarily kill germs on anything it touches. In fact, the sponge may just spread germs around. Nor do healthy adults contract major diseases from ordinary contact with everyday surfaces. As Hanna Rosin put it in an article in the *New Republic*, "Antibacterial products are designed to play into that particularly American inability to process risk" (Rosin 1997, 31).

Rosin also blamed the microbiologist Philip Tierno for starting the "hysteria." Tierno swabbed a number of objects to identify bacteria and published his findings. In his popular book, published in 2001, called *The Secret Life of Germs: What They Are, Why We Need Them, and How We Can Protect Ourselves against Them*, Tierno described some of this swabbing: "When I tested the sample take from a taxicab seat, it contained *Streptococcus viridans*, a common mouth germ probably expelled by a cough; *Enterobacter* sp., found in feces; and *Staphylococcus aureus*, shed from the skin. A movie-theater seat teemed with *S. aureus* as well as group B strep, which is usually found in vaginal fluid, and *Enterococcus*, another fecal germ" (14). And so on. Tierno's alarmist exposure of the prevalence of germs, as well as people's general unwillingness to wash their hands after using the bathroom, makes for a frightening read.

While the avoidance of bacteria and viruses is certainly advised for people with compromised immune systems, most healthy adults do not need to take any more precaution than washing their hands with regular soap and water, especially after using the toilet (Weintraub 2017, D4). This, though, seems beyond Americans' capabilities. While 92 percent of adults say that they always wash their hands after using public restrooms, in one study only 77 percent were observed doing so (Harris Interactive 2007, 6). The numbers in the home are unknown. The response by the marketplace has been to make the bathroom ever more sanitary and easy to clean, associating a sanitary space with personal hygiene. Realistically, a sanitary space does not necessarily ensure personal hygiene, but it is a comfort to consumers.

As an example, Kohler's offerings reflect this concern for cleanliness. As Kohler's catalog copy proclaims: "Kohler toilets are designed to exceed even your high standards of cleanliness. They look clean. They flush clean. They use new technologies to help keep your home clean and to keep you feeling clean and comfortable. Because for your bathroom and you, there's no such thing as too clean" (2016, 127). Kohler offers a one-piece toilet with no seams, instead of a tank produced separately from the bowl. Made out of vitreous china, the toilet is heavier and more expensive than the two-piece version, but its seamless appearance suggests a sanitary surface. The company also has a "touchless flush" on some toilets, requiring just a wave of the hand and eliminating a particularly germ-ridden area, the flush handle (131, 135). A deodorizing toilet seat contains a carbon filter in the seat's hinge; the battery-operated fan moves air over the scent pack. For sinks, Kohler sells an undermount sink in which the counter continues uninterrupted to the edge of the opening, and the basin is mounted underneath, eliminating the visible seam that comes from setting the basin into the counter. And the single-handle faucets, in which the handle is built into the spout, are easy to clean. Even more strikingly, Kohler's offerings are mostly a sanitary white. The company that pioneered bold colors has returned to the classic, "timeless" colors of white, off-white, and other muted shades. White is consistently Kohler's best seller (M. Smith 2017).

One particular threat from the toilet gained the public's attention in the early 21st century. The "toilet plume" refers to microscopic droplets of water, and whatever else, that are cast into the air when the toilet flushes. Some people have measured the distance of dispersed bacteria at 6 feet or even 20, and graphic YouTube videos employ ultraviolet light to track the potentially harmful traces landing on toothbrushes and drinking glasses. Scientific articles on the subject, while acknowledging that toilet flushing produces infectious aerosols, have yet to determine that they actually transmit disease (Johnson et al. 2013, 254–58; Gerba, Wallis, and Melnick 1975, 229–37). The danger of a healthy adult being infected by his or her own fecal matter is negligible, although the concerns about public facilities are more valid. Further, the prevalence of these aerosols depends on the type of flush—a siphonic toilet producing a fraction of the aerosols of a wash-down type—and ultra-low-flow toilets produce even fewer (Johnson et al. 2013, 254).

Despite the unlikelihood of toilet plume presenting a danger in the home, the sanitary-ware industry has developed a clever solution. Kohler offers a "quiet close" seat to encourage the user to put the lid down. The user need not actually lower it; after starting the closing motion, the lid closes slowly and quietly on its own. This has the added benefit of putting the seat down at the same time, thereby encouraging male users to put the seat down after using the toilet, to the relief of the women with whom they share bathrooms.

An interesting recent innovation in the American bathroom is the combination toilet and bidet. Most Americans have never used a bidet, and convincing them they need one is a tough sell. But when it is combined with the toilet and further enhanced with new technology, it has a trendy appeal. The Japanese firm Toto introduced the Washlet in 1980 and started production in the United States in 1989. Other firms have caught on; Kohler offers "intelligent toilets," including its high-end Numi toilet, introduced in 2011, and American Standard markets the SpaLet. The appeal of these "smart" toilets is that they do not require the use of hands for wiping or drying, thus appealing to Americans' fondness for personal hygiene.

The Toto Washlet has a heated seat and a sensor-operated lid that opens when the user approaches the toilet and closes when the user leaves. The bidet function is contained in retractable, self-cleaning wands set into the rim of the bowl. The wand squirts water upward to wash the user's private parts. The user can direct water flow to front or back and then more specifically within that range; the water can

The "smart" toilets of the early 21st century combine a bidet with a toilet, enabling hands-free use. Computerized technology can open and close the lid, change the water temperature, heat the seat, and generally transform the toilet experience. (Sarawut Muensang/Dreamstime.com)

pulse or be in a steady stream; and the pressure of the flow and the temperature of the water can be adjusted. Then, warm air dries the recently washed regions. A deodorizing function sucks air through filters to eliminate odors. Cleaning the bowl has also been considered. Before each use, a "pre-mist" wets down the sides of the bowl for better elimination of waste, and after each use, electrolyzed water, a disinfectant, washes down the bowl. The user controls the fixture's actions by a keypad on a handheld device.

The Washlet, the Numi, and similar smart toilets appeal to several concerns that Americans have about toilets. The user never needs to put hands anywhere near the toilet bowl, thereby ensuring a degree of hygiene. Cleanliness is emphasized not only for the user, but also in automatic cleaning of the bowl and wand. The toilets rely on computer technology, making the toilet seem trendy rather than a design that has been basically unchanged for a century. The new technology and the emphasis on cleanliness succeed in moving the association of bidets away from sex and toward personal hygiene. For people squeamish about the noise they might make on the toilet, some models offer programmed sounds to mask any unpleasantness. The smart toilets are undeniably comfortable, as well, with heated seats and warm water so that they appeal to users' desire for luxury. Also, by combining the toilet with the bidet, the new fixture will fit into any bathroom and not disrupt Americans' familiarity with three fixtures.

The smart toilets also encompass the other trends identified in this chapter. They offer dual flushes, meeting high-efficiency standards of 1.28 or 0.6 gallons per flush, and while they use water for functions other than flushes, the toilets save on toilet paper. Equipped with night and ambient lighting, they provide a measure of safety, while the hands-free nature of the smart toilets means that they accommodate people with limited mobility. And the production of personal hygiene, with little intervention on the part of the user, is a triumph of technology over squeamishness.

While the high-tech toilets produce a luxurious experience, they also address users' concerns about germs through their hands-free features. Once again, contemporary ideas find expression in bathroom fixtures. But despite the electronic sensors, LED lights, automatic faucets, and other flashy high-tech features, the bathroom is essentially the same place it was more than a century ago. Now there may be two sinks instead of one, the shower may be separate from the tub, and the toilet may incorporate a bidet, but the bathroom is still basically three fixtures, very much in a room of its own. And it continues to be an expression of Americans' ideas about cleanliness.

CONCLUSION:
PERSONAL AND PUBLIC

The bathroom is a place for highly personal activities, but its location, furnishings, and accessories are influenced by public actions and social trends. Shifting ideas about sanitation, hygiene, and disease guided the location and makeup of the three-fixture bathroom. Municipal regulations, technological capability, and federal standards outlined what was possible in terms of fixtures and design. Political priorities and personal preferences determined who got bathrooms, explaining why nearly half of Americans did not have a bathroom in the home in 1940. In the 1920s, a consumerist revolution, pushed by advertising, created a demand for more stylish bathrooms and more products to be used in the bathroom. The consequent need for more time and space in the bathroom led, after World War II, to larger bathrooms and more of them. Ever larger and more opulent bathrooms continue to be the trend, despite some interest in water conservation. All of these forces affecting the bathroom take it far beyond the realm of the purely personal.

The bathroom had an enormous impact on the American house. Once it was incorporated into the design, not installed as an afterthought, it rested at the heart of the living space. It offered convenience, cleanliness, and privacy, operating quietly and automatically. It eased burdens, obviating trips to the privy and haulage of water for bathing. In the course of the 20th century, the bathroom insinuated itself into Americans' homes and lives so that a house without a bathroom is unimaginable.

The intersection of societal trends in the American bathroom makes it, to some extent, a microcosm of the larger society. In identifying what is American about the American bathroom, the theories of sanitation and hygiene, the political debates about provision of services, and the hopes and fears presented in bathroom-related advertising all reveal an American ethos. Taking technology imported from Great Britain, Americans adapted and improved it so that American fixtures were high quality. Prosperity after World War II allowed for the construction of an unprecedented number of new houses, most with bathrooms. By the 1960s, the United States was famous for its numerous and efficient bathrooms.

In recent decades, though, improvements have come from other countries. Sweden and Australia led the way in water-conserving fixtures, while the ne plus ultra in convenience, sanitation, and technological achievement, the Toto Washlet, came from Japan. And as the Global South seeks new methods of providing basic sanitation in water-scarce areas, the United States' lavish, water-consumptive bathrooms provide no model. Americans are ceding their leadership in bathrooms.

Nonetheless, the bathroom is a significant American achievement. A small room in the heart of the house with smoothly operating fixtures, bringing water in from outside and removing sewage safely and automatically, the bathroom offers privacy and renewal in a quotidian setting. A place of contradictions, the bathroom is the smallest room in the house but certainly one of the most expensive; named for its cleaning function, it is used more for its toilet; and the most private space in the house is also the most dependent on public infrastructure. Everyone has one, and everyone would be loath to give it up.

GLOSSARY

bathhouse. A building containing bathing facilities for multiple users.

bathroom. A room for personal hygiene activities, generally containing a sink, a toilet, and a bathtub or shower. Written as **bath room** or **bath-room** until first decade of 20th century.

bathtub. Plumbed fixture, large enough in which to submerge the body.

bidet. Plumbed fixture designed for cleaning genital and anal areas.

boiler. Container, usually copper, for water located next to the heat source, usually a coal-fired stove.

cesspool or **cesspit.** Underground reservoir for household sewage.

chamber pot. Vessel, usually porcelain or earthenware, for urination and defecation.

cistern. A reservoir for storing water.

close stool. Lidded portable box with a seat and a removable receptacle for urination and defecation.

comfort height. A toilet seat height of 17 to 19 inches, which is 2 to 3 inches higher than toilets were for most of the 20th century.

compact bathroom. A bathroom that measured five by seven feet, often with the three fixtures aligned along one wall and the bathtub across the short end.

compartmentalized bathroom. A bathroom that is subdivided so that one or more fixtures sits in its own room.

composting toilet. A waterless toilet that uses microorganisms to decompose feces and produce compost suitable for gardens.

curbless or **zero-entry shower.** A shower that has no barrier between the bathroom floor and the shower floor.

earth closet. Modestly popular in the 1860s and 1870s, a seat with a reservoir underneath for excretions, a tank of dirt, and a mechanism to deposit dirt on top of the excretions to absorb liquid and odors.

enameled cast iron. Iron that has been cast and then fired again with a vitreous compound sprinkled on it, used for bathroom fixtures, especially tubs.

ergonomic. Designed for efficient and safe use.

fiberglass-reinforced plastic. A material used for bathtub-showers beginning in the 1960s.

filth or **environmental theory of disease.** Theory popular in the 19th century that putrefaction of substances produces gases, or a miasma, conducive to the spontaneous generation of elements that cause diseases.

germ or **contagionist theory.** The theory, arising in the late 19th century and still accepted, that microscopic organisms cause disease.

high-efficiency toilet. Toilet that consumes no more than 1.28 gallons per flush.

hot tub. A large bathtub designed for more than one person and used for soaking and socializing more than bathing.

hydropathy. A cold-water bathing regimen, popular in the 1840s.

hygiene. Personal cleanliness to achieve and maintain good health.

latrine. Receptacle, such as a pit in the earth, for urination and defecation, especially a communal one.

lavatory. American term of the 19th century for "sink." Also, a two- or three-fixture bathroom.

low-flow toilet. Toilet that consumes no more than 3.5 gallons per flush.

master bathroom. A bathroom designated for the use of the occupants of the master bedroom.

mixer tap. Faucet that combines hot and cold water so that they come out of one spout.

New Public Health or **Hygiene.** Early-20th-century movement to emphasize prevention of contagion in public situations.

powder room or **half-bath.** A room with two fixtures—toilet and sink—usually located so as to be accessible to guests.

privy or **outhouse.** A small structure with a seat and a vault underneath to hold excretions.

sanitarian. A term employed in the late 19th century for a professional trained in medicine, civil engineering, or an allied field, who developed an expertise in sanitation. Sanitarians particularly held to the filth theory of disease.

sanitary ware. Plumbed fixtures for the bathroom.

sanitation. Promotion of health and prevention of disease by maintenance of sanitary conditions.

sauna. A room providing intense heat, either through dry air or steam, to encourage sweating and cleansing of the pores.

septic tank. A receptacle in the ground in which household sewage is disintegrated by bacteria.

sewage. Excremental waste and the water used to move it. A **sewer** is the piping and conduits used to carry sewage away from the house. **Sewerage** is the system of sewers and sewage. A **combined sewer system** accommodates both household waste and street runoff, while a **separate sewer system** segregates the two.

sewer gas. The combination of gases of the putrefying elements in the sewer, which, when introduced in the house, could cause illness and disease, according to now-discarded theories.

shower. Fixture to permit bathing in a standing position by means of an overhead perforated disk that distributes water.

sink. American term of the 20th century for a plumbed fixture, usually placed at waist height, used in the bathroom for cleaning hands and face, and so on. In the 19th century, "sink" referred to a depression in the ground, as well as a latrine.

sitz or **hip bath.** Container in which to sit while water is poured over the bather.

smart toilet. Toilet that uses sensors and mechanisms to open and close the seat, flush, rinse and dry the genital area, provide music as desired, and so on.

soaking tub. A bathtub with slightly higher sides than usual, set at a distance from walls and other fixtures so that it stands alone.

sunken tub. A bathtub whose bottom is lower than floor level, putting the top rim at floor level or slightly above.

toilet. Previously called a "water closet," a plumbed fixture that consists of a seat and a water-flushed bowl, used for defecation and urination.

trap. A device, such as an S- or U-shaped curve in which water stands, in a waste pipe for preventing upward escape of sewer gas.

ultra-low-flow toilet. Toilet that consumes no more than 1.6 gallons per flush.

universal design. Design of fixtures and bathrooms that can be used by the widest range of people.

vitreous china. Earthenware that has been fired and then coated with a vitreous glaze and fired again, used for bathroom fixtures, especially toilets.

water closet. Plumbed fixture that uses water to carry away excretions, now called a toilet.

BIBLIOGRAPHY

"39 Ways to Build a Better Bathroom." 1953. *House and Home* 3 (February): 93–100.

Abbott, Edith. 1936. *The Tenements of Chicago, 1908–1935.* Chicago: University of Chicago Press.

Abramovitch, Ingrid. 1998. "Object Lesson: Soaking Tubs." *House and Garden* 167, no. 5 (May): 65–66.

Adams, Annmarie. 1996. *Architecture in the Family Way: Doctors, Houses, and Women, 1870–1890.* Montreal: McGill-Queen's University Press.

Adamson, Paul, and Marty Arbunich. 2002. *Eichler: Modernism Rebuilds the American Dream.* Salt Lake City: Gibbs Smith.

Adler, Jerry, with Karen Springen. 1998. "Feeling Flush." *Newsweek*, June 22, p. 66.

Aladdin Homes "Built in a Day" Catalog No. 29. 1917. Bay City, MI: Aladdin Company.

Allen, John K. 1907. *Sanitation in the Modern Home.* Chicago: Domestic Engineering.

American Standard. 2016. "Behind the Shower Curtain: New Research from American Standard Reveals Unique Consumer Bathing Habits." Press Release.

Anderson, Alan D. 1977. *The Origin and Resolution of an Urban Crisis: Baltimore, 1890–1930.* Baltimore: Johns Hopkins University Press.

Arnold, Earl. 1951. "Water for the Farm: Your Plumbing Program." *Rural Electrification News* 16 (February–March): 3–5.

Arnold, Eleanor, ed. 1984. *Party Lines, Pumps and Privies: Memories of Hoosier Homemakers.* Privately printed.

Askar, Nadia. 2016. "Shower Safety." *Plumbing and Mechanical* 34, no. 2 (April): 44–46.

Auer, Michael J. 1991. "The Dymaxion Dwelling Machine." In *Yesterday's Houses of Tomorrow: Innovative American Homes, 1850–1950*, edited by H. Ward Jandl, 83–99. Washington, D.C.: Preservation Press.

Bailey, Ilena M., and Melissa Farrell Snyder. 1921. "A Survey of Farm Homes." *Journal of Home Economics* 13 (August): 346–56.

Baldwin, J. 1997. *BuckyWorks: Buckminster Fuller's Ideas for Today*. New York: John Wiley and Sons.

Baldwin, Sidney. 1968. *Poverty and Politics: The Rise and Decline of the Farm Security Administration*. Chapel Hill: University of North Carolina Press.

"Baltimore Sewage Purification Plant." 1909. *Municipal Journal and Engineer* 27, no. 21 (November 24): 769–72.

"Baltimore's Sewerage and Sewage Disposal." 1907. *Municipal Journal and Engineer* 23, no. 23 (December 4): 632–36.

Barre, H. J., and L. L. Sammet. 1950. *Farm Structures*. New York: John Wiley and Sons.

Barron, Hal S. 1997. *Mixed Harvest: The Second Great Transformation in the Rural North, 1870–1930*. Chapel Hill: University of North Carolina Press.

"Bathing in the Falls." 1888. *Baltimore Sun*, July 25, p. 4.

"A Bathroom for the Ages." 2015. *Consumer Reports* (September). Online (restricted access).

"Bathroom Layouts Need Revamping." 1948. *American Builder* 70 (August): 72–85.

"Bathroomology." 1965. *Newsweek* 66 (December 13): 19.

"Bath-Room Fixtures." 1905. *House Beautiful* 17 (April): 44.

Bayer, Ada-Helen, and Leon Harper. 2000. *Fixing to Stay: A National Survey of Housing and Home Modification Issues*. Washington, D.C.: AARP.

Bayles, James C. 1884. *House Drainage and Water Service in Cities, Villages, and Rural Neighborhoods*. New York: David Williams.

Beecher, Catharine E. (1842) 1843. *A Treatise on Domestic Economy for the Use of Young Ladies at Home, or at School*. Boston: Thomas H. Webb and Company.

Bell, Chris. 2017. Personal Interview. Salt Lake City, June 4.

Bethany, Marilyn. 1980. "The Us-Generation Bathroom." *New York Times Magazine*, August 24, pp. 60–61.

Bicknell's Village Builder. (1872) 1976. New York: A. J. Bicknell and Company. Reproduced in *Bicknell's Village Builder: A Victorian Architectural Guidebook*, Watkins Glen, NY: American Life Foundation and Study Institute.

"The Big Swing to the Sunken Tub." 1961. *House Beautiful* 103 (August): 74–77.

Blake, Nelson Manfred. 1956. *Water for the Cities: A History of the Urban Water Supply Problem in the United States*. Syracuse, NY: Syracuse University Press.

Blaszczyk, Regina Lee. 2000. *Imagining Consumers: Design and Innovation from Wedgwood to Corning*. Baltimore: Johns Hopkins University Press.

Blodgett, Richard. 2003. *A Sense of Higher Design: The Kohlers of Kohler*. Lyme, CT: Greenwich Publishing Group.

Bock, Gordon. 2001. "Waterworks: A Look at Faucets and Showers in Historic Bathrooms." *Old House Journal* 29, no. 2 (March/April): 48–51.

Boone, Christopher G. 2003. "Obstacles to Infrastructure Provision: The Struggle to Build Comprehensive Sewer Works in Baltimore." *Historical Geography* 31: 151–68.

Borden, Neil H. 1942. *The Economic Effects of Advertising*. Chicago: Richard D. Irwin.

Brooks, William W. 1948. "How Large Should Your Bathroom Be?" *Better Homes and Gardens* 26, no. 7 (March): 208–12.

Brown, George Preston. 1881. *Sewer-Gas and Its Dangers*. Chicago: Jansen, McClurg and Company.

Brown, Helene. 1970. "Molded Bathrooms Complete in a Package." *American Home* 73 (May): 100–2.

Brown, Kathleen M. 2009. *Foul Bodies: Cleanliness in Early America*. New Haven, CT: Yale University Press.

Brumberg, Joan Jacobs. 1997. *The Body Project: An Intimate History of American Girls*. New York: Vintage Books.

Brusnighan, John M. 1981. "Appraisal of 1978 Conference Case History: Do the Benefits Endure?" In *Proceedings of the National Water Conservation Conference on Publicly Supplied Potable Water*, edited by Dynamac Corporation, 427–32. Washington, D.C.: U.S. Department of Commerce, National Bureau of Standards.

Bryson, Bill. 2010. *At Home: A Short History of Private Life*. New York: Doubleday.

Building Code of Baltimore. 1908. Privately printed.

Busch, Jane C. 2008. "Homes in the Suburban Era, 1946–1970." In *Greenwood Encyclopedia of Homes through American History*, edited by Thomas W. Paradis, 4: 1–155. Westport, CT: Greenwood Press. 4 vols.

Bushman, Richard L. 1993. *The Refinement of America: Persons, Houses, Cities*. New York: Vintage Books.

Bushman, Richard L., and Claudia L. Bushman. 1988. "The Early History of Cleanliness in America." *The Journal of American History* 74, no. 4 (March): 1213–38.

Butterfield, Suzanne. 1981. "Case Study: Distribution of Residential Water Saving Devices." In *Proceedings of the National Water Conservation Conference on Publicly Supplied Potable Water*, edited by Dynamac Corporation, 449–52. Washington, D.C.: U.S. Department of Commerce, National Bureau of Standards.

Byington, Margaret F. (1910) 1974. *Homestead: The Households of a Mill Town*. Pittsburgh: University of Pittsburgh Press.

Capper, John, Garrett Power, and Frank R. Shivers, Jr. 1983. *Chesapeake Waters: Pollution, Public Health and Public Opinion, 1607–1972*. Centreville, MD: Tidewater Publishers.

Carter, W. Hodding. 2006. *Flushed: How the Plumber Saved Civilization.* New York: Atria Books.

"The Case for the Live-In Bathroom." 1972. *House and Garden* 141 (May): 108, 144, 195.

Cassedy, James H. 1962a. *Charles V. Chapin and the Public Health Movement.* Cambridge, MA: Harvard University Press.

Cassedy, James H. 1962b. "The Flamboyant Colonel Waring: An Anti-contagionist Holds the American Stage in the Age of Pasteur and Koch." *Bulletin of the History of Medicine* 36:163–76.

Chapin, Charles V. 1902. "The End of the Filth Theory of Disease." *Popular Science Monthly* 60, no. 3 (January): 234–39.

Chapin, Charles V. 1917. *How to Avoid Infection.* Cambridge, MA: Harvard University Press.

"City Is Throwing in Towel on Last of Public Baths." 1959. *Baltimore Sun,* October 23, p. 44.

"Color Harmony—to Get Greater Retailer Recognition: Martex Color Guide Basis of Towel Merchandising Plan." 1931. *Printers' Ink,* September 10, pp. 108–10.

"Color in Industry." 1930. *Fortune,* February, pp. 85–94.

"Comfortable Stations." 1991. *Time* 138, no. 26 (December 30): 79.

Comstock, William T. (1881) 1997. *Modern Architectural Designs and Details.* New York: William T. Comstock. Reproduced in *Victorian Architecture: Two Pattern Books.* Watkins Glen, NY: American Life Foundation and Study Institute.

Conley, Mikaela. 2011. "CDC Report Shows Bathroom Injuries Cause Thousands of Visits to ER." *ABC News,* June 9.

Cowan, Ruth Schwartz. 1983. *More Work for Mother: The Ironies of Household Technology from the Open Hearth to the Microwave.* New York: Basic Books.

Crane Company. 1926. *Homes of Comfort: How Crane Fixtures Help to Make Them Possible.* Philadelphia: Privately printed.

Crane Company. 1936. *For the Home of Today.* Chicago: Privately printed.

Crane Company. 1939. *How to Plan the Bathroom You've Always Wanted.* Chicago: Privately printed.

Crane Company. 1940. *Plumbing and Heating for the Modern Home.* Chicago: Privately printed.

Crane Limited. 1920. *Plumbing: A Selection of Crane Plumbing Fixtures.* Montreal: Privately printed.

Crooks, James B. 1968. *Politics and Progress: The Rise of Urban Progressivism in Baltimore, 1895–1911.* Baton Rouge: Louisiana State University Press.

Cutler, Martha. 1907. "Modern Bathrooms." *Harper's Bazaar* 41, no. 2 (February): 165–69.

Danbom, David B. 1979. *The Resisted Revolution: Urban America and the Industrialization of Agriculture, 1900–1930.* Ames: Iowa State University Press.

Davidson, Lisa Pfueller. 2005. "Early Twentieth-Century Hotel Architects and
the Origins of Standardization." *Journal of Decorative and Propaganda
Arts* 25: 72–103.

"Design Decade [Bathroom]." 1940. *Architectural Forum* 73, no. 4 (October): 271–72.

Dickinson, Roy. 1931. "Research That Makes Advertising Campaigns." *Printers'
Ink Monthly* 23, no. 2 (August): 33–34, 61–62.

Dolkart, Andrew S. 2006. *Biography of a Tenement House in New York City:
An Architectural History of 97 Orchard Street*. Santa Fe, NM: Center for
American Places.

Downing, A. J. 1842. *Cottage Residences*. New York: Wiley and Putnam.

Downing, A. J. 1850. *The Architecture of Country Houses*. New York: D. Appleton and Company.

Dubrow, Gail Lee. 2002. "Deru Kugi Wa Utareru or The Nail That Sticks Up Gets
Hit: The Architecture of Japanese American Identity, 1885–1942." *Journal
of Architectural and Planning Research* 19, no. 4 (Winter): 319–33.

Dubrow, Gail, and Donna Graves. 2002. *Sento at Sixth and Main: Preserving
Landmarks of Japanese American Heritage*. Washington, D.C.: Smithson-
ian Books.

Duffy, John. 1990. *The Sanitarians: A History of American Public Health*.
Urbana: University of Illinois Press.

Dwyer, Charles P. 1856. *Economic Cottage Builder: or, Cottages for Men of
Small Means*. Buffalo, NY: Wanzer McKim and Company.

Edwards, W. B. 1937. " 'You, Too, Can Be Beautiful': A View of the Modern
Advertiser's Psychology Which, Though Profitable, Lacks Logic and Reason." *Printers' Ink*, October 14, pp. 11, 12, 14.

Ellis, John H. 1964. "Memphis' Sanitary Revolution, 1880–1890." *Tennessee Historical Quarterly* 23, no. 1 (March): 59–72.

Engler, Mira. 2004. *Designing America's Waste Landscapes*. Baltimore: Johns
Hopkins University Press.

Euchner, Charles C. 1991. "The Politics of Urban Expansion: Baltimore and the
Sewerage Question, 1859–1905." *Maryland Historical Magazine* 86, no. 3
(Fall): 270–91.

"Feminism on the Farm." 1921. *The Nation* 113, no. 2937 (October 19): 440.

Fine, Leonore, and Jesse A. Remington. 1972. *The Corps of Engineers: Construction in the Unites States*. Washington, D.C.: U.S. Army, Office of
Chief of Military History.

Fisher, Adam. 2009. "Humanure." *Time* 174, no. 23 (December 14): 74.

"Flush Fact vs. Flush Fiction: The Truth about High-Efficiency Toilets." EPA
WaterSense, June 2008.

Fox, Stephen. (1984) 1997. *The Mirror Makers: A History of American Advertising and Its Creators*. Urbana: University of Illinois Press.

Garb, Margaret. 2005. *City of American Dreams: A History of Home Ownership and Housing Reform in Chicago, 1871–1919*. Chicago: University of
Chicago Press.

Gardner, E. C. (1882) 1896. *The House That Jill Built, after Jack's Had Proved a Failure.* Springfield, MA: W. F. Adams Company.

Geary, Don. 1997. "Low-Flush Toilets." *Consumers Digest* 36 (July–August): 51–52.

General Federation of Women's Clubs. (1926) 2001. "Farm Equipment Survey." In *The Chicago Tradition in Economics*, edited by Ross B. Emmett, 4: 88. New York: Routledge. 8 vols.

Gerba, Charles P., Craig Wallis, and Joseph L. Melnick. 1975. "Microbiological Hazards of Household Toilets: Droplet Production and the Fate of Residual Organisms." *Applied Microbiology* 30, no. 2 (August): 229–37.

Gerhard, Wm. Paul. 1882. *House-Drainage and Sanitary Plumbing.* New York: D. Van Nostrand Company.

Gerhard, Wm. Paul. (1882) 1898. *House-Drainage and Sanitary Plumbing.* New York: D. Van Nostrand Company. 7th ed.

Gerhard, Wm. Paul. 1884. "Sanitary Questions." In *Cottages or Hints on Economical Building*, compiled and edited by A. W. Brunner, 33–54. New York: William T. Comstock.

Gibbs, F. W. 1939. "The History of the Manufacture of Soap." *Annals of Science* 4, no. 2: 169–90.

Giedion, Sigfried. (1948) 2013. *Mechanization Takes Command: A Contribution to Anonymous History.* Minneapolis: University of Minnesota Press.

Gilman, Caroline. 1840. *The Lady's Annual Register and Household Almanac for 1840.* Boston: Otis, Broaders and Company.

Girouard, Mark. 1978. *Life in the English Country House.* New Haven, CT: Yale University Press.

Girouard, Mark. 2000. *Life in the French Country House.* New York: Alfred A. Knopf.

Givens, Ron, with Karen Spingen. 1986. "Splish, Splash, It's More Than a Bath." *Newsweek*, May 5, p. 80.

Gleick, Peter H., Dana Haasz, Christine Henges-Jeck, Veena Srinivasan, Gary Wolff, Katherine Kao Cushing, and Amardip Mann. 2003. *Waste Not, Want Not: The Potential for Urban Water Conservation in California.* Oakland, CA: Pacific Institute.

Good, Chris. 2011. "Rand Paul and the 19-Year Libertarian War on Low-Flow Toilets." *Atlantic*, March 16. https://www.theatlantic.com/politics/archive /2011/03/rand-paul-and-the-19-year-libertarian-war-on-low-flow-toilets/72545/. Accessed July 4, 2017.

Gorman, Christine, and Julie Grace. 1996. "Toilet Wars." *Time* 148, no. 2 (July 1): 59.

Gottfried, Herbert, and Jan Jennings. (1985) 2009. *American Vernacular Buildings and Interiors, 1870–1960.* New York: W. W. Norton and Company.

Gries, John M., and James Ford. 1932. *House Design Construction and Equipment.* Washington, D.C.: President's Conference on Home Building and Home Ownership.

Griffin, Adrian H., and Richard M. Soehren. 1984. *Water Conservation in California.* Department of Water Resources Bulletin 198-84. Sacramento: California Department of Water Resources.

Groth, Paul. 2004. "Workers'-Cottage and Minimal-Bungalow Districts in Oakland and Berkeley, California, 1870–1945." *Urban Morphology* 8, no. 1: 13–25.

Haase, Albert E. 1928. "Cannon's Step-by-Step Advertising Career." *Printers' Ink Monthly* 17, no. 2 (August): 29–30, 86–87.

Hall, John. 1840. *A Series of Select and Original Modern Designs for Dwelling Houses, for the Use of Carpenters and Builders Adapted to the Style of Building in the United States.* Baltimore: John Murphy.

Hall, John. (1840) 1848. *A Series of Select and Original Modern Designs for Dwelling Houses, for the Use of Carpenters and Builders Adapted to the Style of Building in the United States.* Baltimore: John Murphy. 2nd ed.

Handlin, David P. 1979. *The American Home: Architecture and Society, 1815–1915.* Boston: Little, Brown and Company.

Hanger, G. W. W. 1904. "Public Baths in the United States." *Bulletin of the Bureau of Labor, No. 54.* Washington, D.C.: GPO. 1245–367.

Harris Interactive. 2007. *A Survey of Handwashing Behavior.* Washington, D.C.: American Society for Microbiology and the Soap and Detergent Association.

Hauenstein, Heidi, Tracy Quinn, and Ed Osann. 2013. *Toilets and Urinals Water Efficiency.* Sacramento: California Statewide Utility Codes and Standards Program.

"He Grabbed Space for a *Furo* . . . a Japanese Soaking Bath." 1983. *Sunset* 171 (September): 131.

Hellyer, S. Stevens. (1877) 1893. *The Plumber and Sanitary Houses.* London: B. T. Batsford. 5th ed.

Hering, Rudolph. 1887. "Results of Six Years' Experience with the Memphis Sewers." *Engineering and Building Record* 16, no. 26 (November 26): 739.

Hill, Hibbert Winslow. (1916) 1920. *The New Public Health.* New York: MacMillan Company.

Hoagland, Alison K. 2004. *Army Architecture in the West: Forts Laramie, Bridger, and D. A. Russell, 1849–1912.* Norman: University of Oklahoma Press.

Hoagland, Alison K. 2010. *Mine Towns: Buildings for Workers in Michigan's Copper Country.* Minneapolis: University of Minnesota Press.

Hoagland, Alison K. 2011. "Introducing the Bathroom: Space and Change in Working-Class Houses." *Buildings and Landscapes: Journal of the Vernacular Architecture Forum* 18, no. 2 (Fall): 15–42.

Hopkins, Claude C. 1927. *My Life in Advertising.* New York: Harper and Brothers.

"A Hot Fad from Finland." 1963. *Life* 54 (January 18): 93–94.

"How to Plan Your 1956 Bathrooms." 1955. *American Builder* 77 (November): 86–91.

Hoy, Suellen. 1995. *Chasing Dirt: The American Pursuit of Cleanliness.* New York: Oxford University Press.

Hussey, E. C. (1874) 1994. *Cottage Architecture of Victorian America.* New York: Dover Publications.

Ingersoll, John H. 1977. "Bubbly Balm That's Fun." *House Beautiful* 119 (June): 12, 16, 18, 20.

Inman, Marjorie. 1988. "Environmental Stress, Bathroom Spaces and Household Density." *Housing and Society* 15, no. 1: 85–93.

Institute for Human Centered Design. 2016. "History of Universal Design." https://humancentereddesign.org/universal-design/history-universal-design. Accessed July 1, 2017.

"Integrated Bathroom." 1937. *Architectural Record* 81, no. 1: 40–41.

"It Began with the Two-Basin Counter." 1970. *Sunset* 144 (January): 78, 81.

"It Takes More Than Plumbing to Make a Good Bathroom." 1950. *House Beautiful* 92 (March): 115–16, 144–52.

J. L. Mott Iron Works. 1914. *Modern Plumbing*, Number 8. New York: Privately printed.

Jacobs, James A. 2015. *Detached America: Building Houses in Postwar Suburbia.* Charlottesville: University of Virginia Press.

Jacobs, Lewis. 1939. *The Rise of American Film: A Critical History.* New York: Harcourt, Brace and Company.

Jellison, Katherine. 1993. *Entitled to Power: Farm Women and Technology, 1913–1963.* Chapel Hill: University of North Carolina Press.

Jennings, Jan. 2011. "Le Corbusier's 'Naked': 'Absolute Honesty' and (Exhibitionist) Display in Bathroom Settings." *Interiors* 2, no. 3: 307–32.

Johnson, David L., Kenneth R. Mead, Robert A. Lynch, and Deborah V. L. Hirst. 2013. *American Journal of Infection Control* 41, no. 3 (March): 254–58.

Kanner, Bernice. 1989. "Dear John." *New York* 22 (July 17): 12–13.

Kaups, Matti. 1976. "A Finnish Savusauna in Minnesota." *Minnesota History*, Spring, pp. 11–20.

Keating, Ann Durkin. 1988. *Building Chicago: Suburban Developers and the Creation of a Divided Metropolis.* Columbus: Ohio State University Press.

Keene, E. S. 1911. *Mechanics of the Household: A Supplementary Course of Physics Dealing with Household Appliances.* Part I. Privately printed.

Kellogg, Cynthia. 1960. "New Ideas for the Bath." *New York Times Magazine*, June 12, pp. 66–67.

Kelly, Barbara M. 1993. *Expanding the American Dream: Building and Rebuilding Levittown.* Albany: State University of New York Press.

Kira, Alexander. 1966. *The Bathroom: Criteria for Design.* Ithaca, NY: Cornell University Center for Housing and Environmental Studies.

Kira, Alexander. (1966) 1976. *The Bathroom.* New York: Viking Press. New and expanded edition.

Kirkpatrick, Ellis Lore. 1929. *The Farmer's Standard of Living.* New York: The Century Company.

Klein, Jessi. 2016. "The Bath: A Polemic." *New Yorker*, May 23, pp. 36–37.

Kline, Ronald R. 2000. *Consumers in the Country: Technology and Social Change in Rural America.* Baltimore: Johns Hopkins University Press.

Kohler Company. 1928. *Color Charm Enters the Bathroom*. Kohler, WI: Privately printed.

Kohler Company. 1929. *Modern Beauty and Usefulness in Plumbing Fixtures.* Kohler, WI: Privately printed.

Kohler Company. 1936. *Planned Plumbing and Heating for Better Living.* Kohler, WI: Privately printed.

Kohler Company. 1939. *Planned Plumbing and Heating*. Kohler, WI: Privately printed.

Kohler Company. 2016. *Bathroom Products*. Kohler, WI: Privately printed.

Koloski-Ostrow, Ann Olga. 2015. *The Archaeology of Sanitation in Roman Italy.* Chapel Hill: University of North Carolina Press.

Lafever, Minard. 1856. *The Architectural Instructor.* New York: G. P. Putnam and Company.

Lambert, Gerard B. 1956a. *All out of Step: A Personal Chronicle.* Garden City, NY: Doubleday and Company.

Lambert, Gerard B. 1956b. "How I Sold Listerine." *Fortune*, September, pp. 111, 166, 168, 170, 172.

Langford, Marilyn. 1965. *Personal Hygiene Attitudes and Practices in 1000 Middle-Class Households.* Ithaca, NY: Cornell University Agricultural Experiment Station.

Lanspery, Susan, James J. Callahan, Jr., Judith R. Miller, and Joan Hyde. 1997. "Introduction: Staying Put." In *Staying Put: Adapting the Place Instead of the People*, edited by Susan Lanspery and Joan Hyde, 1–22. Amityville, NY: Baywood Publishing Company.

Lawlor, Drue, and Michael A. Thomas. 2008. *Residential Design for Aging in Place*. Hoboken, NJ: John Wiley and Sons.

Lears, Jackson. 1994. *Fables of Abundance: A Cultural History of Advertising in America*. New York: Basic Books.

Lees, Al. 1974. ". . . and What of the Seamless Bathroom?" *Popular Science* 204 (May): 111, 144.

Lennen, Philip W. 1926. "In Memoriam: An Appreciation of Milton Feasley—a Real Advertising Man." *Printers' Ink*, October 14, pp. 25–26, 28.

Levitt and Sons. 1961. *Belair at Bowie Maryland*. Privately printed.

Lewis, Sinclair. (1922) 1950. *Babbitt*. New York: Harcourt, Brace and World.

Lief, Alfred. 1958. *"It Floats": The Story of Procter & Gamble*. New York: Rinehart and Company.

Lockwood, Yvonne R. 1977. "The Sauna: An Expression of Finnish-American Identity." *Western Folklore* 36, no. 1 (January): 71–84.

Loos, Adolf. (1898) 1982. "Plumbers." *Neue Freie Presse*, July 17. In *Spoken into the Void: Collected Essays, 1897–1900*, 45–49. Cambridge, MA: MIT Press.

Lubove, Roy. 1962. *The Progressive and the Slums: Tenement House Reform in New York City, 1890–1917*. Pittsburgh: University of Pittsburgh Press.

Lumsden, L. L. 1918. *Rural Sanitation: A Report on Special Studies Made in 15 Countries in 1914, 1915, and 1916*. U.S. Treasury Department, Public Health Service, Public Health Bulletin no. 94. Washington, D.C.: GPO.

Lupton, Ellen, and J. Abbott Miller. 1992. *The Bathroom, the Kitchen, and the Aesthetics of Waste: A Process of Elimination*. Cambridge, MA: MIT Visual Arts Center.

Lyman, Joseph B., and Laura E. Lyman. 1859. *The Philosophy of Housekeeping: A Scientific and Practical Manual*. Hartford, CT: S. M. Betts and Company.

Lynd, Robert S., and Helen Merrell. 1929. *Middletown: A Study in American Culture*. New York: Harcourt Brace and Company.

Maddock, Archibald M., II. 1962. *The Polished Earth: A History of the Pottery Plumbing Fixture Industry in the United States*. Privately printed.

Maddock, Thomas. 1910. *Pottery: A History of the Pottery Industry*. Privately printed.

Malcolm, Janet. 1972. "On and off the Avenue." *New Yorker*, September 9, pp. 112–14.

Marchand, Roland. 1985. *Advertising the American Dream: Making Way for Modernity, 1920–1940*. Berkeley: University of California Press.

Marsh, Margaret. 1989. "From Separation to Togetherness: The Social Construction of Domestic Space in American Suburbs, 1840–1915." *Journal of American History* 76, no. 2 (September): 506–27.

Martin, Ann Smart. 1993. "Makers, Buyers, and Users: Consumerism as a Material Culture Framework." *Winterthur Portfolio* 28, nos. 2/3: 141–57.

McClary, Andrew. 1980. "Germs are Everywhere: The Germ Threat as Seen in Magazine Articles, 1890–1920." *Journal of American Culture* 3, no. 1 (Spring): 33–46.

McMahon, Michal. 1988. "Makeshift Technology: Water and Politics in 19th-Century Philadelphia." *Environmental Review* 12, no. 4 (Winter): 20–37.

Melosi, Martin V. 2000. *The Sanitary City: Urban Infrastructure in America from Colonial Times to the Present*. Baltimore: Johns Hopkins University Press.

Melosi, Martin V. 2011. *Precious Commodity: Providing Water for America's Cities*. Pittsburgh: University of Pittsburgh Press.

Melvin, Bruce L. 1935. "Housing Standards for Subsistence Homesteads." *Architectural Record* 77 (January): 9–11.

Metropolitan Museum of Art. 1929. *The Architect and the Industrial Arts: An Exhibition of Contemporary American Design*. Privately printed.

Michael, Jerrold M. 2011. "The National Board of Health, 1879–1883." *Public Health Reports* 126 (January–February): 123–29.

"Model Cottages." 1846. *Godey's Magazine and Lady's Book* 33 (September): 133–35.

"Modern Laving." 1963. *Time* 82 (December 27): 56.

Mok, Michael. 1966. "Blame the Outmoded U.S. Bathroom." *Life* 60 (May 20): 84C–86.

Monarch Water Heater Company. Ca. 1905. *The Monarch Water Heater: The Automatic Instantaneous Heating of Water.* Privately printed.

"The Morals of the Bathtub." 1896. *Ladies' Home Journal.* 13 (November): 14.

Moskowitz, Marina. 2004. *Standard of Living: The Measure of the Middle Class in Modern America.* Baltimore: Johns Hopkins University Press.

Mulrooney, Margaret M. 1989. *Legacy of Coal: The Coal Company Towns of Southwestern Pennsylvania.* Washington, D.C.: U.S. Department of the Interior, National Park Service, Historic American Buildings Survey/Historic American Engineering Record.

Murdoch, Guy. 1994. "Outhouse Blues." *Consumers' Research Magazine* 77, no. 1 (January): 2.

Murphy, Kate. 2006. "For the Busy Couple, a Bathroom Break." *New York Times*, New York edition, July 20, F1.

National Association of Home Builders. 2016. *Remodeling Market Index: Special Questions on Aging-in-Place.* Washington, D.C.: National Association of Home Builders, Economics and Housing Policy Group.

National Association of Home Builders and House and Garden Magazine. 1964. "Housing Design and the American Family." Washington, D.C.: NAHB Journal of Homebuilding.

National Board of Health. 1880. "Report on the Sanitary Survey of Memphis, Tenn." *Annual Report of the National Board of Health.* H.Ex.Doc.8, 46th Cong., 3rd sess. Washington, D.C.: GPO.

"National Marketing Meeting." 1967. *People: Published at Kohler, Wisconsin by and for the Members of the Kohler Co. Organization* 16, no. 29 (January 12): 1.

Neth, Mary. 1995. *Preserving the Family Farm: Women, Community, and the Foundations of Agribusiness in the Midwest, 1900–1940.* Baltimore: Johns Hopkins University Press.

"New Orders of the Bath." 1927. *Vogue*, November 15, pp. 91–93, 138, 140.

Nordskog, Michael. 2010. *The Opposite of Cold: The Northwoods Finnish Sauna Tradition.* Minneapolis: University of Minnesota Press.

Nye, David E. 1990. *Electrifying America: Social Meanings of a New Technology, 1880–1940.* Cambridge, MA: MIT Press.

Odell, Frederic S. (1881) 1977. "The Sewerage of Memphis." *Transactions of the American Society of Civil Engineers* 9, no. 216 (February). In *Sewering the Cities*, edited by Barbara Gutmann Rosenkrantz, 23–52. New York: Arno Press.

Offit, Avodah K. 1981. "The Bathroom: Your House's Erogenous Zone?" *House and Garden* 153 (August): 84–87.

Ogle, Maureen. 1996. *All the Modern Conveniences: American Household Plumbing, 1840–1890.* Baltimore: Johns Hopkins University Press.

Osterud, Grey. 2012. *Putting the Barn before the House: Women and Family Farming in Early-Twentieth-Century New York.* Ithaca, NY: Cornell University Press.

"Party-Time Tubs." 1972. *Life* 72 (January 14): 40–42.

Paxton, Edward T. 1955. *What People Want When They Buy a House: A Guide for Architects and Builders.* U.S. Department of Commerce, Housing and Home Finance Agency. Washington, D.C.: GPO.

Penner, Barbara. 2013a. *Bathroom.* London: Reaktion Books.

Penner, Barbara. 2013b. "Designed-In Safety." *Places Journal* (October). doi:10.22269/13105. Accessed April 13, 2017.

Peterson, Jon A. 1979. "The Impact of Sanitary Reform upon American Urban Planning, 1840–1890." *Journal of Social History* 13, no. 1 (Autumn): 83–103.

Pickett, Clarence E. 1934. "The Social Significance of the Subsistence Homestead Movement." *Journal of Home Economics* 26 (October): 477–79.

Plunkett, Mrs. H. M. 1885. *Women, Plumbers, and Doctors: or, Household Sanitation.* New York: D. Appleton and Company.

Potter, David M. 1954. *People of Plenty: Economic Abundance and the American Character.* Chicago: University of Chicago Press.

Quincy, Josiah. 1898. "Playgrounds, Baths, and Gymnasia." *Journal of Social Science* 36 (December): 139–47.

Radford's Modern Homes: 200 House Plans. 1909. Chicago: Radford Architectural Company.

Report of the Sewerage Commission of the City of Baltimore. 1897. Privately printed.

Rodengen, Jeffrey L. 1999. *The History of American Standard.* Privately printed.

Rodriguez, Juan. 2017. "Get ADA Guidelines for Accessible Bathrooms." *The Balance.* https://www.thebalance.com/ada-construction-guidelines-for-accesible-bathrooms-844778. Accessed January 24, 2018.

Rosin, Hanna. 1997. "Don't Touch This." *New Republic,* November, pp. 24–31.

"Rub a Dub Dub." 1998. *New Yorker,* July 13, p. 27.

Sando, Linnea C. 2014. "The Enduring Finnish Sauna in Hamlin County, South Dakota." *Material Culture* 45, no. 2: 1–20.

Schoenfeld, Margaret H. 1940. "Progress of Public Housing in the United States." *Monthly Labor Review* 51, no. 2: 267–82.

Schultz, Stanley K., and Clay McShane. 1978. "To Engineer the Metropolis: Sewers, Sanitation, and City Planning in Late-Nineteenth-Century America." *Journal of American History* 65, no. 2 (September): 389–411.

Scott, Linda M. 2015. "Woodbury Soap: Classic Sexual Sell or Just Good Marketing?" *Advertising and Society Review* 16, no. 1. doi:10.1353/asr.2015.0008. Accessed March 8, 2017.

Seale, William. 1986. *The President's House: A History.* Washington, D.C.: White House Historical Association. 2 vols.

"Seamless Bathrooms." 1968. *Popular Science* 193 (October): 162–64.

Sears, Roebuck and Company. (1926) 1991. *Honor Bilt Modern Homes.* Mineola, NY: Dover Publications.

"Sewage Pollution of Water Supplies." 1903. *Engineering Record* 48, no. 4 (August 1): 117.

Shannon, J. Lewis. 1992. "Thomas Worker Housing." Washington, D.C.: Library of Congress, Prints and Photographs Division, Historic American Engineering Record.

Shryock, Richard Harrison. (1957) 1977. *National Tuberculosis Association, 1904–1954.* New York: Arno Press.

Simon, Roger D. 1996. *The City-Building Process: Housing and Services in New Milwaukee Neighborhoods, 1880–1910.* Philadelphia: American Philosophical Society.

Sipe, Brian M. 1988. "Earth Closets and the Dry Earth System of Sanitation in Victorian America." *Material Culture* 20, no. 2/3 (Summer/Fall): 27–37.

Sivulka, Juliann. (1998) 2012. *Soap, Sex, and Cigarettes: A Cultural History of American Advertising.* Boston: Wadsworth.

Sivulka, Juliann. 2001. *Stronger Than Dirt: A Cultural History of Advertising Personal Hygiene in America, 1875 to 1940.* Amherst, NY: Humanity Books.

Skow, John. 1965. "The Importance of Being Poached." *Saturday Evening Post* 238 (May 8): 88–91.

Smillie, W. G. 1943. "The National Board of Health." *American Journal of Public Health* 33, no. 8 (August): 925–30.

Smith, Bertha. 1905. "The Public Bath." *Outlook* 79 (March 4): 567–77.

Smith, Michael, Manager, Design Center, Kohler Company. 2017. Personal Interview, June 26. Kohler, Wisconsin.

Smith, Virginia. 2007. *Clean: A History of Personal Hygiene and Purity.* New York: Oxford University Press.

Sprackling, Helen. 1928. "Rainbow Bathrooms." *House Beautiful* 63 (June): 750–51, 793–94, 796–97.

Sprackling, Helen. 1933. "The Modern Bathroom." *Parents Magazine* 8 (February): 25, 50–52.

Standard Sanitary Manufacturing Company. 1901. *Modern Bath Rooms and Appliances.* Pittsburgh: Privately printed.

Standard Sanitary Manufacturing Company. 1903. *Modern Bath Rooms and Appliances.* Pittsburgh: Privately printed.

Standard Sanitary Manufacturing Company. 1904. *"Standard" Porcelain Enameled Baths and Sanitary Appliances.* Catalog P. Pittsburgh: Privately printed.

Standard Sanitary Manufacturing Company. 1906. *Modern Bath Rooms.* Pittsburgh: Privately printed.

Standard Sanitary Manufacturing Company. 1909. *Modern Bathrooms.* Pittsburgh: Privately printed.

Standard Sanitary Manufacturing Company. 1923. *"Standard" Plumbing Fixtures for the Home.* Pittsburgh: Privately printed.

Standard Sanitary Manufacturing Company. 1927. *"Standard" Plumbing Fixtures for the Home.* Pittsburgh: Privately printed.

Standard Sanitary Manufacturing Company. Ca. 1930. *"Standard" Plumbing Fixtures for the Home.* Pittsburgh: Privately printed.

Standard Sanitary Manufacturing Company. Ca. 1935. *Planning Your Plumbing Wisely.* Pittsburgh: Privately printed.

Stern, Marc Jeffrey. 1994. *The Pottery Industry of Trenton: A Skilled Trade in Transition, 1850–1929.* New Brunswick, NJ: Rutgers University Press.

Stone, May N. 1979. "The Plumbing Paradox: American Attitudes toward Late Nineteenth-Century Domestic Sanitary Arrangements." *Winterthur Portfolio* 14, no. 3 (August): 283–309.

Storke, E. G. 1859. *The Family and Householder's Guide.* Auburn, NY: Auburn Publishing Company.

Strasser, Susan. (1982) 2000. *Never Done: A History of American Housework.* New York: Holt Paperbacks.

Sullivan, C. C. 2008. "Precious Water: Sustainable Indoor Water Systems." McGraw-Hill Construction Continuing Education. https://www.construction.com/CE/articles/0801water-3.asp. Accessed July 10, 2017.

Tarr, Joel A. 1979. "The Separate vs. Combined Sewer Problem: A Case Study in Urban Technology Design Choice." *Journal of Urban History* 5, no. 3 (May): 308–39.

Tarr, Joel A. 1988. "Sewerage and the Development of the Networked City in the United States, 1850–1930." In *Technology and the Rise of the Networked City in Europe and America,* edited by Joel A. Tarr and Gabriel Dupuy, 159–85. Philadelphia: Temple University Press.

Tarr, Joel A., with James McCurley III, Francis C. McMichael, and Terry Yosie. 1984. "Water and Wastes: A Retrospective Assessment of Wastewater Technology in the United States, 1800–1932." *Technology and Culture* 25, no. 2 (April): 226–63.

Tarshis, Barry. 1979. *The "Average American" Book.* New York: Atheneum/SMI.

Tierno, Philip M., Jr. 2001. *The Secret Life of Germs: What They Are, Why We Need Them, and How We Can Protect Ourselves Against Them.* New York: Atria Books.

Tobin, Mitch. 2001. "The Low Flow's False Flush." *E: The Environmental Magazine* 12, no. 2 (March/April): 15–16.

Tomes, Nancy. 1998. *The Gospel of Germs: Men, Women, and the Microbe in American Life.* Cambridge, MA: Harvard University Press.

Tomes, Nancy. 2000. "The Making of a Germ Panic, Then and Now." *American Journal of Public Health* 90, no. 2 (February): 191–98.

"Two Years Old, Going on Three." 1922. *Domestic Engineering* 101: 369.

U.S. Access Board. 2017. "History of the Access Board." https://www.access-board.gov/the-board/board-history. Accessed July 1, 2017.

"U.S. Builders Get New Handle on Bathrooms." 1968. *Business Week,* July 6, p. 100.

U.S. Department of Agriculture. 1915a. *Domestic Needs of Farm Women.* Report No. 104. Washington, D.C.: GPO.

U.S. Department of Agriculture. 1915b. *Economic Needs of Farm Women.* Report No 106. Washington, D.C.: GPO.

U.S. Department of Agriculture, Farm Security Administration. 1939. *Small Houses.* Washington, D.C.: GPO.

U.S. Department of Commerce, Bureau of the Census. 1931. *Biennial Census of Manufactures.* Washington, D.C.: GPO.

U.S. Department of Commerce, Bureau of the Census. 1963. *U.S. Census of Housing, 1960.* Vol. 1: States and Small Areas, Part I: United States Summary. Washington, D.C.: GPO.

U.S. Department of Commerce, Bureau of the Census. 2011. "Historical Census of Housing Tables: Plumbing Facilities." https://www.census.gov/hhes /www/housing/census/historic/plumbing.html. Accessed April 24, 2017.

U.S. Department of Commerce, Bureau of the Census. 2013. "American Housing Survey." C-02-AH, Rooms, Size, and Amenities. https://factfinder.cen sus.gov/faces/tableservices/jsf/pages/productview.xhtml?pid=AHS_2013 _C02AH&prodType=table. Accessed April 24, 2017.

U.S. Department of Commerce, Bureau of Standards. 1929. *Recommended Minimum Requirements for Plumbing.* Washington, D.C.: GPO.

U.S. Department of Commerce, Bureau of Standards. 1930. *Staple Vitreous China Plumbing Fixtures.* Washington, D.C.: GPO.

U.S. Federal Emergency Administration of Public Works Housing Division. 1937. *Homes for Workers.* Housing Division Bulletin No. 3. Washington, D.C.: GPO.

Vale, Lawrence J. 2005. "Standardizing Public Housing." In *Regulating Place: Standards and the Shaping of Urban America,* edited by Eran Ben-Joseph and Terry S. Szold, 67–101. New York: Routledge.

Vickers, Amy. 1989. "New Massachusetts Toilet Standard Sets Water Conservation Precedent." *Journal of the American Water Works Association* 81, no. 3 (March): 48–51.

Vigarello, Georges. 1988. *Concepts of Cleanliness: Changing Attitudes in France since the Middle Ages.* Trans. Jean Birrell. Cambridge: Cambridge University Press.

Vinikas, Vincent. 1992. *Soft Soap, Hard Sell: American Hygiene in an Age of Advertisement.* Ames: Iowa State University Press.

Von Furstenberg, Diane. 1993. *The Bath.* New York: Random House.

Wagner, W. Sydney. 1917. "The Statler Idea in Hotel Planning and Equipment." *Architectural Forum* 27. Part I, "Introduction," no. 5 (November): 115–18. Part II, "The Development of the Typical Floor Plan," no. 6 (December): 165–70.

Ward, Florence E. 1920. *The Farm Woman's Problems.* U.S. Department of Agriculture Circular 148. Washington, D.C.: GPO.

Waring, George E., Jr. 1870. *Earth-Closets and Earth Sewage.* New York: The Tribune Association.

Waring, George E., Jr. 1882. "The Death-Rate of Memphis." *American Architect and Building News* 11, no. 326 (March 25): 142–43.

Waring, George E., Jr. 1884. "The Memphis Sewers after Four Years' Use." *American Architect and Building News* 16, no. 447 (July 19): 27–28.

Waring, George E., Jr. 1894. "Out of Sight, Out of Mind: Methods of Sewage Disposal." *Century Illustrated Monthly Magazine* 47: 939–48.

Wasch, Diane Shaw, Perry Bush, Keith Landreth, and James Glass. 1988. *World War II and the U.S. Army Mobilization Program: A History of 700 and 800 Series Cantonment Construction*. Washington, D.C.: U.S. Department of the Interior, National Park Service, Historic American Buildings Survey/Historic American Engineering Record.

Webster, Richard. 1930. "Sales Assortments—Model Stocks for Customers." *Printers' Ink Monthly* 20, no. 3 (March): 34–35, 90–100.

Weintraub, Karen. 2017. "Do Hand Sanitizers Really Cut Down on Illness?" *New York Times*, May 16, p. D4.

"The Well-Equipped Bathroom." 1921. *House and Garden* 40 (August): 58–59.

"What the 'Take a Bath Every Day' Campaign Means to the Plumbing and Heating Industry." 1920. *Domestic Engineering* 93, no. 9 (November 27): 397–400.

Whipple, George C. 1911. "Principles of Sewage Disposal." *Engineering Record* 63, no. 1 (January 7): 20–23.

Wilhelm, Albert. 1913. "Americanization by Bath." *Literary Digest* 47 (August 23): 280–81.

Wilkie, Jacqueline S. 1986. "Submerged Sensuality: Technology and Perceptions of Bathing." *Journal of Social History* 19, no. 4 (Summer): 649–64.

"Will It Be a Dream House?" 1949. *Ladies Home Journal* 66 (October): 206–7, 231.

Wingate, Charles F. 1883. "The Unsanitary Homes of the Rich." *North American Review* 137 (August): 172–84.

Winkler, Gail Caskey. 1989. "Introduction." In *The Well-Appointed Bath: Authentic Plans and Fixtures from the Early 1900s*, edited by Charles E. Fisher III, 11–25. Washington, D.C.: National Trust for Historic Preservation.

"Words That Sing to Your Pocketbook." 1919. *Atlantic Monthly* 124 (October): 572–75.

"Work of Standardization." 1905. *Domestic Engineering* 33, no. 5 (November 4): 34.

Worthington, William, Jr. 1990. "The Privy and the Pump: The Matthewman & Johnson Excavating Device." *Technology and Culture* 31, no. 3 (July): 451–55.

Wrenn, Lynette B. 1985. "The Memphis Sewer Experiment." *Tennessee Historical Quarterly* 44, no. 3 (Fall): 340–49.

Wright, Gwendolyn. 1980. *Moralism and the Model Home: Domestic Architecture and Cultural Conflict in Chicago, 1873–1913*. Chicago: University of Chicago Press.

Wright, Gwendolyn. 1981. *Building the Dream: A Social History of Housing in America*. Cambridge, MA: MIT Press.

Wright, Lawrence. (1960) 2000. *Clean and Decent: The Fascinating History of the Bathroom*. London: Penguin.

Yee, Roger. 1975. "Dear John." *Progressive Architecture* 56, no. 7 (July): 70–78.

Yegül, Fikret. 2010. *Bathing in the Roman World*. Cambridge: Cambridge University Press.

Yezierska, Anzia. 1919. "Soap and Water and the Immigrant." *New Republic* 18, no. 225 (February 22): 117–19.

Youmans, Edward L. 1858. *The Hand-Book of Household Science*. New York: D. Appleton and Company.

Zola, Irving Kenneth. 1997. "Living at Home: The Convergence of Aging and Disability." In *Staying Put: Adapting the Place Instead of the People*, edited by Susan Lanspery and Joan Hyde, 23–54. Amityville, NY: Baywood Publishing Company.

INDEX

Page numbers in *italics* indicate photographs.

About the Author

Alison K. Hoagland is professor emerita at Michigan Technological University, where she taught history and historic preservation, after having served as the senior historian at the Historic American Buildings Survey of the National Park Service. She is the author of *The Log Cabin: An American Icon* (University of Virginia Press, 2018) and *Mine Towns: Buildings for Workers in Michigan's Copper Country* (University of Minnesota Press, 2010), among other works.